First published in the UK and the USA in 2003 by Earthscan Publications Ltd

Copyright © World Water Council and Japan Water Resources Association, 2003

World Water Council
10, place de la Joliette
Les Docks de la Joliette, Atrium 10.3
13002 Marseille, France
Tel: +33 (0) 491994100
Fax: +33 (0) 491994101
Email: wwc@worldwatercouncil.org
Web: **www.worldwatercouncil.org**

Reproduction of this publication for educational or other noncommercial purposes is authorized without prior permission from the copyright holder. Reproduction for sale or other commercial purposes is prohibited without the prior written permission of the copyright holder.

The views of the authors expressed in this publication, and the presentation of the material, do not necessarily reflect the views or policies of the World Water Council or the Japan Water Resources Association.

The boundaries, colours, and other information shown on any map in this volume do not imply any judgement on the legal status of any territory or the endorsement or acceptance of such boundaries.

ISBN   1-84407-078-6 paperback
          1-84407-085-9 hardback

Printed and bound in the UK by Cambrian Printers, Aberystwyth
Substantive editing, design, and prepress production by Communications Development in Washington, DC, with art direction by its UK partner, Grundy & Northedge.
Typesetting by MapSet Ltd, Gateshead, UK
Cover by Yvonne Booth based on original design by Grundy & Northedge
Cover photographs © Richard Mas

For a full list of publications, please contact:

Earthscan Publications Ltd
120 Pentonville Road, London, N1 9JN, UK
Tel: +44 (0)20 7278 0433
Fax: +44 (0)20 7278 1142
Email: earthinfo@earthscan.co.uk
Web: **www.earthscan.co.uk**

22883 Quicksilver Drive, Sterling, VA 20166-2012, USA

Earthscan is an editorially independent subsidiary of Kogan Page Ltd and publishes in association with WWF-UK and the International Institute for Environment and Development

A catalogue record for this book is available from the British Library

Library of Congress Cataloging-in-Publication Data

World water actions : making water flow for all / François Guerquin ... [et al.].
      p. cm.
   Includes bibliographical references and index.
   ISBN 1-84407-078-6 (pbk. : alk. paper) — ISBN 1-84407-085-9 (hardback : alk. paper)
    1. Water-supply—Management. 2. Water-supply—Management—International cooperation. I. Guerquin, François.

TD345.W65 2004
363.6'1—dc22

2003017716

Printed on elemental chlorine-free paper

world WATER actions

Making Water Flow for All

François Guerquin
Tarek Ahmed
Mi Hua
Tetsuya Ikeda
Vedat Özbilen
Marlies Schuttelaar

World Water Council
3rd World Water Forum

**World Water Council
Water Action Unit**

Earthscan Publications Ltd
London • Sterling, VA

Foreword from the President of the World Water Council

On our blue planet, water is life.

No water, no life.

To manage water properly, in a sustainable manner for the benefit of all, including the poorest, is a major challenge. For people living in arid regions, the challenges of water have long been obvious. Now the rest of the world is starting to look at water from a similar perspective. The global discussions initiated 26 years ago at the First International Conference on Water in Mar del Plata sparked the growing interest and involvement of a broad range of stakeholders in finding solutions to the worsening water crisis. Soon it was clear that "Water is everybody's business".

The absolute necessity of building bridges between all elements of the water sectors and all the key actors motivated the creation of the World Water Council in 1996. Since then, the World Water Council has been fully committed to creating an environment to encourage the emergence of a strong and united water community.

The process began at the First World Water Forum in Marrakech, Morocco, in 1997, where participants mandated the World Water Council to develop a "Long-Term Vision for Water, Life, and Environment in the 21st Century", referred to simply as the *World Water Vision*. A bold undertaking from the start, the scope grew more ambitious over time as the exercise triggered powerful interest within many diverse groups who saw the urgent need for a holistic discussion about water.

Their opinions and aspirations were expressed through the hundreds of local, national, and regional preparatory meetings leading to the publication of two global documents, *World Water Vision: Making Water Everybody's Business* and *Towards Water Security: A Framework for Action*, which were presented and discussed at the Second World Water Forum at The Hague in 2000. At that forum His Royal Highness the Prince of Orange characterized the forum as the "birthplace of the water movement".

As announced at the Second World Water Forum, the World Water Council has established a monitoring team to survey the efforts of the global water community in converting the Vision to actions and to report to the Third World Water Forum on what is being done. *World Water Actions* is the outcome of this. It is a unique report: it aims to demonstrate that all around the world people are working to address critical water issues—and often with considerable success.

Following up on the objectives of the *World Water Vision*, *World Water Actions* presents an encouraging picture of the wide range of actions worldwide to improve water resources management and water services. It also identifies gaps and emerging priorities. We hope that it will motivate people to continue working, on scales both large and small, towards safe water for all. When completed, shared, and multiplied, all these actions can lead to achievement of the Vision.

I wish to thank the staff of the Water Action Unit. Coming from diverse backgrounds around the world, they worked as a team to produce this report under the constant supervision and dedicated guidance of William J. Cosgrove, vice president of the World Water Council. I also want to thank the technical advisors and the staff of the Secretariat of the World Water Council, who provided administrative support.

Their work would not have been possible without the generous financial support of the Japan Water Resources Association and the Dutch Ministry of Foreign Affairs. Special thanks are extended to Groupe des Eaux de Marseille, the Southeastern Anatolia Project (GAP) Regional Development Administration in Turkey, and the Egyptian Ministry of Water Resources and Irrigation. Our gratitude also goes to Hideaki Oda, Secretary General of the Secretariat of the Third World Water Forum, and Kenzo Hiroki, Vice Secretary General for Finance, Planning, and General Affairs of the Secretariat of the Third World Water Forum. Many other organizations made either financial or intellectual contributions to *World Water Actions*, and these are greatly appreciated.

This work is dedicated to our friend Anil Agarwal, who sadly left us in December 2001. The indefatigable efforts and enlightened commitment of this pioneer of the water community live on and were a great source of inspiration to those who worked on the production of *World Water Actions: Making Water Flow for All*.

Dr. Mahmoud Abu-Zeid
President of the World Water Council
Minister of Water Resources and Irrigation, Egypt

Contents

Foreword	iv
List of figures, tables and boxes	ix
About the authors	xii
Preface	xiv
Background	xviii
Acknowledgements	xxv
Overview: Recording actions, identifying gaps	**2**

Assessing Challenges, Initiating Change

1	Water's many values	**14**
2	Water management	**19**
3	Transboundary basins	**37**
4	Water and gender	**48**
5	Water-related risks	**55**
6	Financing water infrastructure and services	**73**

2

Focusing on Key Areas, Promoting Change

7	**Water supply and sanitation**	88
8	**Water for energy**	104
9	**Water for health**	113
10	**Water for agriculture**	122
11	**Water, ecosystems, and biodiversity**	137

Taking Stock, Advancing Change

12	The Third World Water Forum and the future agenda	**154**

Photo credits	167
References	168
Index	172

viii **World Water Actions**

List of figures, tables and boxes

Figures

O.1	Number of actions collected, excluding global actions	2
1.1	Types of values associated with water	15
2.1	Water actions involving country-level reforms	27
2.2	Water actions involving local reforms	29
2.3	Water actions involving awareness raising and capacity building	33
6.1	Breakdown of financing in the water sector	74
6.2	International aid to water by source, 1990–2001	75
6.3	Annual investment in infrastructure projects with private participation in developing countries by sector, 1990–2001	76
6.4	Net private long-term financial flows to developing countries, 1991–2001	76
6.5	Ratio of potential to actual water service revenues in selected developing country cities, 2001	84
11.1	Actions to protect ecosystems, by type	140
11.2	Actions to protect ecosystems, by region	141

Tables

2.1	Water actions that aim to share water among potentially conflicting uses	31
4.1	Water actions that promote women's involvement in water management	51

Boxes

B.1	The Millennium Development Goals	xix
O.1	Linking water and WEHAB	4
O.2	Integrated water resources management	5
2.1	Decentralization in Mexico	28
3.1	Definitions	38
3.2	Sharing the benefits of better water management	40
3.3	Using a decision support system to jointly define more rational use of shared groundwater (action 1315)	44

4.1	Gender issues and Gujarat's water and sanitation vision (action 1075)	53
5.1	Definitions of key terms	56
5.2	Floods in Mozambique: impacts, consequences, and responses	61
5.3	Community disaster response committees in the Philippines	70
6.1	Financing water management in South Africa	80
6.2	The Soozhal initiative (action 3093)	81
6.3	Output-based payments for catchment restoration in Brazil (action 1008)	82
6.4	Main recommendations from the World Panel on Financing Water Infrastructures	83
7.1	Voluntary Action for Development, Uganda (action 3512, one of three winners of the Water Action Contest)	97
7.2	Connecting slums to water and sanitation networks: India's experiences	98
7.3	Technology Transfer Division, Bombas de Mecate (action 3047, one of three winners of the Water Action Contest)	100
8.1	All energy sources affect the environment and human health	106
8.2	Karnataka, India: generating benefits by combining efficiency gains and greater reliance on renewable energy	107
9.1	Water, health, and climate change	114
10.1	"121" project (action 2604, one of three winners of the Water Action Contest)	129
11.1	Key messages in the *Vision for Water and Nature*	138
11.2	Snowy River Inquiry (action 579)	144

About the authors

Tarek Ahmed

Education: PhD, University of Southampton

Professional experience: researcher in various institutes in Egypt and the United Kingdom

Expertise: irrigation management, economics of water projects

François Guerquin

Education: Ecole Polytechnique, Ecole Supérieure d'Electricité, INSEAD

Professional experience: technical director, Marseilles Water Supply Company

Expertise: urban water supply and sanitation service management

Mi Hua

Education: Epidemiologist, Guangxi Medical College

Professional experience: project officer, Public Health Bureau of Guangxi, China

Expertise: rural water supply, sanitation and health project management

Tetsuya Ikeda

Education: Master of Engineering, University of Tokyo

Professional experience: deputy director of various Japanese ministries

Expertise: disaster management, water quality monitoring and pollution regulation

Vedat Özbilen

Education: Middle East Technical University, Ankara

Professional experience: urban and regional planner and project coordinator, Southeastern Anatolia Project Regional Development Administration, Turkey

Expertise: community participation , integrated approach to water development projects, environment protection, public–private participation

Marlies Schuttelaar

Education: Ecole Centrale de Paris, Ecole Nationale du Génie Rural, des Eaux et des Forêts

Professional experience: consultant engineer in the Netherlands and France

Expertise: public consultation and river basin management

Preface

The growing sense of community among water professionals that led to the shared authorship of this report can be traced to the World Water Council's commitment to organizing world water forums every three years. Although the First World Water Forum—held in Marrakech, Morocco, in 1997—was dominated by the most powerful water actors (water companies, international donors, government agencies), it set an important precedent for broad discussion and debate. That forum also called on the World Water Council to develop a global vision for water, life, and the environment.

Participation in the Second World Water Forum—held in The Hague, the Netherlands, in 2000—was more diverse, drawing on representatives of labour groups, civil society organizations, and non-governmental organizations (NGOs) as well as social activists, consumer advocates, and others. An input into the second forum was *World Water Vision: Making Water Everybody's Business* (written by William J. Cosgrove and Frank R. Rijsberman for the World Water Council), which offered recommendations and solicited commitments to action by governments and international organizations. Among the commitments made at the second forum was for the World Water Council to establish a monitoring system to assess progress towards the Vision by collecting and cataloguing world water actions at all levels—international, national, local, and individual.

The Third World Water Forum—held in Kyoto, Shiga, and Osaka, Japan, in March 2003 (www.world.water-forum3.com)—expands civil society participation through a "Virtual Water Forum", through the collection of "Water Voices" at the grass-roots level (such voices are used to illustrate this report), through the Water Action Contest, and through an open process for proposing session topics at the actual forum.

This report is one element of the World Water Council's efforts to document innovative global water actions that address the priorities identified at the second forum and that respond to the challenges of integrated water resources management. The CD-ROM that accompanies this report contains a searchable Actions Database of the more than 3,000 actions on which the report is based as well as a User Guide. The continually updated database is also available at www.worldwatercouncil.org/search_actions.php. These actions include on-going projects (planning, preparation, or implementation), applied research and studies, awareness-raising campaigns, and policy, legal, and institutional reforms—all designed to improve water management. The actions are categorized by geographical situation, key challenges, and thematic keywords.

A first version of this report, prepared by the Water Action Unit of the World Water Council, was the main input to the Ministerial Conference at the Third World Water Forum. The third forum complemented this effort by eliciting as many commitments to additional actions as possible. The results are described in the last chapter of this report.

Information about the actions described in this report and in the Actions Database came from the water community through interviews, Internet research, mailed suggestions and questionnaires, papers and proceedings from water-related conferences, and broad appeals to stakeholders—who volunteered more information. The gathering and refining of information have been constrained by the need to finalize this report for publication, but the information base will continue to grow and improve. During much of the analysis, the database contained around 2,000 actions. By the time of the Third World Water Forum, the number was almost 3,000. By the time the report was completed, it rose to 3,200.

Despite efforts to make the Actions Database broadly representative, the actions recorded are only a small percentage of the total activity which took place between the Second and Third World Water Forum. But they do illustrate the wide range of activity presently underway in the water sector. One of the main challenges in preparing this report was capturing the many small-scale actions implemented by local governments and NGOs. Such actions are often innovative and add to the understanding of water issues. Moreover, while the Actions Database includes initiatives from both industrial and developing countries, some chapters of the report focus on developing countries, where most action is needed.

This report was written by the Water Action Unit on behalf of the international water community—individuals and organizations whose work is related to the management and use of water and who share an interest in ensuring safe, reliable, sustainable water resources for current and future generations. Transforming the many individuals who work on water into a community that shares a common purpose is a matter of self-perception and self-awareness as well as group perception and group awareness. The hope is that the interaction involved in creating this report will reinforce that sense of community and common purpose—transcending individual interests.

This report is also intended to reach the media and others who influence decisions on water policies and investments. Showing them the actions being taken—by communities large and small, near and far—should demonstrate conclusively that where there is will to deal with water issues, there are ways.

Parallel to this report is the *World Water Development Report*, a wide-ranging assessment of the world's freshwater presented in the Third World Water Forum by the United Nations World Water Assessment Programme. Background material from the World Water Assessment Programme is cited throughout this report. Readers interested in learning more about the world's water challenges should also read the *World Water Development Report*.

Many other international activities and organizations have generated reports and statements for the Third World Water Forum. The Water Action Unit has tried to keep pace with these initiatives and incorporate them into this report as much as possible.

The staff of the Water Action Unit participated in the Third World Water Forum, which has enriched this report in several ways:

- the version of this report presented at the forum received a valuable range of direct contributions, remarks and comments

- the various debates at the forum took forward thinking on a number of key issues

- a number of organizations announced commitments to launch new projects, initiatives and action.

Most of this new material is included in the final chapter of this report.

The Water Action Unit hopes that this report will contribute to the water movement now under way around the world—building bridges between water professionals and offering practical insights and solutions to make water flow for all.

Water Action Unit
Marseilles, France
June 2003

Background

Water is central to human development and poverty alleviation.

Water is no longer taken for granted as a plentiful resource, always available. More and more people in more and more countries are experiencing water differently—as individuals in their day-to-day life and as communities and nations.

Population growth and increasing living standards are putting heavy pressure on water resources. Many countries are already suffering a water crisis that affects their people and the ecosystems we all depend on. More than 1 billion people lack access to safe drinking water. More than 2 billion lack access to sanitation. Several countries lack sufficient water to produce food. About half of the world's wetlands were destroyed in the last century. With current practices, the degradation of ecosystems and the loss of biodiversity will threaten the lives of future generations. It is clear that we must change our ways (Cosgrove and Rijsberman 2000).

A new water agenda

People have come to realize that water, as a limited resource, must be carefully managed for the benefit of all people and the environment to ensure water security today and in the future. This concept of water security, which considers the future of water in present-day planning, also implies ensuring access to water by poor and marginalized groups and empowering them to represent their interests. The World Water Forum series gives people from all regions and of all groups and convictions the opportunity to share their views on these issues, to advocate actions for better water resources management at all levels, from local to international, and to promote access to water as a human right.

These principles were reinforced at the Third World Water Forum in Kyoto, Shiga, and Osaka, Japan, in March 2003, the largest and most representative meeting on water ever organized.

This report is the result of an inventory of water actions and implementation of commitments of governments and organizations, from the international to the grass-roots level, since the Second World Water Forum in The Hague, the Netherlands, in 2000. It demonstrates how this world water community has progressed in the better use and management of water and water resources. There has been significant progress in creating a more enabling environment for water use and management. Much is happening at the community level.

> **Box B.1 The Millennium Development Goals**
>
> The 2000 United Nations General Assembly established the Millennium Development Goals, with 2015 as the horizon (action 1948). One of the targets for assessing progress towards these goals is to halve the proportion of people without access to safe drinking water. A number of the other targets also depend on sound water management. As shown throughout this report, water plays a role in many of these targets, such as:
>
> - Halving the proportion of people living on less than $1 per day.
> - Halving the proportion of people suffering from hunger.
> - Ensuring that all children, boys and girls equally, can complete a course of primary education.
> - Reducing maternal mortality by three-quarters and under-five mortality by two-thirds.
> - Halting and reversing the spread of HIV/AIDS, malaria, and other major diseases that affect humanity.
>
> In August 2003 the World Summit on Sustainable Development approved a supplementary target:
>
> - Halving the proportion of people without access to sanitation facilities.
>
> All the Millennium Development Goals have to be achieved while, at the same time, protecting the environment from further degradation. The World Summit Plan of Implementation asks to "develop integrated water resources management and water efficiency plans by 2005, with support to developing countries, through actions at all levels".
>
> *Sources:* United Nations 2000; 2002a.

But much more effort is needed to combat the problems of hunger and water-related diseases by improving access to water, water supply, and sanitation. And progress is slow when measured against the task of meeting the Millennium Development Goals, a set of eight goals agreed by the United Nations General Assembly in 2000, for development and poverty eradication by 2015 or before (box B.1). One target directly concerns water: to halve the proportion of people without access to sustainable drinking water (United Nations 2002a). Other targets, such as halving the proportion of people who are hungry, will also require improved water management.

The visioning process: The world water forums

The First World Water Forum, in Marrakech, Morocco, in 1997, emerged from the commitment of the World Water Council to organize global water summits every three years. This first forum established the important precedent of convening water professionals and others concerned with water issues for discussion and debate. The forum was followed up by the development of a "long-term vision for water, life, and environment in the 21st century", an intensive, top-down and bottom-up review of past experience and scenario building about the future. The vision exercise stimulated hundreds of local, national, and regional preparatory meetings, strengthening the sense of community among the many participants and resulting in the release of two global documents: *World Water Vision: Making Water Everybody's Business* (Cosgrove and Rijsberman 2000) and *Towards Water Security: A Framework for Action* (Global Water Partnership 2000), presented at the Second World Water Forum in 2000.

Making water everybody's business

The Second World Water Forum was a landmark event in the evolution of global water consciousness. The visioning exercise and related water vision documents prepared for the forum engaged many thousands of people from around the world and mobilized people and resources to an extent not previously seen in the water domain. The forum attracted more than 5,700 participants from 156 countries, including 120 ministers, international water specialists, politicians, officials, journalists, and representatives of civil society.

Through an intensified participatory process, the second forum produced a set of recommendations and imbued stakeholders with the strong sense that water is "everybody's business".

The documents and participatory processes of the first and second forums were an important input for the Third World Water Forum in 2003. Those preparations took participation even further—to an ongoing Internet "Virtual Water Forum", a Water Action Contest, and the collection of "water voices"—a recounting of actions, experiences, and perceptions at the grass-roots level around the word—a selection of which are quoted throughout this report.

The Hague Ministerial Declaration

Concurrent with the second forum was a Ministerial Conference, whose key outputs were an official declaration and commitments for practical actions to advance water security. The Ministerial Declaration listed seven key challenges (Council of Ministers 2000):

- *Meeting basic needs:* to recognize that access to safe and sufficient water and sanitation are basic human needs and are essential to health and well-being, and to empower people, especially women, through a participatory process of water management.
- *Securing the food supply:* to enhance food security, particularly of the poor and vulnerable, through

the more efficient mobilization and use, and the more equitable allocation, of water for food production.
- *Protecting ecosystems:* to ensure the integrity of ecosystems through sustainable water resources management.
- *Sharing water resources:* to promote peaceful cooperation and develop synergies between different uses of water at all levels, whenever possible, within and, in the case of boundary and transboundary water resources, between states concerned, through sustainable river basin management or other appropriate approaches.
- *Managing risks:* to provide security from floods, droughts, pollution, and other water-related hazards.
- *Valuing water:* to manage water in a way that reflects its economic, social, environmental, and cultural values for all its uses, and to move towards pricing water services to reflect the cost of their provision. This approach should take account of the need for equity and the basic needs of the poor and the vulnerable.
- *Governing water wisely:* to ensure good governance, so that the involvement of the public and the interests of all stakeholders are included in the management of water resources.

Making commitments for practical action

During the second forum and the Ministerial Conference many organizations and country delegations committed themselves to specific actions. The Global Water Partnership declared its commitment to pursuing key priorities emerging from the Framework for Action and incorporating them into its work plan. Many country delegations made commitments, ranging from statements of intent to monetary pledges. Among them:

- *Mali* set a target of meeting 80 percent of its water needs by 2025.
- *The Netherlands* committed to doubling its funding for water-related activities in developing countries over a period of four years.
- *The United Kingdom* committed to doubling its bilateral support to water and sanitation over a period of three years.
- *Vietnam* set a target of ensuring domestic water supply for its entire population and providing irrigation water for 7 million hectares of cultivated land by 2025.
- *Zambia* set a target of achieving 75 percent coverage of water service in rural areas and 100 percent in urban areas by 2015.

The Netherlands Ministry of Foreign Affairs sent out questionnaires in 2001 to the 39 countries and organizations that had made formal pledges or had released statements of intent at the Ministerial Conference on the actions they were taking. The responses were encouraging, considering the long and complex process of developing new policies, laws, and programmes that reflect national circumstances and of shepherding them successfully through legal and administrative channels.

In many cases the main focus has been on integrating the approach and concepts that came out of the second forum into ongoing policy and programme developments. The broad influence on national policies in such a short time reflects the fact that the Ministerial Declaration was a synthesis of emerging trends and opinions at the global level. It also reflects the fact that an active process of developing water policies is already taking place. In most cases the declaration has had the greatest impact in areas where policy development was already taking place.

Many responses noted the need for more effective international collaboration. For example, Morocco and other African countries are stepping up collaboration on transboundary basins, while the European Union (EU) countries are developing new forms of collaboration to implement the EU Water Framework Directive. Similarly, Germany, the Netherlands, Norway, and the United Kingdom, already active in assisting international collaboration on water in different parts of the world, have adopted expanded programmes since the second forum. Japan, as host of the third forum in 2003, has developed an active programme of international collaboration and assistance. The increasing prominence of formal processes such as the Mekong River Commission and the Nile Basin Initiative also reflects the growing importance of international collaboration.

There has also been widespread adoption of integrated water resources management principles in national policy frameworks. While already under way before the second forum, the trend received additional impetus from the emphasis it received at the second forum. FYR Macedonia credited that emphasis for providing guidance to its policy reform. China has focused on developing institutional processes for promoting conservation in water crisis areas, a departure from the technical approaches previously emphasized. Oman reports the merging of two ministries (Water Resources and Regional Municipality and Environment) as a step towards promoting integrated decision-making in water resources management, ecosystems, and municipality affairs.

Many other issues being incorporated in national policies mirror those identified in the Ministerial Declaration: the importance of providing basic services to those most in need; the inclusion of explicit environmental dimensions in water policies; and the need to improve water governance. The responses to the questionnaires suggest overall that the declaration has been instrumental in clarifying and providing external reference points for issues that were already emerging as vital for policy development at the national level.

The responses also make clear that while many steps are being taken to develop strategies and programmes to implement the commitments, the process cannot be hurried because it entails fundamental changes in policy and in the legal and institutional framework within which water resources are managed. This indicates that the approaches laid out in the Ministerial Declaration are of such structural significance that they are being translated into fundamental, rather than cosmetic changes. The need to tailor the broad and sometimes abstract concepts in the Ministerial Declaration to the specific circumstances of each country is also apparent. This calls for a level of debate and analysis to ensure that particular conditions are reflected and to develop the broader understanding and consensus among professionals and society that are an essential driver of change. Keeping the debate alive on these issues is a key to building this consensus.

Individual analysis of the follow-up of commitments made during the second forum is available on the CD-ROM accompanying this report.

Debates of the Second World Water Forum

The key issues raised by participants of the second forum were privatization, charging the full cost price for water services, rights to access, and participation. Globalization and trade could be considered as emerging issues from The Hague.

Privatization

The second forum infused the whole spectrum of participants with the notion that water is everybody's business and not the exclusive business of governments and water professionals. Much less agreement was obtained on the model that should replace this government monopoly. What was clear is that nobody proposed that the government monopoly should be replaced by a private monopoly, nor that water resources should be privatized. On the contrary, the participants endorsed the *World Water*

Vision's proposal that water resources are a common heritage and should be treated as a common property resource.

Charging the full cost price for water services

That water resources are a common property resource does not imply that water services should be free of charge. The Vision emphasized the needs of users, through managers accountable to users or managed directly by the users themselves, and that users should be charged the full cost of the service—with appropriate subsidies made available to the poor and with recognition of the resources the poor do have: their labour. Many, though certainly not all, supported this recommendation of the Vision.

Right to access

The need to recognize explicitly access to drinking water and sanitation as a basic human right was crucial to most of the participants because water is not only considered essential for human health, it is also desperately needed by millions of poor people in rural areas for productive reasons: to grow the family's food or generate income. Rights to land and use of water are key determinants for people's potential to break out of the poverty trap. When rights are redistributed or new rights are assigned, this must be done on an equitable basis, recognizing the rights of women and men.

Participation

Users not only have the right to access to water services, but should also participate in decision-making on the management of resources. User participation has become an accepted principle but this should include the sharing of power: democratic participation of citizens in elaborating and implementing water policies and projects and in managing water resources. This should include the right of communities to develop their own projects if they can do so without government intervention and without harming upstream or downstream communities and environment.

Globalization and private sector involvement

Globalization concerns and the true nature of private sector involvement were issues that came up repeatedly at the second forum. A careful evaluation of all options, ranging from public to public–private partnership to privatized service provision, should determine which option is most attractive given the local circumstances. Considerations should include participatory and transparent management and an appropriate representation of local communities.

Acknowledgements

The work on *World Water Actions* was initiated by the World Water Council as follow-up to the commitment it made during the Second World Water Forum. Overall guidance on the report was provided by William J. Cosgrove, vice president of the World Water Council. Production was managed by François Guerquin, coordinator. Along with François Guerquin (France), the report's core authors are Tarek Ahmed (Egypt), Mi Hua (China), Tetsuya Ikeda (Japan), Vedat Özbilen (Turkey), and Marlies Schuttelaar (the Netherlands).

World Water Actions benefited from the advice of senior professionals who provided fundamental assistance in developing the report: Ramesh Bhatia, Gunilla Bjorklund, Ashoke Chatterjee, Gourishankar Gosh, David Groenfeldt, Michael Jefferson, Guy Lemoigne, Peter Rodgers, Albert-Louis Roux, Satoru Ueda, James Wimpenny, and Aaron Wolf. The team acknowledges the special contributions of Tony Milburn, who directed the efforts in preparing the final drafts of the report, and of Paul Van Hofwegen, who brought his experience to the team during the last months.

The involvement of Jamil Al-Alawi and Daniel Zimmer, the former and current executive directors of the World Water Council, and of the members of the Council was particularly valuable. Members of the Bureau of the World Water Council provided ongoing advice: Mahmoud Abu-Zeid, Minister of Water Resources and Irrigation, Egypt; René Coulomb, Suez SA; Loïc Fauchon, Groupe des Eaux de Marseille; Hideaki Oda, Secretary General of the Secretariat of the Third World Water Forum, Japan; Olcay Unver, Southeastern Anatolia Project (GAP) Regional Development Administration, Turkey. Permanent collaboration went on with the Secretariat of the Third World Water Forum staff, especially its Vice Secretary General for Finance, Planning, and General Affairs, Kenzo Hiroki.

Many people provided extensive and thoughtful comments on all four drafts of the report, as individuals or as representatives of their organization:

Safwat Abd-el-Dayem, World Bank; Chika Abe, Japan Sewage Works Agency; Ahmed Mohamed Adam, Ministry of Physical Planning and Public Utilities, Sudan; Ahmed Ahmedzadeh, Amelioration and Water Farm Committee, Azerbaijan; Mohamed Ait-Kadi, General Council for Agricultural Development, Morocco; Arthur Askew, World Meteorological Organization, Switzerland; Alice Aureli, United Nations Educational, Scientific, and Cultural Organization, International Hydrological Programme; Luc Averous, Lehman Brothers; Ivaylo Avramov, Bulgaria.

Ahmed Belhadi, CTI Engineering, Japan; Julia Benn, Organisation for Economic Co-operation and Development; Ger Bergkamp, IUCN–The World Conservation Union; Per Bertilsson, Global Water Partnership; Akhissa Bhari, National Institute of Urbanisation, Waters, and Forests (INRGREF), Tunisia; Jeremy Bird, Dams and Development Project; Maarten Blokland, International Institute for Infrastructural, Hydraulic, and Environmental Engineering, the Netherlands; Janos Bogardi, United Nations Educational, Scientific, and Cultural Organization; Olivier Bommelaer, Seine-Normandy Water Agency, France; Gabrielle Bouleau, French Institute of Forestry, Agricultural, and Environmental Engineering (ENGREF); Benito Braga, National Agency for Water Resources, Brazil; Mokhtar Bzioui, Ministry of Public Works, Morocco.

Belinda Calaguas, WaterAid; Margaret Catley-Carlson, Global Water Partnership; Tabeth Chiuta, IUCN–The World Conservation Union, Regional Office for Southern Africa, Zimbabwe; Abdelhafid Debbarh, Ecole Nationale d'Agriculture de Meknes, Morocco; Jerome Delli Priscoli, U.S. Army Corps of Engineers; Ariel Dinar, World Bank; Bert Diphoorn, Ministry of Foreign Affairs, the Netherlands; Jean-François Donzier, Office International de l'Eau (OIEAU); Viktor Dukhovny, Interstate Commission for Water Coordination of Central Asian States, Scientific Information Center, Uzbekistan; Mona El-Kady, National Water Research Center, Egypt; Lucy Emerton, IUCN–The World Conservation Union; Andrew Fenemor, Tasmanian District Council; Jennifer Francis, Gender and Water Alliance.

Santosh Gosh, Centre for Built Environment, India; Abdelkader Hamdane, Ministry of Agriculture, Tunisia; Atef Hamdy, Centre for Advanced Mediterranean Agronomic Studies (CIHEAM), Italy; Brian Hammond, Organisation for Economic Co-operation and Development; Masaki Hirowaki, Shiga Prefectural Government, Japan; Tomoo Inoue, Ministry of Land, Infrastructure, and Transport, Japan; Yumio Ishii, CTI Engineering, Japan; Mikio Ishiwatari, Ministry of Land, Infrastructure, and Transport, Japan; Jan Janssens, World Bank; Torkil Jonch-Clausen, Global Water Partnership; Tapio S. Katko, Tampere University of Technology, Finland; Adje Kerkhof, Cap-Net; Jacques Labre, Suez SA.

Jacques Lecornu, International Commission on Large Dams, Central Office; Christophe Lefebvre, IUCN–The World Conservation Union, France; James Lenahan, Global Water Partnership; Shrikant D. Limaye, Groundwater Institute, India; Wouter T. Lincklaen Arriens, Asian Development Bank, Philippines; C. Maksimovic, Imperial College, United Kingdom; Philippe Marin, International Finance Corporation; Luis Martinez Cortina, Spain; Charles-Louis de Maud'huy, Vivendi Environnement; Chew Oi May, River Basin Initiative Secretariat, Malaysia; Ann Milton, Global Water Partnership; Esther Monier-Illouz, World Bank; Danielle Morley, WaterAid; Takao Murakami, Japan Sewage Works Agency.

Pradi Kumar Nandi, Bhoj Wetland Project, India; Ravi Narayanan, WaterAid; Ceylan Orhun, Tüstas Sinai Tesisler A.S., Turkey; Hikmet Ozgobek, Ministry of Energy and Natural Resources, Turkey; Alberto Palombo, Florida Center for Environmental Studies, Center for Patanal Research, Brazil; Juan-Miguel Picolotti, Centre for Human Rights and the Environment (CEDHA), Argentina; John Pigram, Centre for Ecological Economics and Water Policy Research, Australia; Leonor Pintado Cortina, Comision Nacional del Agua, Mexico; Hervé Plusquelleq, United States; Kristina C. Prasad, International Water Management Institute; Shammy Puri, International Shared Aquifer Resource Management.

Paul Reiter, International Water Association; Daniel Renault, Food and Agriculture Organization of the United Nations; Frank Rijsberman, International Water Management Institute, Sri Lanka; Pierre-Alain Roche, Seine-Normandy Water Agency, France; John Rodda, International Association of Hydrological Sciences; Jacques Rousset, International Union of Technical Associations and Organizations, France; Jamal Saghir, World Bank; Léna Salame, United Nations Educational, Scientific, and Cultural Organization; Luis Santos Pereira, Superior Institute of Agronomy (ISA), Portugal; Jennifer Sara, World Bank; Darren Saywell, Water Supply and Sanitation Collaborative Council; Bart Schultz, Ministry of Transport, Public Works and Water Management, the Netherlands; Aly Shady, Canadian International Development Agency; Mandira Shrestha, International Centre for Integrated Mountain Development, Nepal; David Smith, United Nations Environment Programme; John Soussan, University of Leeds, United Kingdom; Pierre Strosser, France; Andras Szöllösi-Nagy, United Nations Educational, Scientific, and Cultural Organization.

Akatsuki Takahashi, United Nations Educational, Scientific, and Cultural Organization; Yutaka Takahashi, Construction Project Consultants Inc., Japan; Kuniyoshi Takeuchi, Yamanashi University, Japan; Henri Tardieu, Compagnie d'aménagement des coteaux de Gascogne, France; Richard Taylor, International Hydropower Association; Alberto Tejada-Guibert, United Nations Educational, Scientific, and Cultural Organization; Chandrakant D. Thatte, International Commission on Irrigation and Drainage; Shah Tushaar, International Water Management Institute, India; Ryuji Uematsu, Ministry of Land, Infrastructure, and Transport, Japan; Hans Van Damme, the Netherlands; Annette Van Edig, Federal Ministry for Economic Cooperation and Development, Germany; Thomas Van Wayenberge, Suez SA; Pamela Wallace, Dams and Development Project; Uno Winblad, consultant; Yoshiaki Yamanaka, Shiga Prefectural Government, Japan; Kenji Yoshinaga, Food and Agriculture Organization of the United Nations; and Gordon Young, World Water Assessment Programme.

The report benefited from the steady support of the team's assistants, Laetitia Chassefiere and Madeleine Lavastre, and from the editing, design, and prepress production of Communications Development's Bruce Ross-Larson, Meta de Coquereaumont, Paul Holtz, Elizabeth McCrocklin, Jo Anne Moncrief, Alison Strong, and Elaine Wilson. It also benefited from the ongoing collaboration of the Secretariat of the Third World Water Forum.

Funding was provided by the Japan Water Resources Association, the Netherlands Ministry of Foreign Affairs, Groupe des Eaux de Marseille, the Egyptian Ministry of Water Resources and Irrigation, and the Southeastern Anatolia Project (GAP) Regional Development Administration in Turkey. Support was also provided by the Public Health Bureau of Guangxi Province (China), Ville de Marseille, and the United Nations Educational, Scientific, and Cultural Organization. The Water Action Unit has been hosted in the World Water Council's headquarters and benefited from the tireless support of its administrative and communication services.

It is impossible to properly acknowledge and thank everyone who made contributions. To all who contributed and cannot find their names here, and to all who made possible the thousands of actions that are the pride of this report and of the water movement—our warmest thanks.

Overview:
Recording actions, identifying gaps

Among commitments made during the Second World Water Forum in The Hague in 2000, the World Water Council pledged to set up a monitoring system on actions that are bringing its *World Water Vision* to reality. It established the Water Action Unit to spearhead that work. This report highlights the fruits of those efforts. It presents an overview and analysis of actions around the world—projects (planning, preparation, or implementation), applied research and studies, awareness-raising campaigns, and policy, legal, and institutional reforms—that are addressing the urgent priorities identified in the Vision. More than 3,000 actions have been collected in this effort, documenting numerous water success stories and suggesting many elements of the water future. (An annotated database of these actions is available on the CD-ROM accompanying this report and also at www.worldwatercouncil.org/search_actions.php.) The map in figure O.1 shows the global distribution of actions.

In addition, countries followed the initiative taken by Egypt to prepare their own report of water actions and sent them as a contribution to the Water Action Unit. Such national water actions reports from China, Egypt, France, Germany, Indonesia, Japan, Mali, and Turkey are included on the companion CD-ROM.

The actions recorded in the Actions Database were active after the forum—even if initiated before—and are innovative in character. They recognize that whether the work is on urban water supply or village irrigation systems, the way to improved livelihoods and water security now and in the future is through better management of water resources.

Activities which—for some countries—are normal and routine, such as maintenance of infrastructure or monitoring of water quality, are thus not included in the database.

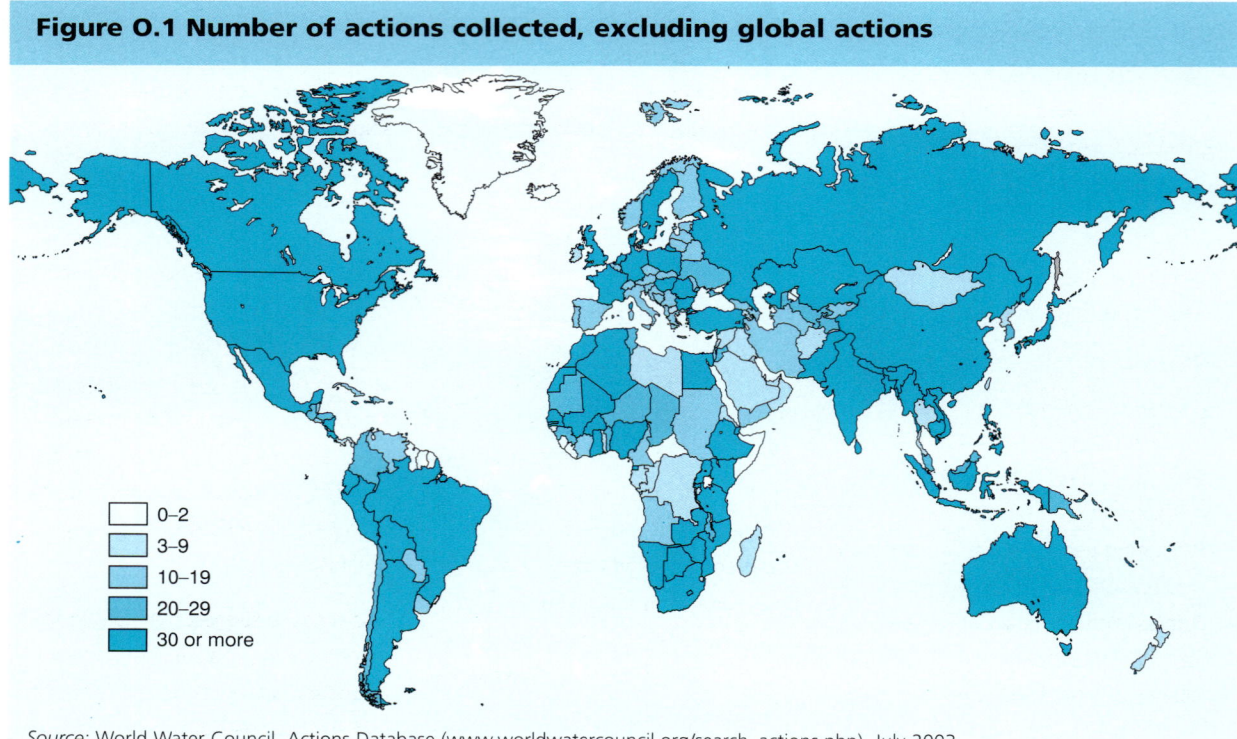

Figure O.1 Number of actions collected, excluding global actions

0–2
3–9
10–19
20–29
30 or more

Source: World Water Council, Actions Database (www.worldwatercouncil.org/search_actions.php), July 2003.

Overview: Recording actions, identifying gaps

There are many challenges to water management. But there are also many solutions

However, it should be emphasized that these activities are also critically important for meeting the challenges of water security.

Characterizing the actions taken in every country by thousands of organizations in the many diverse sectors that comprise the world water community is a difficult undertaking. To help make the task tractable and to give it coherence, the *World Water Vision* and the recommendations that emerged from the second forum were initially taken as points of reference. However, as the inventory made progress, the framework of analysis was renewed to take into account the thinking developed at the International Conference on Freshwater in Bonn in December 2001 and the World Summit on Sustainable Development in Johannesburg in August 2002 and to better highlight the issues still needing attention.

Part 1 of this report, Assessing Challenges, Initiating Change, exposes the urgent overall management needs:

- Recognizing water's many values.
- Managing water more efficiently.
- Strengthening international cooperation.
- Promoting gender equity in water decision-making.
- Addressing the impact of climate variability and change.
- Financing water development.

Part 2, Focusing on Key Areas, Promoting Change, examines the special needs of the water supply and sanitation, energy, health, agriculture, and biodiversity (WEHAB) sectors (box O.1):

- Ensuring sustainable access to water supply and sanitation.
- Managing water and energy to benefit both.
- Improving health outcomes through better water projects and management.
- Increasing agricultural production while protecting the water supply for humans and ecosystems.
- Ensuring water for biodiversity and ecosystems.

How are the identified priorities being addressed in current actions? Which priorities are being addressed most fully, and which need more attention? Each of the following chapters provides answers to these questions for one aspect of freshwater management. They begin by exposing the current situation and the issues, and then elaborate the generally agreed solutions that have been proposed and promoted within the water community. Next they present a picture of what has been happening in the field in recent years—with illustrations from the Actions Database (the action ID is quoted to allow for easy reference)—and conclude by analysing the challenges that remain.

World Water Actions suggests priorities for action based on what is already being done and identifies areas where improved approaches may be needed. By inventorying the thousands of actions under way around the world, this report can serve as a guide to individuals and organizations working on common themes, introduce them to each other, and facilitate synergies and partnerships. An earlier version of this report's conclusions on emerging priorities was discussed in a special session of the Third World Water Forum in Kyoto, Shiga, and Osaka in March 2003.

Exploring water actions for 2000–2003 and beyond

There are many challenges to water management. But there are also many solutions, as this report and the thousands of global water actions show. For every water problem it seems that someone somewhere has devised a solution or is developing one. Though not necessarily applicable in other socio-economic and physical environments, these solutions can still reveal many lessons. For that reason—and because of the infinite potential of the human spirit—*World Water Actions* is cautiously optimistic.

This is not to suggest that solving the world's water problems will be easy. Ultimately, the politicians and decision-makers who will have to take risks are

O World Water Actions

The world today is much more aware of the full range of values water offers to humanity

faced with two choices: action or inaction. With water, the risks of inaction increase every day. Thus politicians who have to risk reform and decision-makers who have to commit resources have little to fear. As this report shows, the odds definitely favour water reform and investment.

Recognizing water's many values

The world today is much more aware of the full range of values water offers to humanity, from livelihoods to recreational, aesthetic, religious, and cultural values. This recognition is clearly reflected in recent international conferences on water and development (the International Conference on Freshwater in Bonn in 2001 and the World Summit on Sustainable Development in Johannesburg in 2002). In Johannesburg, countries identified the importance to sustainable development of five key sectors—water supply and sanitation, energy, health, agriculture, and biodiversity—collectively referred to as WEHAB. *World Water Actions* shows that water is central for each of these sectors. In particular, awareness of the value of water for ecosystems has grown tremendously though it is still not universal. The water actions clearly show that even with broad awareness of the many values of water, finding solutions remains very difficult when interests and associated values conflict.

Box O.1 Linking water and WEHAB

Much of the report's focus and structure derives from the five sectors identified at the World Summit on Sustainable Development in Johannesburg in 2002 as essential to alleviating poverty and achieving sustainable development: water supply and sanitation; energy; health; agriculture; and biodiversity—together referred to as WEHAB. Water is essential to all these sectors and central to poverty alleviation and socio-economic development.

The main water challenges facing the WEHAB sectors include:

- *Water supply and sanitation:* the vast numbers of people unserved or underserved by water and sanitation services; the doubts about official data on coverage (which understate the problem); the related health and livelihood problems; and the growing problem of water pollution.
- *Energy:* the large share of people unserved by reliable and affordable energy; the impact on livelihoods and development; the unexploited potential of hydropower in developing countries; the environmental problems of fossil fuel energy and hydropower; and the close links between energy and water.
- *Health:* the widespread illness and death resulting from water-related diseases, which affect mainly children under five; the harmful impacts on well-being and livelihoods and the links to poverty; and the neglect of public health services and preventive approaches to water-related diseases.
- *Agriculture:* the unconscionably large number of hungry people and the challenge of feeding growing populations; the central role of water use; and the water pollution resulting from agrochemicals.
- *Biodiversity and ecosystems:* the water stress and biodiversity loss in ecosystems; the impacts of pollution; the challenge of balancing ecosystem and human water needs; and the need for conservation and sustainable use of biodiversity.

Note: For more details on each of these issues, see chapters 7 to 11.

Managing water more efficiently

The water crisis has been called a crisis of management. In most countries reforms to improve management in the water sector are under way, often beginning with adjustments in the legal, institutional, and regulatory frameworks. The most visible change is towards greater coordination of water concerns across sectors. Other significant changes are greater user participation; a broader range of providers, from private sector

Overview: Recording actions, identifying gaps

Among the major challenges facing water management are developing and properly maintaining infrastructure, improving water efficiency, and reducing water pollution

to community-based organizations to public utilities; and greater interest in river basin management and decentralization.

But much remains to be done, especially in successfully applying the principles of integrated water resources management (box O.2). Implementation and enforcement are key. While nearly everyone applauds the principles, applying them properly requires strong institutions, sufficient know-how and commitment, and adequate financial resources. Among the major challenges facing water management are developing and properly maintaining infrastructure, improving water efficiency, and reducing water pollution. The impact of water on development is enormous, argument enough for governments to make improved water management a top priority.

Strengthening international cooperation

The water actions show a move towards new cooperative arrangements for transboundary water systems, towards more multi-purpose approaches, and towards greater involvement of non-state actors. Ecosystem protection and risk management are replacing purely economic considerations as new drivers for transboundary cooperation. New arrangements are emerging, thanks in large measure to the broker role played by international organizations. The emphasis is on reducing the risk of conflict and improving the capacity to reach shared solutions. Decentralized cooperation—cooperation between local authorities—is also emerging as a promising solution for managing transboundary water systems. But actions on transboundary water systems are still far from integrated water resources management. And integrated water resources management, which focuses on water even as it considers the land and the people in the catchment, should be viewed as only one element of broader cooperation in regions that are connected by water systems.

Promoting gender equity in water decision-making

Integrating gender concerns in water decision-making is important not only for greater equity but also for greater efficiency. Accelerating poverty alleviation and socio-economic development depends on mobilizing every available skill, thereby increasing natural resilience and empowering people to improve their own lives. The will to change is growing nationally and internationally, and there are some replicable examples of successful measures for promoting gender equity in decision-making. Still needed is a better understanding of what has to be done, what can be done, and how to do it. Practical methods, such as gender budgeting and gender analysis

Box O.2 Integrated water resources management

Integrated water resources management is coordinated, sustainable development and management of water, land, and related resources to maximize equitable economic and social development while protecting ecosystems. Integrated management has to be applied through a complete rethinking of water management institutions—putting people at the centre.

of programmes and projects, need further development.

Addressing the impact of climate variability and change

A range of actions are devoted to water-related disasters such as floods and droughts. Among the outstanding issues needing attention are strengthening the institutional framework for disaster forecasting and management, enhancing people's capabilities for coping with them, and promoting and sharing knowledge among all concerned with water-related risks. Necessary changes are under way but progress is slowed by the lack of capacity, financial resources, and the political or institutional will to push ahead. Greater advances in disaster

World Water Actions

Very few countries have an overall framework linking laws, regulations, institutions, and financing mechanisms. The absence of such an integrated framework indicates that water is not yet of high enough priority for many governments

management are required to achieve a safer world in the 21st century. The impact of the increased variability in climate will almost certainly lead to more extreme water-related hazards and consequently to large socio-economic losses which will disproportionately hurt the poor. There is a pressing need to learn how this change in climate will affect people's livelihoods and opportunities and to identify what initiatives are needed at local, regional, and international levels to cope with them.

Financing water development

New commitments for international assistance in the water sector are growing, and some countries are encouraging private investment in the water sector. Many countries and communities around the world have found creative ways to increase tariffs to pay for sustainable operation and maintenance of water services, including guaranteed minimum quantities of free water, water stamps, and a variety of subsidies. Many initiatives are funding operation and rehabilitation improvements or are linking funding with results, dramatically improving the efficiency of investments. National strategies to match funding and costs need to be improved, however, and the financing needs of the water sector have to be better understood. While a range of water actions include financing components, very few countries have an overall framework linking laws, regulations, institutions, and financing mechanisms. The absence of such an integrated framework indicates that water is not yet of high enough priority for many governments.

Ensuring sustainable access to water and sanitation

Water and sanitation is a basic need, its importance clearly recognized in the Millennium Development Goals. Many international, national, and community organizations are working to meet this need through a variety of projects: utility sector reform; international programmes on water, sanitation, and hygiene; and hand-washing campaigns. Gender dimensions receive considerable attention in these activities. There has also been a noticeable expansion in rainwater harvesting. The World Summit on Sustainable Development recommended new types of partnerships to alleviate poverty. The water sector has many such partnerships at the global, regional, national, and local levels, a considerable number of them facilitated by the Global Water Partnership. Additional networks, such as community groups working with local authorities and professional operators, offer great potential for helping to achieve the Vision goals and should be encouraged.

Managing water and energy to benefit both

The link between water management and energy management is increasingly recognized. Population growth and changing consumption patterns both result in a substantial increase in the demand for water and energy. Some actions aim at energy demand management and improving decision-making on water and energy through multistakeholder processes, demand-management initiatives, and national processes. Where more is needed, actions seek to improve the use of existing infrastructure, reverse the decline in the stock of infrastructure, and design new projects in a way that allows public expression and the selection of optimized solutions for society. Other actions focus on comparing the effects of energy production approaches, assessing environmental impacts, and using cleaner technologies. Energy professionals at all levels (including governments and non-governmental organizations (NGOs)) must give more thought to water, and water professionals must give more thought to energy.

Improving health outcomes through better water projects and management

A small number of water actions explicitly use water management as a tool to address health issues, but a

Overview: Recording actions, identifying gaps

Facing world water problems is essential because of water's unique nature and irreplaceable role in so many aspects of human life

much larger number of actions provide indirect health benefits. Some actions provide access to water supply for domestic uses (drinking, washing, cooking) or for food production, thus reducing water-related illnesses and malnutrition. Others deal with pollution and water quality issues. Other health benefits derive from an improved environment. Fundamental components are participation, local management of water resources, awareness raising, and education to improve domestic behaviours linked to water. Because the health benefits of water actions are often indirect, they need to be emphasized in political discussions on water investment and incorporated in the planning and decision-making process.

Increasing agricultural production while protecting the water supply for humans and ecosystems

Several countries, especially in arid areas, are engaged in long-term planning and strategy formulation for sustainable agricultural development. Other actions include demand management, enhanced productivity of water for agriculture, and increased storage, harvesting, and reuse of water. Less conventional approaches include lower cost desalination and the development of more salt-tolerant crop species. Institutional and other reforms are directed at more sustainable water use. Awareness raising and information systems for water and soil conservation, protection of water resources, better irrigation practices, and adaptation to the effects of climate change are widespread at all levels, community to international. Participatory approaches and attempts to reorient traditional agencies towards greater people and service orientation has made considerable progress, especially in irrigation management. Stakeholders are participating more in decision-making and user group activism is growing, including efforts to remedy the under-representation of women in water resources management. Many actions focus on capacity building initiatives and research and development. Solutions are being developed for sustainable ecosystem use, where food production and ecosystem preservation coexist.

Ensuring water for biodiversity and ecosystems

Many actions are being taken to protect, conserve, and restore water resources, and many local, national, and international participatory ecosystem-based management and pollution control initiatives are underway. Knowledge is increasing on ecosystem water requirements. Actions for wetland restoration, coastal zone management, and river management are significant worldwide. Environmental impact assessments are increasingly required for infrastructure development proposals. Overall, beneficial reform is under way, motivated by the growing understanding and appreciation of ecosystem benefits and services and the dangers of ecosystem destruction. But more must be done in establishing minimum water flow requirements for ecosystems for conservation and protection, abating water pollution, building a systems approach to water management, and integrating the management of land, water, and ecosystems (including biodiversity). And serious reforms are required to regulate the allocation of water between human needs and ecosystem needs.

Accelerating actions

Solving the world's water problems will not be quick or easy. But as the water actions show, it can be done. And facing those problems is essential because of water's unique nature and irreplaceable role in so many aspects of human life. Water problems—and their solutions—challenge people to work together in new ways and partnerships and to respond to new opportunities for change.

Beneficial reform is under way in all the key areas but more attention is required to the reforms at the local level. The burden on developing countries is immense. Not only are they challenged to reform water while caring for the environment—

World Water Actions

The Millennium Development Goals will not be met by 2015 without accelerating the pace of reform and raising the rate of investment

something developed countries did not do—they are asked at the same time to radically reform water services management and expand delivery in a fraction of the time that industrial countries needed. It is a tall order. And analysis of the water actions suggests that the Millennium Development Goals will not be met by 2015 without accelerating the pace of reform, raising the rate of investment, strengthening institutions, and building the necessary capacity in the water sector. The priorities coming out of this analysis, presented by the authors for discussion by the Third World Water Forum participants, are for:

1. Governments and local authorities to acknowledge the importance of water to development and poverty reduction by mainstreaming water in strategies and master plans for all WEHAB sectors.

Governments have an obligation to provide sufficient water to all to meet their basic needs. Furthermore, water is essential to development in many economic sectors and should therefore receive priority in all development agendas. That requires mainstreaming water in all other sector policies, especially recognizing water's contribution in health, food, environment, and energy.

2. Governments and local authorities to increase investments for water development.

Water laws, strategies, and plans have to be translated into budget estimates and financing plans for water in all WEHAB sectors. Greater investments in expansion and improvements of water infrastructure are necessary to meet the Millennium Development Goals. Primary responsibility for such investments rests with national governments. If responsibility is delegated to lower levels, so must the means to invest.

3. International financial institutions and bilateral donors to prioritize support to countries that face their responsibilities towards water, as stated above.

In allocating support, international agencies and multilateral and bilateral donors should give priority to countries that are establishing strategies for integrating and coordinating water issues for all water-related sectors and that are increasing investments based on sound planning.

4. Governments and international financial institutions to adopt measures to attract financing for infrastructure.

Measures to reduce risk and improve cost recovery are necessary to encourage investment. Governments and the international community need seriously to consider the most promising recommendations of the Panel on Financing Water Infrastructure and to implement appropriate measures quickly.

5. International institutions to deepen understanding and expand public awareness of the benefits of water and improved water management.

The benefits of water and good water management should be quantified so that they may be considered in priority setting, planning, development, management, and budgeting for the water sector. International financial institutions, United Nations agencies, international NGOs, and research institutions could develop methodologies for such analysis.

6. Service providers to improve the quality and efficiency of service provision, operation, and maintenance.

Management of water infrastructure should be improved, especially for water for people and agriculture. Safe

Overview: Recording actions, identifying gaps

Effective implementation requires empowering local authorities and user groups

and continuous water delivery should be ensured through efficient systems operated and maintained to optimize their life and performance.

7. The United Nations, in preparing the declaration for the Decade of Education for Sustainable Development, to take account of the important role of water in sustainable development.

Changing the attitude and behaviour of people towards water means increasing their awareness and knowledge. This insight underlies the statement of the Plan of Implementation of the World Summit on Sustainable Development, "recommend[ing] to the United Nations General Assembly that it consider adopting a Decade of Education for Sustainable Development starting in 2005". Local-language information packages should be developed for primary and secondary school students and extension programmes to promote water values and ethics and to inform people about water's many vital functions, about the causes and impacts of pollution, and about solutions. Water should have the place it deserves during this Decade of Education.

8. Governments to focus on capacity building activities for the new institutions created by decentralization and their newly assigned roles and tasks.

Effective implementation requires empowering local authorities and user groups. Attention thus has to shift to capacity building of the decentralized agencies in their new institutional context, so that they can work effectively in a participatory, people- and service-oriented approach with user groups, communities, and households. Central agencies also have to be transformed, so that they can take up their new roles and responsibilities.

9. Governments, industry, agriculture, and people in their daily lives to contribute to eradicating existing pollution and ensuring that economic development does not increase pollution.

Economic and domestic activities should be optimized to reduce pollution at source. When waste is unavoidable, the most acceptable way of treating it should be designed in consideration of concerns for human and environmental health. More resources should be invested in wastewater treatment and sanitation, with preference for small-scale and local solutions. This requires technology innovation and transfer

between all countries. Responsibility for pollution should be more clearly defined in national legislations, and more consistently enforced. The polluter-pays principle should be applied.

10. Community organizations, NGOs, private and public sectors, local administrations, and national governments to work in partnership for the best in water management—because water is everybody's business.

Optimum use should be made of the options available. This requires regulation (for both public and private organizations) and operation in an accountable and transparent way under public oversight. Public–private partnerships offer a full range of options—including services provided by community and user organizations—that can be adapted to social, economic, and geographic conditions. Objective benchmarking and performance monitoring systems have to be an integral part of any operation.

11. International institutions to facilitate cooperation in the joint management of transboundary water systems.

Cooperation in transboundary river basins and groundwater systems should be enhanced so as to develop shared basin-wide strategies that

World Water Actions

The Third World Water Forum demonstrated clearly the intense interest in water issues worldwide

allocate available water to optimize benefits for all. Involvement of non-state actors should be encouraged. An independent international facility should be established to share experience on transboundary water management and provide countries, on their request, with advice or mediation. The next round of World Trade Organization negotiations should take into account the impact of water resources availability on countries' trading positions.

12. Water managers, in collaboration with climate and water scientists, to develop ways to better adapt to climate variability and to reduce the human suffering caused by floods and droughts.

Through collaboration between water managers and water and climate scientists better tools could be developed for coping with and adapting to the effects of climate variability today, thus creating resilience to adapt to the effects of climate change in the future. Both structural and other kinds of measures are required. Models should be strengthened to permit improved prediction of the effects of climate change on water management at regional and basin levels.

13. International institutions to establish a global monitoring system covering the state of water resources, activities in the water sector, and progress toward the Millennium Development Goals.

The water actions, especially those resulting from commitments made at the world water forums and the Word Summit on Sustainable Development, should be monitored to encourage all stakeholders to initiate and sustain such efforts. Monitoring the condition of global water resources is essential for ensuring that new management practices effectively improve the situation. A global Web-based monitoring network and system of indicators should be developed as a cooperative endeavour by international and independent institutions.

Outcomes of the Third World Water Forum

More then 24,000 people, including some 1,200 journalists, attended the Third World Water Forum in Kyoto, Shiga, and Osaka in March 2003, making it the largest meeting on water ever convened. This enormous gathering demonstrated clearly the intense interest in water issues worldwide and the success of the World Water Forum series in highlighting water as a major concern of this century. The gathering validated the third forum's three foundation principles: an open forum; a forum created by its participants; and a forum for actions and commitments.

Participants dealt with all aspects of freshwater in a rich and open debate. Prominent among the topics discussed at the forum were:

- Water as a human right.
- Financing water infrastructure.
- Private sector participation.
- Governance.
- Storage.
- Integrated water resources management.
- Groundwater.
- Water and ecosystems.
- Water and climate variability and change.

The forum launched more than 100 new initiatives for improved water management and served as a valuable platform for networking and information exchange. Not all issues received the attention they merited, but the forum raised awareness about many issues and set the path for future work. Progress on these issues will be reported on at the Fourth World Water Forum in 2006.

1

Assessing Challenges,
Initiating Change

1. Water's many values

The "Ministerial Declaration of The Hague Conference on Water Security in the 21st Century" (Council of Ministers 2000) recognized "valuing water" as one of the seven key challenges for the global community, proclaiming that we have to "manage water in a way that reflects its economic, social, environmental, and cultural values for all its uses, and move towards pricing water services to reflect the cost of their provision. This approach should take account of the need for equity and the basic needs of the poor and vulnerable."

Present situation

As the Ministerial Declaration affirms, water has many values. Some of the values commonly associated with water are shown in figure 1.1.

Water values are both economic (see chapter 6) and non-financial. While the economic values influence how well water services are provided, the non-financial values are also important for establishing the foundation of a more just and equitable management of the world's water. These values shape the institutions through which water is managed.

Institutions here encompasses the full range of policies, laws, regulations, standards, and norms by which actions and behaviours are governed, as well as the organizations through which these principles are put into practice in the management of water. All of this is embedded in the overall institutional framework in which people live and the cultural, religious, and socio-economic factors that reflect their basic values.

The range of water values

Many of the services water provides are irreplaceable and thus invaluable. From practical uses (livelihood, food production, sanitation, energy, transport) to recreational, aesthetic, religious, and cultural values, water affects nearly every aspect of life. In the extreme it is the sine qua non of life on Earth, and humanity has not been an adequate steward of this precious resource. The implications of that hard truth are finally dawning on us.

For centuries, but much intensified in the past 100 years, humanity has had a free ride in its use of water. Those days are over. Ecosystems are telling us that, loud and clear. It is time to start repaying our water debts, to recognize the value of all the services that water provides, and to ensure that the services are equitably shared by humanity and ecosystems alike, based on a set of agreed values that should shape water institutions.

Life-giving value. Water may well be accepted as a basic human right, but reliable provision of safe water supplies is far from universally available. It is clear from the "compensation culture" that pervades the high-income world that the value of an individual human life in an industrial country is many hundreds of thousands of dollars. Yet if the millions of children who die annually

Water's many values   1

In addition to water's importance as a basic human right, water is central to socio-economic development and poverty alleviation

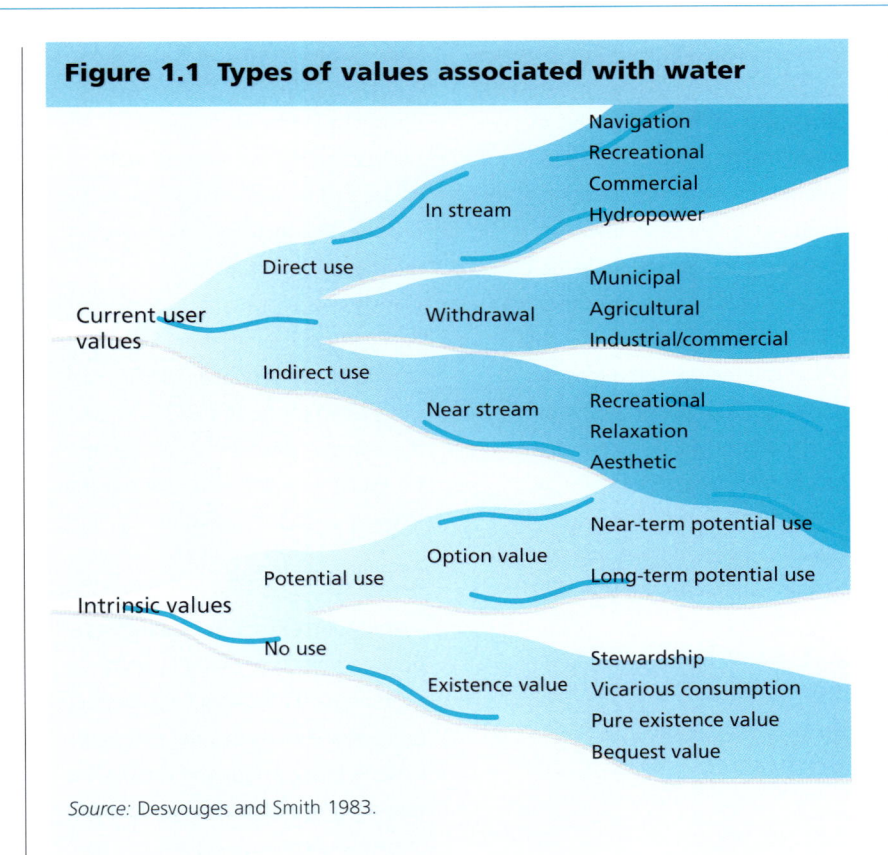

Figure 1.1 Types of values associated with water

- Current user values
  - Direct use
    - In stream
      - Navigation
      - Recreational
      - Commercial
      - Hydropower
    - Withdrawal
      - Municipal
      - Agricultural
      - Industrial/commercial
  - Indirect use
    - Near stream
      - Recreational
      - Relaxation
      - Aesthetic
- Intrinsic values
  - Potential use
    - Option value
      - Near-term potential use
      - Long-term potential use
  - No use
    - Existence value
      - Stewardship
      - Vicarious consumption
      - Pure existence value
      - Bequest value

Source: Desvouges and Smith 1983.

from preventable water-related disease in developing countries are taken as an indicator, the value accorded to a human life in developing countries is very low. These deaths are both indefensible and unnecessary, since so many of the causes are readily preventable.

Social value. In addition to water's importance as a basic human right, water has other important roles in development. As this report emphasizes in many ways, water is central to socio-economic development and poverty alleviation. For many decades it has been clear that good water resources development and management plus the establishment of sound water supply and sanitation systems in all communities constitute a key foundation of growth. Every community, large or small, urban or rural, must have a safe and reliable water supply for the health, well-being, and development of its residents. That we seem to be relearning this lesson again in the 21st century is one of the mysteries of modern life.

Value to ecosystems. Only in the past few decades have people started to explicitly recognize the enormous range of values provided by ecosystems, including their irreplaceable services, their monetary value, and their role in sustaining human and other life on the planet. The services include producing food, decomposing organic waste, purifying water and air, storing and recycling nutrients, preventing floods and regulating run-off, absorbing human and industrial wastes and converting them to beneficial uses, and storing, cycling, and distributing freshwater. In addition to their practical benefits, ecosystems provide amenity and recreational values.

Ecosystems are essential to civilization, and their services operate on a vast scale in little-known ways that cannot be replicated by technology. The practical benefits of ecosystem services have an estimated worth of $36–$58 trillion a year, compared with gross world product of $39 trillion in 1998 (Hawken, Lovins, and Lovins 1999).

Economic value. Water has an economic value in some of its uses because of its contributions to many

1 Assessing Challenges, Initiating Change

Ethics should have a key role in water management, as should recognition of the importance of the unquantifiable values of water. Preserving the life-giving value of water should always be a priority in water allocation

> ' I notice the dreadfulness of water and my gratefulness for it only when floods and shortages come. Yet we have many other opportunities to think about water.
> —Japan '

economic activities. Water enables agriculture, fishing, navigation, and hydropower generation, and it is an input for many industries. Water also receives and carries away waste. It is possible to estimate the economic value of water for all these uses, and also to determine the price that people, industries, and governments are ready to pay for these services. Furthermore, because businesses value healthy workers and healthy customers, water's contribution to health has an additional value to industry. Businesses also values freedom from environment-related threats and are reluctant to invest where such threats—many allied to widespread water-related diseases—are prevalent.

Essential values are missing. Missing from this partial catalogue of water's values are the human values of justice and equity. Crucially, access to adequate and safe water supplies by the disadvantaged and frequently undeerrepresented – the poor (among whom the burden falls disproportionately on women, children and the elderly) and natural ecosystems – is still far from equitable and just. While attitudes toward these values are changing, they are still not adequately reflected in the way the water community and water institutions work. These attitudes are not changing fast enough to preserve the social order and ecosystems in the future.

What needs to be done?

Ethics should have a key role in water management, as should recognition of the importance of the unquantifiable values of water. Preserving the life-giving value of water should always be a priority in water allocation. Only when these values are incorporated into our thinking about water and water management will our institutions function to provide fairly for all water needs and enable economic values to be used more productively to help rationalize the use of water.

What is being done?

Efforts are under way to better understand the full range of water values and translate them into practice. Research projects by the International Institute for Infrastructural, Hydraulic, and Environmental Engineering in Delft seek to clarify the understanding of these concepts (action 2481), while the Water Academy's Social Charter for Water is working on their practical application (action 2362).

Life-giving value

Water is increasingly recognized as a human right. The United Nations Committee on Economic, Cultural, and Social Rights declared access to water a human right and established it as a social and cultural good, not merely an economic commodity (UN CESCR 2002). The World Health Organization published in 2003 a book on this issue (WHO 2003). Drinking water is a vital resource for human beings, and inadequate quantities of water or unsafe water can gravely impair health (chapter 9). South Africa, which inscribed the basic right to water in its Constitution, is working to put this principle into practice (box 6.1 in chapter 6).

Water's many values

> **I still remember the sound of the streaming brook and the smell of grasses. . . . Now a paved road covers the brook, and many cars run over it.**
> —Jamaica

Water plays a role in reaching most of the other Millennium Development Goals

Value to ecosystems

Attempts to quantify the value of aquatic ecosystems services can be spotted in Haiti (action 2064), in Japan (action 1841), and in Costa Rica (action 1810). These few examples cannot readily be replicated widely, because these efforts are time-consuming and should be undertaken only when necessary to improve decision-making. But it is important to point out that the knowledge exists, particularly within international organizations, such as IUCN–The World Conservation Union, that can guide such calculations where and when needed (Barbier, Acreman, Knowler 1997). Universities and research institutes are working to improve these methodologies, as in the United States (action 2477) and the Netherlands (Seyam and others 2001).

Social value

Water is rising higher on the international political agenda. Once viewed largely as a technical sector, it now gets greater recognition as central to poverty alleviation and sustainable development. One of the Millennium Development Goals is to halve the proportion of people without reliable access to drinking water by 2015. But as shown throughout this report, water plays a role in reaching most of the other Millennium Development Goals as well.

The 2001 Bonn International Conference on Freshwater contributed to global awareness that water is essential for human development and for sustaining ecosystems (Ministerial Session of the International Conference on Freshwater 2001). The conference also underscored problems of corruption and identified measures that governments, financial institutions, and other organizations can take to eliminate it.

The recent World Summit on Sustainable Development identified water and sanitation, energy, health, agriculture, and biodiversity (together referred to as WEHAB) as integral to a coherent approach to sustainable development and affirmed that water is essential to all of these. The World Summit approved a supplementary target for the Millennium Development Goals: to halve by 2015 the proportion of people without access to sanitation facilities.

All of this emphasizes strongly how central water security is to social cohesion and move out of poverty.

Economic value

It is widely accepted that water has an economic value. The 1992 Dublin International Conference on Water and the Environment established the four "Dublin Principles" for sound water management. Among them was that water should be treated as an economic good. This principle and the concept of water's economic value is a very contentious issue. Many people in lower-income countries view water as a gift from God and can see no reason to pay for it. On the other hand, it is increasingly recognized that water delivery systems are unsustainable without pricing the water supplied – but also that not everybody can afford to pay for it. The debate on what are the economic values of water and how to apply them to facilitate better water management is continuing, and different countries and communities still hold a wide range of different views on the subject. All of this complicates the challenge of financing the much needed expansion of the water sector, a topic which is dealt with in more details in chapter 6.

1 Assessing Challenges, Initiating Change

Water management is an issue of politics and human relationships, and as such may have to reconcile conflicting values

> Water and air are the blessings of God to the planet for all of humanity. Let us make them pure and clean and see that they are easily available to all.
> —Pakistan

What remains to be done?

Water management is an issue of politics and human relationships, and as such may have to reconcile conflicting values. But there is a basic set of principles that, if applied, can improve the way we live with water:

1. Water is essential for all life—for human beings and for ecosystems.
2. Access to water is a human right.
3. Cooperation and dialogue on water issues yield the greatest benefits in the long run.
4. Solidarity should be fostered between rich and poor and between upstream and downstream users of water.
5. Transparency is essential when dealing with issues as sensitive as those integral to water.
6. Providing water to all in a sustainable way has a cost, which should be recovered from all those who benefit: direct users, indirect users, and society at large.

Education is essential for promoting these principles. That includes awareness raising among policymakers and decision-makers. And because appreciation of the value of water grows over a lifetime, formal and informal education is needed to accelerate the process. Water and its values should become part of the curriculum for primary and secondary education. The impact of formal education is enhanced if the family and wider social institutions reinforce the lessons with good practice, good example, and good incentives.

Much research has been done on the many values of water, and efforts are under way to link the values and to provide decision-makers with the background, understanding, and tools needed to make informed and justified decisions based on an appreciation of the whole range of water's values. Now the values need to be put into practice. That becomes easier if the commitment of policymakers to incorporate the whole spectrum of values in their decision-making is formalized by the institutional requirement to do so. And that can happen by making the analysis of the whole water value spectrum an integral part of already obligatory environmental impact assessments.

2. Water management

Competition for freshwater resources is increasing because of increased demand, a greater variety of uses and users, and depletion of some resources and loss of others because of pollution. However, the view expressed in *World Water Vision: Making Water Everybody's Business* (Cosgrove and Rijsberman 2000) is that all uses could be served in the future, without depleting the Earth's natural capital, if everybody committed to improving water management.

Politicians and decision-makers must be the ones to initiate change. This should start with a management environment that enables the emergence of new tools, institutions, and capacities. Many countries have already started to adjust their approaches to water, introducing decentralization and participation and empowering communities and user groups. Water management requires clear definitions of water ownership and use and of responsibilities regarding water pollution. It requires transparent and participatory decision-making on investments, cost recovery, and service delivery. Above all it requires effective accountability and enforcement mechanisms that give voice and choice to users and societies.

More and more countries are reforming their water management. However, financial issues often remain unresolved, approaches remain sectoral, and investment is often inadequate. The challenge of improving water management is especially daunting in countries with weak institutions and endemic corruption. Countries that lack a good educational system are also severely disadvantaged. In all countries reform will take time and so needs to begin now. Dialogue, debate, and exchange of experience at all levels will help to steer the process in the right direction and to keep it going.

Present situation

In many countries water management systems have changed little in recent decades despite enormous population growth and increasing awareness of ecosystem deterioration. Water management problems include:

- A lack of national strategies for water development.
- Fragmented management of water-using activities.
- Overly centralized management.
- Limited political and public awareness of water issues.
- Pervasive corruption.
- A severe shortage of capacity to manage water resources and provide water services.
- Poorly adapted institutions.
- Failure to involve all stakeholders in decision-making and management.
- Failure to appreciate fully the key role of water in poverty alleviation and socio-economic development.

2 Assessing Challenges, Initiating Change

Few countries have water institutions adapted to equitable, efficient water management

> Every one of us should think of ourselves as water managers.
> —India

Insufficient awareness of water's importance

The WEHAB (water supply and sanitation, energy, health, agriculture, and biodiversity) sectors, addressed individually in chapters 7–11 of this report, are central to alleviating poverty and advancing socio-economic development. Given water's importance in these sectors, it follows that sound water management is essential to national planning and budgeting. Yet water rarely figures at this level in developing countries:

- Efforts to analyse the poverty effects of water interventions are often weak, making it hard to make a case for such initiatives.
- Different water subsectors—water supply and sanitation, irrigation, ecosystems—have failed to form the strong alliances needed to make a collective case for water investments.
- Water advocacy skills tend to be limited, and the sector has weak relationships with the ministries and local authorities responsible for planning and setting priorities.

Moreover, national planning and budgeting fail to take into account the potential for water-related diseases and climate-related hazards to undermine poverty alleviation and socio-economic development. Water's potential for improving international cooperation is not appreciated, nor is the enormous and irreplaceable value of ecosystem services. Water's many values are not fully recognized (see chapter 1).

Outdated institutions and approaches

Few countries have water institutions adapted to equitable, efficient water management. Most institutions are rooted in an outdated culture of centralized, supply-driven management and service delivery, with fragmented, subsector approaches to management. Few water managers view water holistically, as central to development. And scientists and engineers rarely have the skills needed to work with communities.

Daunting financial challenges

Low water prices and limited cost recovery compromise the efficient operation and maintenance of all kinds of water systems. Low prices also encourage misallocation and waste. Water investments are generally perceived as offering low returns over long periods, and insufficient financing leads to poor maintenance and decaying infrastructure (see chapter 6).

Inadequate knowledge and data

The lack of information and data on sound water management is a serious problem, and is exacerbated by falling investments in national water management systems. Knowledge about groundwater is especially inadequate. Many water managers seem unaware of growing expertise to credibly forecast the effects of climate changes on water resources. There is also extensive experience with solving water problems in developing countries—information that is not being adequately shared worldwide.

Water management | 2

Governments everywhere must acknowledge the central role that water plays in alleviating poverty and advancing socio-economic development

Old problems—still without solutions

The challenges of water management and financing apply to all water subsectors and are dealt with in part 1 of this report. Part 2 focuses on operational issues for each subsector. Some of these operational issues are worrisome because they crop up in all subsectors and remain unsolved—yet have existed for decades. Among the most pressing of these, discussed later in this chapter, are poor management of infrastructure, low water use efficiency, and water pollution. Awareness of these problems should increase, and water institutions should be encouraged to resolve them.

Recent lessons about water reform

All of the foregoing points to an urgent need for widespread reforms of water management. Fortunately, much has been learned about water reform in recent years:

- It is typically a second- or third-generation reform, often following power sector reform and frequently coinciding with political and economic liberalization. Reforms in other sectors often provide momentum for water reform.
- Reforms should be driven by reform-minded politicians, community and political pressures, or both—not by idealized notions of how water should be managed.
- Politicians and civil servants should be given assistance to understand the importance of reform, with timely advice and access to best international practices.
- Advising and investing in reform-minded countries encourages other countries to follow suit.
- The reforming country must set the agenda for reform.

What needs to be done?

Governments everywhere must acknowledge the central role that water plays in alleviating poverty and advancing socio-economic development. They must also recognize the need for integrated water resources management, which promotes coordinated, sustainable development and management of water, land, and related resources to maximize equitable economic and social development. Integrated water resources management has to be applied through a complete rethinking of water management institutions—putting people at the centre.

The Plan of Implementation developed at the 2002 World Summit on Sustainable Development proposes that integrated water resources management and water efficiency plans be developed by 2005, with support for developing countries provided through actions at all levels (United Nations 2002). In addition, countries should exploit the potential that water provides for improving cooperation and relations between riparian countries—especially through collaboration on water management and infrastructure development.

2 Assessing Challenges, Initiating Change

Sound water management should be integrated in national planning and budgeting

Integrating water management with national planning and budgeting

Sound water management should be integrated in national planning and budgeting. Water management must recognize the potential threats and opportunities that changes in climate present to communities and water resources (see chapter 5), focus investments on infrastructure designed to alleviate poverty and accelerate socio-economic development, and pursue measures that provide for the water needs of communities, agriculture, and industry as well as for the long-term protection of ecosystems.

Reforming water institutions

Fragmented, subsector approaches to water management need to change to integrated efforts—based on widespread international agreement—that:

- Develop effective water policies and action programmes in every country.
- Create a mechanism in every country—such as a national water council—to oversee water reform and coordination and to encourage the creation of river basin and other decentralized organizations.
- Put people at the centre by switching to demand-responsive approaches, harnessing the potential of communities, involving users—including women—in planning and operation, and developing their resilience.
- Improve the delivery of water services by opening the sector to a wide range of service providers—large and small, public and private—and ensuring that they are autonomous, well-regulated, and accountable.
- Establish frameworks for efficient, equitable, sustainable water use and conservation by promoting participatory, ecosystem-based management.
- Establish frameworks for the mutually beneficial uses of shared water resources. Though national and transboundary water resources pose different challenges, many of their water management needs are the same.
- Improve management structures and institutions through learning and capacity building, accompanied by systematic evaluations.

These efforts should be guided by the following principles:

- Accountability—in water management, conservation, and service delivery.
- Participation by all stakeholders—whether public or private, communities or non-governmental organizations (NGOs), with special attention to the problems of women and poor people.
- Predictability—all laws and regulations should be applied fairly and consistently.
- Financial sustainability—through recovery of both operational and capital costs.
- Transparency—clear policies, rules, regulations, and decisions, with information available to the public.
- Decentralization and subsidiarity—delegation of responsibility and authority for water management to the lowest feasible level.

Water management

Land and water resources should be managed at the basin level to maximize and share water benefits

Strengthening basin and groundwater management

Decentralization involves managing surface waters at the catchment level with the involvement of all stakeholders. Land and water resources should be managed at the basin level to maximize and share water benefits.

Groundwater. Groundwater aquifers represent a huge water resource. For example, the total volume of groundwater is much greater than the water that flows through the world's rivers in a year. But not all groundwater is renewable, and some can be renewed only over long periods.

Because a layer of soil and rock protects it from direct human impacts, a lot of groundwater is of high quality and suitable for drinking. But more and more aquifers—mainly shallow ones, which are the most accessible and so the most used—are too polluted for safe use. And in some areas overexploitation of groundwater has led to soil subsidence—that is, lowering of the soil surface. Even if all negative impacts were stopped, it could take hundreds of years for the aquifers to recover.

Some desert areas may have huge volumes of unused water under the ground. In addition, some brackish groundwater may be usable for agriculture or suitable for desalination at lower costs than seawater. Moreover, deep groundwater can provide geothermal energy. Thus groundwater is an enormous potential resource for development—but also a very fragile one that requires special care to preserve.

Assessing the quantity and quality of groundwater is a complex, costly exercise beyond the capacity of some countries. As a result accurate knowledge of groundwater is lacking in many parts of the world. There is also a serious lack of aquifer management expertise.

Integrated surface and groundwater management. Groundwater and surface water should be managed in an integrated way. This means taking into account both their physical links—when one flows into the other—and the full range of water resources available through planning. This may pose a problem for geographical planning. The surface catchment will generally not correspond to the aquifer recharge area. The river basin should be the basis for planning because it is recognized by most users and because surface water has more uses—sometimes conflicting—than groundwater.

Users feel less involved with groundwater. Because it is generally invisible, a collective sense of responsibility for it is lacking. It is difficult to create local, decentralized management bodies for groundwater because few people are aware that they use the same groundwater body. Thus it is recommended that groundwater management be the responsibility of high-level authorities such as governments and water agencies. They should ensure that groundwater issues are tackled in river basin planning and, if needed, organize cooperation on groundwater management among organizations at lower levels.

2 Assessing Challenges, Initiating Change

A wide range of options for service delivery is available in the water subsectors

> It will be much cheaper for them to buy my water rights than to construct a dam. And what's more, it will not destroy nature.
> —Japan

Expanding training and capacity building

Training of water professionals should be reoriented towards holistic water management and promotion of partnerships in management, including working with communities. In addition, university research should address the technical and socio-economic challenges of water management in developing countries.

Developing countries have acquired valuable skills and experience with water management. For example, associations of water professionals offer enormous knowledge and know-how. These resources need to be shared more extensively across developing countries, to build up best practices for all aspects of water management.

Addressing international issues

The two main types of international cooperation on water management are donor and agency activities in developing countries and collaboration among these countries. There is a strong need for countries that share a river basin or groundwater system to tackle integrated water resource management at that level (see chapter 3).

Although donors and various agencies have done some excellent work on water in developing countries, some of their activities have been criticized. Most donor activities are poorly coordinated. Moreover, donors often focus more on their own priorities than those of recipient countries. Finally, some countries have become too dependent on large donor contributions to water supply and sanitation.

This all points to a need for donors to:

- Help ensure that water issues are fully represented in planning processes in developing countries.
- Continue to fund essential water projects but improve coordination, both with one another and with national and local planning priorities.
- Facilitate exchanges between water professionals in developing countries and help improve the poverty analysis, collaboration, and advocacy skills of water workers in these countries.
- Seek to reduce, where possible, any over-reliance on donor contributions, and enhance self-reliance.

Using a variety of options to deliver water services

Water services concern a variety of subsectors, mainly agriculture (for irrigation and drainage) and households and industry (for water supply and sanitation). Different challenges and concerns for these services and subsectors are addressed in various chapters of this report. A full range of options is available, and the best one depends on local conditions.

A wide range of options for service delivery is available in the water subsectors. One of the challenges facing water users in the lower-income countries is to choose the most appropriate option for their particular local circumstances. More work needs to be done by the international community to improve the quality of this guidance, by suitable decision-support systems or other appropriate means.

The delivery of water services need not be a natural monopoly. Competition is increasingly possible, whether among small independent providers, by benchmarking and regulating utilities, or by fostering an environment that enables NGOs and communities to provide services. This requires decentralizing service provision (giving power and resources to local authorities), establishing appropriate regulation, and building

Water management

Many water problems could be prevented by rehabilitating and properly maintaining existing infrastructure

the capacity of communities and small independent providers.

The concepts of private sector involvement and public–private partnerships often create significant misunderstandings. The wider range of non-governmental initiatives (including local, community-based entrepreneurship) is often ignored because of a preoccupation with large-scale corporate interventions. But to increase efficiency, the number and competence of public and private service providers of all sizes should be greatly increased.

There is no best model for providing water services, and debates on whether to use public or private providers miss the point. The goal is achieving the most efficient, effective operation based on the local situation. Most water utilities are still public, and there are good and bad ones—just as there are good and bad private companies. But introducing efficient private companies may raise service standards, influencing other providers. Moreover, applying the same benchmarks and regulations to public and private providers helps counter the inefficiency inherent in the monopoly nature of water services (as in agricultural and urban systems) and encourages the adoption of good practices. Regulators must be strong, independent, and well-funded.

Transparency and accountability in water management institutions help eliminate corruption, but they are not enough. Governments must also enact and enforce anticorruption laws, monitor public and private organizations, and develop codes of conduct to ensure probity. Financial organizations must play a full part in efforts to combat corruption.

Developing, managing, and maintaining infrastructure

The chapters on water supply and sanitation (chapter 7), energy (chapter 8), and agriculture (chapter 10) all point to a serious shortage of large-scale water infrastructure—networks of pipes, dams for storage, systems for irrigation, and plants for water treatment—as well as small-scale infrastructure such as individual sanitation systems and household rainwater harvesting equipment.

Many water problems could be prevented by rehabilitating and properly maintaining existing infrastructure. Recent reforms of water utilities prove this point. Thus all service providers must rehabilitate run-down systems and perform systematic maintenance, following approved standards. Monitoring such maintenance will be an important task for regulators. Some existing infrastructure is inappropriate, however, because its benefits are too small relative to the environmental and social damage it causes (see chapter 11).

In all water subsectors inappropriate management and maintenance of infrastructure cause infrastructure losses; waste money, water, and energy; and increase pollution and threats to human health and security. Effective infrastructure requires training operational staff, clearly defining responsibilities, and devoting sufficient financial resources to proper management. Such efforts often go unnoticed because they are considered routine or "business as usual"—but they are tremendously important. Good infrastructure management could save much of the financing needed to achieve the Millennium Development Goals (see chapter 6).

Emphasis should be given to low-cost solutions (such as rainwater harvesting and eco-sanitation) and new technologies (see also chapters 7, 8, and 10). Desalination is becoming cheaper as new technology emerges and energy costs fall. Once-unusable brackish water can now be purified, and seawater treatment for coastal communities and effluent treatment and reuse are becoming more cost-effective.

2 Assessing Challenges, Initiating Change

Joint planning and development of water supplies for agricultural, municipal, and industrial applications help achieve the most efficient water use and allow for the best possible reuse

Increasing water use efficiency

Delivery systems for agricultural, industrial, and municipal water are often extremely inefficient, with large losses and waste. Irrigation, which uses 70–80 percent of the world's freshwater, is the biggest culprit. Thus even small savings there can free up large amounts of water for use elsewhere. Municipal distribution systems also waste a lot of water: losses of 50 percent or more are common. In addition, huge amounts of electricity are used to pump water for irrigation and municipal water supplies—much of which is then wasted.

Different water users can accommodate water of different quality. The highest-quality water must be reserved for human consumption; industry and agriculture sometimes can get by using lower-quality water, if appropriate. With safeguards, treated effluents from municipalities can be used by both industry and agriculture. In addition, some industrial effluents, subject to adequate treatments and controls, can be used by agriculture. Systematic wastewater treatment and reuse will likely become an essential element of water strategies in many areas. Joint planning and development of water supplies for agricultural, municipal, and industrial applications help achieve the most efficient water use and allow for the best possible reuse.

Jointly optimizing various uses, including through demand management, is an essential first—not last—step in achieving the most efficient water use. New resources should not be developed until existing ones have been optimized.

Tackling water pollution

It is possible to unlink socio-economic development and environmental degradation—but only by tackling water pollution with rules and regulations, economic tools, wastewater treatment, incentives for clean production by industry, and other mechanisms.

Two key points need to be made from the outset. Firstly, nature does not possess an infinite self cleansing capacity. Secondly, large, sophisticated wastewater plants are not the only treatment option. A wide range of alternative wastewater treatment systems, including natural ones, is available and the application of these is growing rapidly. To achieve locally acceptable water quality, the challenge is to balance treatment processes with the capacity of communities or businesses to commission and operate them and with the capacity of the receiving water to absorb the treated effluents. But this approach is achievable, as shown by a growing number of communities and businesses.

Industrial pollution can be addressed with a combination of incentives and penalties. But the first need is to reduce pollution at its source, by applying cleaner technology (see chapter 6 for financial tools and chapter 11 for cleaner production techniques). Governments should do more to encourage the spread of cleaner technology by providing education and incentives and by applying the polluter-pays principle. There is a growing body of expertise in clean production suitable for both large and small companies.

Finding solutions to agricultural pollution is more complex because of the vulnerability of some farmers. Farming is not just a business; for some people it is a complete livelihood. At any rate, neither agricultural nor industrial pollution can be solved without involving the agricultural and industrial sectors that cause it.

Water management 2

Countries have created bodies representing stakeholders to produce national water plans, make proposals for and review new policies and regulations

What is being done?

The Actions Database contains hundreds of actions involving water management and institutional reform. These actions have been categorized as follows: promoting country-level reforms, developing local reforms, raising awareness and building capacity, and advancing international dialogues and assessments.

Promoting country-level reforms

Reforms of national water policies, laws, and regulations involve a wide range of activities (figure 2.1). The creation of apex water bodies includes representative and consultative bodies as well as executive agencies. Water policy initiatives involve both sector and subsector (such as water supply and sanitation) policies. They include both countries and states in large countries (such as Uttar Pradesh in India). Partnerships offer many examples of how countries have created bodies representing stakeholders to produce national water plans, make proposals for and review new policies and regulations, and so on. Establishing a water plan helps change the framework for better water management.

Highlights. Brazil's new National Water Agency (action 389) will develop a wide range of water management expertise given the enormous diversity of the country's hydrogeographical conditions, including transboundary watercourses and states (such as Ceará) that are pioneers in water reform. In Chile water sector reform (action 139) was driven by the government's overall commitment to developing an open, export-oriented economy. Now it is in the latest stage of its numerous reforms, as is Mexico (box 2.1). They are among the many countries (others include Honduras and FYR Macedonia) that are decentralizing water management based on the subsidiarity principle. Jordan's new National Security Council for Water (action 170), chaired by the prime minister, is a response to the country's water stress and location in a region of political unrest. And China has introduced new regulations governing the construction and administration of new water projects, including bidding procedures, contract supervision, and strong anticorruption measures (action 356).

Figure 2.1 Water actions involving country-level reforms

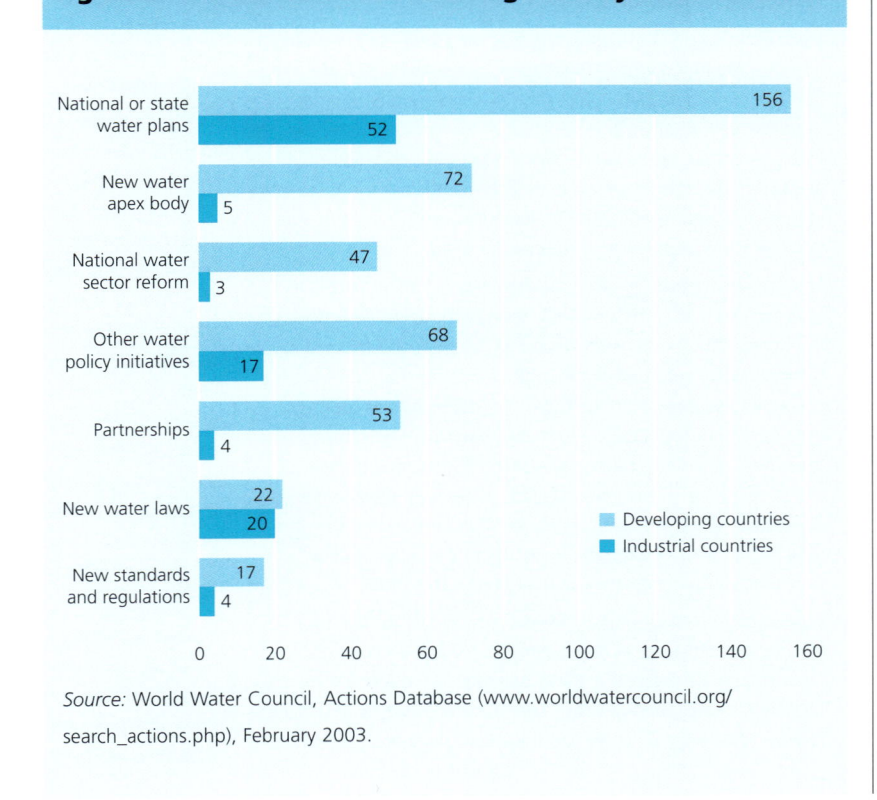

Category	Developing countries	Industrial countries
National or state water plans	156	52
New water apex body	72	5
National water sector reform	47	3
Other water policy initiatives	68	17
Partnerships	53	4
New water laws	22	20
New standards and regulations	17	4

Source: World Water Council, Actions Database (www.worldwatercouncil.org/search_actions.php), February 2003.

2 Assessing Challenges, Initiating Change

> *Inconsistent city planning systems led to flooding. The drainage system was altered, and the water absorption area was reduced, so the water could not be contained.*
> —Indonesia

Box 2.1 Decentralization in Mexico

The first decentralization phase 1989–2000

In 1989 the National Water Commission (CNA) was created in Mexico as a decentralized agency of the Ministry of the Environment and Natural Resources to manage and preserve national waters and establish sustainable water use, with the participation of civil society. Among its main responsibilities are: to update every six years the National Water Plan; to assist state and municipal governments; and to foster the development of water supply and sanitation systems.

In 1992 the National Water Law was enacted. The Law regulates water management, mandates a water rights system sustained on a Public Registry of Water Rights and allows users to sell their rights. The Law set the basis for decentralized water planning and management, for which purpose the country has been divided into 13 regions, each encompassing one or more watersheds. As at June 2003 the regions comprise a total of 26 river basin councils, 7 basin commissions, 5 basin committees, and 48 technical committees for groundwater.

Thereafter, irrigation infrastructure was transferred to 80 irrigation districts, integrated with 443 modules to manage 3,325,855 hectares, to benefit 500,000 users. The users conditioned the reception to the satisfactory situation of the infrastructure, besides their poor organizations since they did not have enough human and economic resources to operate and maintain this infrastructure efficiently; therefore the CNA implemented specific programmes to improve the infrastructure and assist the users.

The municipalities were given responsibility for water supply and sewerage services (1983) without having the means and capacity to address issues such as low efficiency, population unserved in marginal areas and rural communities, or tariffs that do not cover costs. With support from the CNA, 350 municipalities took up their new responsibilities and installed water utilities; some of them have an administration council in which representatives of civil society have a vote. Nevertheless, integrated management of water at local level was not on the agenda of municipalities, especially since they were not in charge of sanitation until a Constitutional amendment corrected this in the 1990s.

Despite important progress made during this first decade of reforms, the efficiency of the water services is still as low as 35 percent, only 27 percent of the wastewater produced in the country is treated, and the coverage of water supply is 88 percent and for sewerage 76 percent. Moreover, while agriculture is the country's main water user (78 percent), irrigation efficiency is only 46 percent.

New actions in response to initial difficulties

In order to empower users' organizations and municipalities in the irrigation districts, and to encourage more efficient use of water, several national policies have been in put in place.

For agriculture, a National Alliance (action 3524) allows the state and federal governments (CNA and the Ministry of Agriculture) and water users to work jointly. The programmes implemented by the CNA—Modernization and Rehabilitation of Irrigation Districts; Parcels Development; Efficient Use of Water and Energy (action 3525), among others—lend support to the national policy.

For municipalities, in 2001 the CNA, together with the Ministry of Finance and the National Bank for Works and Services (Banobras), initiated the Programme for the Modernization of Water Utilities (action 3498) and the Programme for the Devolution of Water Rights (action 3499). The former provides a supplementary source of funding to local authorities in their process of reform, while the latter entitles them as beneficiaries of budgets resulting from water right taxes.

Today the National Water Law is under reform in order to give more autonomy to the CNA. Its regional offices will be transformed into basin organizations, to assist the river basin councils (action 125) maintain their own management systems and capacitate the local authorities in their new role. The overall guidance comes from the government through the *National Water Plan 2000–2006* (action 3500) and the *Hydraulic Sector Vision for Mexico-2025* (action 3501), which set specific targets: reduce water leaks in water supply and irrigation, increase coverage of water supply and sewerage services, and of treated wastewater; modernize and create new irrigated areas, increase the crops production; warrant certainty in the National Water Rights and increase the water public budget. The water policies need different institutional arrangements, deconcentration, decentralization, public–private participation and social participation (action 615). Access to information is provided by a new legislation (action 1675).

The national policies have resulted in a number of successful local initiatives, for example: participative planning at the hydraulic regional level (actions 1671 and 2020); integrated and sustainable water management in watersheds (actions 1756 and 3502); capacity building in the sector (action 2755); and support to public

Water management 2

> *We try to preserve the forests in our river basins to protect our water supply, but the owners of the forests exploit them. We must promote other ways for them to earn an income.* —Argentina

A number of countries have developed regulations for allocating water to different purposes

participation in the projects, especially through the Temporary Employment Programme (action 1228). Furthermore, some local authorities manage federal programmes such as the Efficient Use of Water and Energy, Full Use of Hydro-Infrastructure in Agriculture, and Modernization of Irrigated Areas; operate wells and aqueducts; have in custody riverbeds; and manage shores.

Where do we stand?

The process has not been easy; it has demanded time, planning, legal and institutional reforms, cooperation from local governments, political will, and civil society participation. Locally power relations remain a constraint for the active participation of all categories of stakeholders and principally the poorest ones. However today many federal programmes and activities have been transferred to the local level, and some water utilities (like Monterrey and Tijuana) and irrigation districts have achieved international standards.

Source: Leonor Pintado Cortina, Comisión Nacional del Agua, and World Water Council, Actions Database (www.worldwatercouncil.org/search_actions.php), February 2003.

Partnerships fostered by the Global Water Partnership (several dozen are in the Actions Database) offer new ways to involve stakeholders and improve decision-making. Governments can also initiate such stakeholder involvement. In Colombia, committees set up by ministries to improve coordination within the administration were open to Colombian academics, the private sector and civil society as well as agencies of international cooperation, strengthening considerably the process (action 1813). In Armenia, a Law on Water Users' Association and Unions of Water Users' Association was passed in 2002 (action 1897). Water plans have been especially common in Asia, and their follow-up activities stimulate additional actions.

Regulating water allocations. A number of countries have developed regulations for allocating water to different purposes. Such regulations should be flexible, reflecting the weather, season, and socio-economic situation. India's National Water Policy (action 833) provides some interesting ways of prioritizing water uses. General approaches in these regulations include:

- Increasing allocations for the environment and for poor people, with selective use of pricing mechanisms to facilitate this.

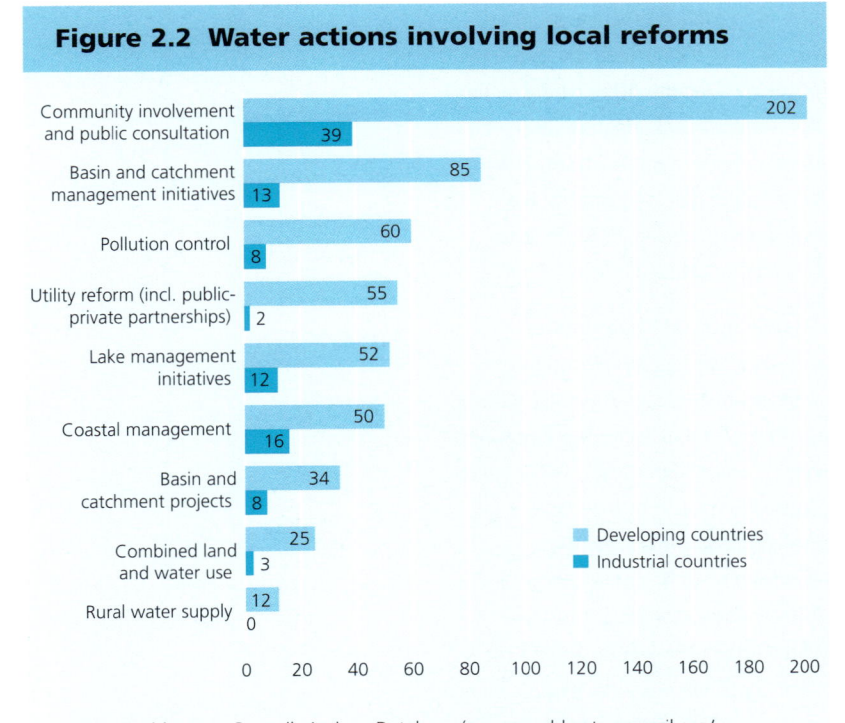

Figure 2.2 Water actions involving local reforms

Category	Developing countries	Industrial countries
Community involvement and public consultation	202	39
Basin and catchment management initiatives	85	13
Pollution control	60	8
Utility reform (incl. public-private partnerships)	55	2
Lake management initiatives	52	12
Coastal management	50	16
Basin and catchment projects	34	8
Combined land and water use	25	3
Rural water supply	12	0

Source: World Water Council, Actions Database (www.worldwatercouncil.org/search_actions.php), February 2003.

2 Assessing Challenges, Initiating Change

Setting up a basin organization is a long process

- Relying in some countries on guidelines rather than on hard and fast rules.
- Implementing pollution control policies, including the polluter-pays principle.
- Giving priority to specific water uses in times of water stress—for example, the diversion of irrigation water to urban water supplies in Jordan (action 1394).

Implementing water markets and allocating water rights and entitlements. Implementing water markets, in which rights are allocated, is a way of allocating water among sectors and uses. Tradable water rights have long existed in some countries. New actions in this area are occurring in Australia (action 595), China (action 384), and Sri Lanka (action 292). In addition, a new approach involves allocating water use rights to the environment (action 1076, in Texas, the United States).

Whether a market-based system ensures a satisfactory allocation of water is uncertain. In Australia trade in water is regulated by the Water and Rivers Commission (action 595), which can refuse deals that may have unacceptable impacts on the environment or on other users; simultaneously the Pilot Interstate Water Trading Project (action 3138) is a first try to learn and facilitate future permanent interstate trade of water entitlements, thus improving the efficiency of consumptive water use..

Creating an environment for better water services. The actions recorded to create an environment for better water services all concern the water supply and sanitation sector and are discussed in chapter 7.

Regional water management. Regional economic groups are proposing water policies at the regional level (see chapter 4). The European Union's Water Framework Directive (action 1169) provides the most comprehensive regional water legislation, to be translated into national laws by 2004. The Southern African Development Community is also tackling water issues at the regional level (actions 320, 792, 1861). The New Partnership for Africa's Development has pledged to accelerate water resources projects (action 423).

Developing local reforms and basin and aquifer management

Local institutional and project reforms range from creating river basin and lake management organizations to reorienting water supply and sanitation services (see chapter 7) to developing community awareness and public consultation projects (figure 2.2). Pollution control initiatives have also been observed, as have programmes dealing with links between coastal zones and freshwater systems.

Creating river basin organizations and promoting basin-level management. Since 2000, more countries have added the principle of managing water at the basin level to their water legislation, mainly in Africa, Asia, and Eastern Europe. Though this principle is widely accepted, it is not a priority in all countries. New basin organizations have been created in more than 25 countries, often as pilot organizations. Most basin committees have been created by governments within institutional frameworks, but there are a few examples of local, multistakeholder approaches. Brazil has used both approaches: water agencies are being created to support basin-level municipal organizations (actions 866, 1712).

Setting up a basin organization is a long process (action 955 on Paranaiba Basin, Brazil), particularly if it involves getting all stakeholders to talk to each

Water management

> With no land development projects planned, water is a major problem in our country.
> —Iran

Financing mechanisms are being implemented to share upstream-downstream costs and benefits

other. The presence of a neutral body willing to invest time and energy is an important factor in this process (action 389 on Brazil's National Water Agency, action 1963 on the role of a basin agency in France). This process is even more complicated at the transboundary level (see chapter 3).

Many river basin organizations are still searching for financing. Experience in France shows that basin agencies do well as legislative bodies and in agreeing on long-term management objectives, but that other systems have to be found to finance and execute plans and projects (usually local authorities take that role). There is little evidence in the Actions Database on how basin organizations have moved from consultation to action. Still, financing mechanisms are being implemented to share upstream-downstream costs and benefits (action 1810 in Costa Rica, action 1841 in Japan, action 1941 in the Republic of Korea).

Planning water management. Most of the multipurpose water management plans in the Actions Database have been developed at the basin level. These plans range from small watersheds to international rivers, including lake basin management. Approaches vary in their levels of stakeholder participation and in their responses to the challenge of integrated water resource management.

Australia's Murray-Darling Basin Initiative (action 460) is one of the world's largest, most sophisticated integrated catchment programmes. But community-based approaches to small watershed management have also proven successful (action 3026 in Rio Bolo Watershed, Colombia) — and have even been scaled up in India (action 1525). For large river basins, actions tend to focus on defining general objectives and guidelines for action. At all levels, investments in collecting data, raising awareness, and building confidence are important (action 1845, management of Peru's Moquegua-Osmore river basin).

Detailed knowledge of a river basin is a prerequisite for efficient management. Many actions to improve such knowledge are under way, though only those involving the largest basins are included in the Actions Database (such as action 53, on the Oka Basin Water Management Unit in Russia). In Belgium basin knowledge was improved and participation stimulated by letting inhabitants of a basin collect needed data in catchments (action 635).

Various initiatives are developing methodologies and tools for river basin planning. A working group is addressing this issue in the

Table 2.1 Water actions that aim to share water among potentially conflicting uses

Uses	Number of actions
Ecosystems and agriculture	46
Agriculture and drinking water production	35
Ecosystems and drinking water production	21
Ecosystems and energy production	15
Social functions and energy production	10
Agriculture and recreation	9
Ecosystems and multifunctional dams	7
Ecosystems and recreation	5
Agriculture and energy production	5
Cultural functions and multifunctional dams	3

Note: Social functions include the provision of local livelihoods. Economic production refers to mining, industry, and the like. These data do not indicate how many win-win situations have ultimately been achieved.

Source: World Water Council, Actions Database (www.worldwatercouncil.org/search_actions.php), February 2003.

2 Assessing Challenges, Initiating Change

> *Efforts are being made to find more environmentally friendly and socially acceptable small-scale solutions or to better use existing infrastructure*

implementation process of the EU Water Framework Directive (action 1169). Decision support systems are being developed for many catchments, enabling the simulation of different water management measures on a particular river basin, aquifer, or lake (action 1323, in Guanabara Bay, Brazil).

Developing and managing large-scale water infrastructure. Many countries are involved in large water development projects for irrigation, hydropower, or interbasin transfers. Examples include Algeria (Taksebt Dam, action 972), China (Yellow River and North-South Water Diversion Projects, actions 361 and 382), Egypt (El-Salam Canal, action 189), Morocco (Oujda Water Supply, action 1200), Lesotho (Lesotho Highlands Water Project, action 315), Spain (National Hydrological Plan, action 34), and Syria (Damascus Water Supply, action 838). Chapter 8, Water for Energy, presents a comprehensive view on infrastructure issues, including the work of the World Commission on Dams (action 73) and the Dams and Development Project (action 826).

Large infrastructure projects are intended to allocate water in accordance with perceived overall national benefits. But local resistance to these projects is increasing, organized and supported by local and international NGOs. Because of this vocal resistance, regional development banks have become cautious about lending money to such projects.

A movement is under way to have water rights reconsidered to give communities more entitlement to use water in all its values (action 1532, Right to Water Initiative). In addition, environmental impact assessments are being used more widely to mitigate the negative impacts of large infrastructure. Other actions have tried to mitigate the negative impacts of existing infrastructure, especially by restoring environmental flows (see chapter 11). Mediation between parties has also been attempted by NGOs (action 133 on Yacyreta Dam in Argentina, action 1622 on Ewaso Floodplains in Kenya).

Still, it is difficult to reach mutually acceptable solutions (see efforts around Bujagali Dam in Uganda, action 289). Efforts are being made to find more environmentally friendly and socially acceptable small-scale solutions or to better use existing infrastructure (actions 1525 in India and 1815 in Japan on community-based watershed management, including construction of small dams; action 1554 in Nepal on small hydropower; and action 1839 in Japan on efficient use of existing infrastructure). Such approaches may be preferable when all costs and benefits are taken into account, including discounting of future ones. Equally important are ongoing dialogue, education, and awareness among proponents and opponents of large projects so that everyone has an objective understanding of their benefits and drawbacks.

Sharing water among various uses. Different uses of water may be in conflict, and the challenge is to preserve different functions in acceptable ways.

An example is when agriculture conflicts with ecosystem functioning or flood protection. For instance, deforestation and poor tillage practices in mountain watersheds lead to soil erosion, ecosystem destruction, and higher flood risk. But it is possible to develop sustainable agriculture on such catchments, allowing agricultural protection to be combined with ecosystem conservation and flood risk reduction. Examples include watershed restoration programmes in South and Central America (actions 124, 1833, 2124), Asia (actions 491, 3154), and France (action 2451).

Some actions have tried to share water between seemingly conflicting uses (table 2.1). Most are designed to restore ecosystem functioning, and many are aimed at reconciling agriculture and the environment. Some try to reconcile more than two functions. For instance, the International Water Management Institute's research programme RIPARWIN (action 1366) seeks to

Water management   2

Considerable efforts are being made to put people at the centre when it comes to water issues

develop ways to combine irrigation water systems with provision of water for energy, ecosystems, drinking, and recreation.

Improving aquifer management. Awareness of the need to manage groundwater sustainably has arisen later than for surface water, though user associations for irrigation were founded many years ago in some countries (Mexico, Spain). Some new river basin organizations include groundwater management, with the aim of integrated water resources management. But this approach might not be appropriate if several river basins are located over the same aquifer. The Indus Delta Water Partnership in Pakistan (action 276) includes a specific objective to manage shallow groundwater quantity and quality. The Beauce aquifer in France (action 1966) is one of the few examples of shared groundwater management.

Pursuing integrated water management in urban areas. The concept of integrated water resources management in urban areas (sometimes called integrated urban water management) is gaining ground. Several water actions combine such activities as water demand management, water recycling, household and industrial wastewater management, restoration or creation of natural areas, improvement of living standards, and urban rainwater and stormwater management (action 734 in Australia, action 1663 in France, action 1937 in the Republic of Korea, action 2151 in the Netherlands).

Promoting decentralization and participation. Around the world, considerable efforts are being made to put people at the centre when it comes to water issues—especially in water supply and sanitation, ecosystem management, and basin management. Many water actions try to decentralize water management and increase user participation. They combine action at the national level (regulatory and institutional changes) with training and empowerment of local communities. In India the Maharashtra government is ceding control of irrigation management to the state's farmers (action 235)—a first for water user associations in India. In Angola, Botswana, and Namibia the Okavango river basin project is increasing riparian communities' participation in basin planning and management (action 316). In Peru a National

Figure 2.3 Water actions involving awareness raising and capacity building

Category	Developing countries	Industrial countries
Studies, research, and assessments	88	20
Campaigns and programmes	61	8
Information systems	46	16
Management aids (incl. capacity building)	44	3
Education	17	4

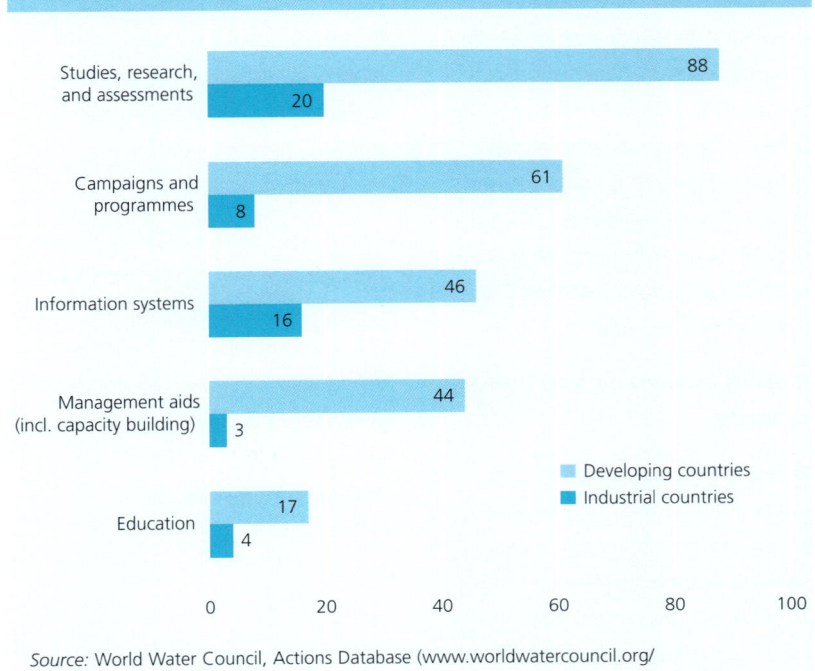

Source: World Water Council, Actions Database (www.worldwatercouncil.org/search_actions.php), February 2003.

2 Assessing Challenges, Initiating Change

A common problem with decentralization is that while the local level is given more duties, it is not given more resources

Project for Rural Water and Sanitation Services validates decentralized and community contracting models, based on an NGO-led pilot project (action 2942).

A common problem with decentralization is that while the local level is given more duties, it is not given more resources. Moreover, participatory approaches have not lived up to their promise. It is not enough for stakeholders to sit at the same table and talk with one another. First, there is a risk that one group of stakeholders will be too powerful or too vocal, undermining the general balance of interests. Second, many stakeholders lack sufficient negotiating capacity to reach agreements and make joint decisions. To improve this capacity, water managers must be trained to be efficient moderators, and all participants must be trained in strategic debating. Knowledge from the social sciences and tools such as decision support systems are available to assist such efforts, but their use needs to be promoted.

Raising awareness and building capacity

Initiating and maintaining momentum on the many needed water reforms will require a wide range of additional activities. This includes campaigns and programmes to raise awareness about reform and the education that must go with them: studies, research, assessments, and information to identify problems and priorities and to efficiently allocate resources to these. It also includes tools and devices to improve water management, including capacity building, institutional strengthening, best practices, and benchmarking.

Many such actions are already under way (figure 2.3). Awareness campaigns and programmes have included big initiatives on household hygiene and environmental protection. Studies, research, and assessments have covered a variety of issues, including groundwater, irrigation, salinity, rainwater harvesting, demand management, biosafety, and sewerage systems. Management aids include capacity building, benchmarking, and management techniques.

Among the many management aids, the Global Water Partnership's Toolbox for integrated water resources management (action 64) and the World Bank's irrigation and drainage benchmarking project (action 441) provide valuable, practical management techniques.

Advancing international dialogues and assessments

Developing countries face not only internal pressures for water reform, but also external pressures from multilateral and bilateral agencies, international NGOs, and other sources. But these external organizations do more than just apply pressure for change. They also provide opportunities to bring people together to exchange experiences and improve understanding of water problems and how to respond to them. Twenty-six actions (21 of them in developing countries) involved dialogue and 19 involved assessments and international reports.

Expanding dialogues. International dialogues on water are an interesting development because they bring together people with different views on the subject, allowing them to share and compare data, intelligence, and ideas, and thereby provide guidance on how to move forward. For example, the Dialogue on Water and Climate (action 71) aims for the water sector to better exploit the expertise of Earth scientists in managing risks (see chapter 5).

The Dialogue on Water, Food, and Environment (action 70) considers how to provide adequate calories and nutrition for everyone. The United Nations Food and Agriculture Organization is confident that future

Water management

Are the reforms moving water to a central role in national planning and priority setting?

food needs can be met, but this apparently will require using an even large share of the world's freshwater for agriculture—which already uses 70–80 percent (see chapter 10). The Dialogue on Effective Governance (action 607) aims to facilitate communications between politicians, other decisionmakers, water managers, and water users and to show that integrated water resources management is practical.

Issuing assessments. Several global assessment initiatives have been launched recently, including the United Nations World Water Assessment Programme (action 61), the Global International Waters Assessment (action 63), and the Millennium Ecosystem Assessment (action 62). The Water Supply and Sanitation Global Assessment (action 88) of the World Health Organization and the United Nations Children's Fund's Joint Monitoring Programme, is an attempt to better understand the share of the world's population still lacking acceptable water and sanitation services. But like many international assessments, it faces questions about the quality and reliability of some of its data. In another attempt linked to the Millennium Development Goals (action 1948), the United Nations has created a task force to recommend plans for implementation of best strategies to achieve these goals (action 2361).

What remains to be done?

Although a great deal of water management reform is under way, these efforts raise some serious questions—and the analysis in this chapter suggests the answers:

- Will the reforms produce the changes needed to accelerate water management improvements in developing countries? It is too early to say. Experiences with organizational change indicate that it takes at least five years—and often longer—for a reorganized entity to become effective.
- Are the reforms moving water to a central role in national planning and priority setting? In some countries, yes. But in others—especially where it may be needed most—probably not.
- Does the know-how generated by international activities filter down to the people in developing countries who really need it? It is hard to know for sure, but there are strong reasons to doubt that it does so effectively enough.
- Is the world making the best use of valuable local experiences with water reforms, in terms of sharing them with countries facing similar challenges? Not as much as it could and should, though there are plenty of success stories showing how things can be done.
- Do developing countries really have the capacity to radically improve their water management? Opinions vary, but in general countries do not have as much capacity as they should.
- Are donor activities in developing countries appropriate to country needs and priorities? Not really, though good work is being done.

So, although reform is occurring, there is no assurance that there is enough of it or that it is timely or effective enough to meet priority needs—including the Millennium Development Goals. Thus more needs to be done, and more quickly. Donor activities need to be more focused, better coordinated, and geared entirely to the priority needs of recipient countries. Moreover, capacity shortfalls need to be addressed by a coordinated and radically expanded donor programme that:

- Provides rapid, comprehensive, coordinated briefings on water's central role in development for key people and organizations involved in national planning and priority setting.

2 Assessing Challenges, Initiating Change

The international community needs to work with centres of excellence in developing countries

- Helps developing countries conduct poverty analysis in water supply and sanitation and in water for agriculture, livelihoods, and ecosystems.
- Helps design water strategies and plans, set in the framework of the overall planning process and incorporating gender mainstreaming. The plans should incorporate the latest predictions of how climate hazards could affect water resources.
- Builds capacity for the two priority objectives above and for the longer-term needs of water management in these countries.
- Assists with needed financing and fundraising.
- Facilitates the exchange of sound experiences and good practices in developing countries on reform, national planning that incorporates all water subsectors, and community empowerment and involvement.

A comparable programme is required for transboundary waters (see chapter 3).

Given these considerable demands, thought should be given to setting priorities and clustering donor activities. Efforts should focus on countries where poverty and water-related diseases and hazards are particularly bad, but where the potential for improvement looks promising. In addition, donors should seek situations where reasonably rapid poverty alleviation and socio-economic development could be achieved with increased assistance. Finally, rather than focusing on single countries when developing capacity, donors should try to work with groups of professionals from different countries—though ideally with similar social, economic, and cultural backgrounds—and to create networks through which they can share their experiences.

Extensive retraining is required for water professionals to convey new approaches to water and development, holistic water management, financial management, regulation, operation and maintenance, and working with communities. Much training is also required to help local governments improve their water management and increase community involvement. Efforts to promote gender mainstreaming also still have a long way to go.

The international community needs to work with centres of excellence in developing countries, helping them identify best practices, appropriate benchmarks, and expanded training programmes—and then disseminating these widely. Some countries have experience and training materials that they have used to strengthen the capacity of their water personnel. This type of solid, practical expertise should be compiled and applied elsewhere.

Finally, successful community empowerment projects for the water sector should be widely publicized and programmes developed to help national and local governments implement best practices based on these experiences.

3. Transboundary basins

Almost half the world is situated in transboundary river basins. From time to time actions in a broader interest require cooperation from the countries sharing those basins. Typical examples are the development of navigation on a river or the protection of downstream ecosystems from upstream pollution. But cooperation is not always easy to obtain, because the benefits may not accrue equitably to the riparian countries involved or may not even be evident.

Land and water resources of transboundary river basins should be managed in an integrated way at the catchment level, just as is the case for national rivers. This means making the most of social, economic, and environmental benefits related to the water, and sharing the benefits equitably among all parties. This requires establishing institutions—agreements, laws, organized procedures, and joint commissions and administrations. And it requires the cooperation of national organizations and administrative bodies that usually do not even talk to one another.

New cooperation arrangements for transboundary water systems are emerging, thanks largely to the broker role played by international organizations. The trend is to reduce the risk for conflicts and improve the capacity to reach shared solutions through training and better access to negotiation methods. Ecosystem protection and risk management are new drivers for transboundary cooperation. There is a clear move from a mono-sectoral approach towards a more multi-purpose one. Non-state actors are also gradually becoming more involved.

But actions on transboundary water systems are still far from integrated water resources management. And integrated water resources management should be viewed as only one element of broader cooperation in regions that are connected by water systems.

Present situation

Managing water systems that cross national boundaries poses a unique challenge. Many of the managerial and institutional concepts developed in chapter 2 apply to such transboundary rivers, lakes, and aquifers—with one crucial distinction. Waters contained entirely within one country are subject only to that country's administrations. But transboundary waters are subject to the politics, cultures, stages of development, and development goals of various riparian countries, and there is no recognized international authority or judicial system for reconciling any differences (box 3.1).

World Water Vision (Cosgrove and Rijsberman 2000), presented at the Second World Water Forum in 2000, calls for increased cooperation in transboundary river basins, noting that almost half the world is situated in nearly 300 such basins. Like this chapter, the Vision recognizes that shared waters offer more potential for cooperation than for conflict. For cooperation to flourish, the Vision argues that efforts are needed to:

- Build confidence between countries that share rivers, gradually leading to the time when countries are willing to work together and allocate resources to solve collective problems.

3 Assessing Challenges, Initiating Change

Shared waters offer more potential for cooperation than for conflict

> "Countries that share rivers or water resources need to work in close coordination and cooperation."
> —Nepal

- Develop international treaties, laws, and dispute resolution mechanisms, all of which usually require long negotiations.
- Encourage voluntary limits on national sovereignty, to allow the principles of integrated water resources management to be applied to transboundary waters.

Potential for cooperation, not conflict

There is now general agreement that shared waters offer more potential for cooperation than for conflict. This finding has been confirmed by an examination of the history of water-related treaties (Beach and others 2000). On many rivers the needs of economic development have traditionally led to some form of cooperation. Still, while conflicts are generally unlikely, disputes can arise over water quantities and infrastructure. An important finding is that establishing transboundary water institutions helps minimize such conflicts—even when riparian states are engaged in armed conflict (UNESCO IHP and Green Cross International 2003). But the big issue remains that, absent direct benefits, governments are not sufficiently aware of the need for solidarity inside transboundary basins or of the regional benefits from cooperation.

Box 3.1 Definitions

The words *international*, *transboundary*, and *shared* are often used to describe water systems located in more than one country.

A *transboundary water system* crosses at least one boundary—whether defined by land or water. In this chapter specifically, "transboundary water system" designates a water system that crosses national boundaries and that provides resources to more than one nation or country.

An *international water system* traverses more than one country. Meanwhile, *international waters* is sometimes understood to mean waters available for use by all nations. Some countries are reluctant to use *international waters*, fearing that such a designation could encourage interference by the international community.

In this chapter *shared water system* is used to mean shared between countries, similar to *transboundary water system*, even though the basic definition of *shared* is much broader—meaning a water system of potential interest to any two or more parties, including non-human parties such as the ecosystem.

A *water system* comprises connected waters such as rivers, lakes, aquifers, or even wetlands. It is not a river basin or groundwater basin, which would also include land. Current transboundary water management generally applies only to the water system itself.

Subsidiarity means that decision and action take place locally, at the lowest level appropriate. In the case of transboundary water management, the subsidiarity principle would require that local authorities in each country cooperate directly with their counterparts on managing the water systems they have in common, as long as involvement from the state authorities is not expressively required.

Inadequate institutions

No comprehensive body of internationally agreed legislation is specific to shared water systems. In addition, there are few well-trained, internationally recognized experts available to help resolve differences. Finally, current water institutions almost exclusively involve national governments and deal little with the principle of subsidiarity in water management.

Some international organizations are involved in water management, but they play a minor role in policy-making and have no official

Transboundary basins 3

> *There is a general lack of expertise when it comes to aquifer management, and even less law on transboundary aquifers than on transboundary rivers*

responsibilities for managing water. They mainly propose new ideas, disseminate knowledge, foster networks, set targets and standards, and monitor development.

Several thousand treaties have been signed for transboundary water systems. The first treaties fixed certain rivers as national boundaries. As commercial navigation developed, treaties were signed to ensure freedom of navigation on shared rivers, such as the treaty on the Rhine in 1815. More recently, treaties have been signed to enable the building of dams, mainly for hydropower and sometimes to allocate quantities of water from the river to the different riparian countries—such as the 1959 treaty allocating Nile water between Sudan and Egypt.

Finally some recent treaties are agreements between upstream and downstream states to cooperate on flood and pollution control, and protection of transboundary ecosystems. But as the *World Water Development Report* shows, many treaties suffer from significant shortcomings (WWAP 2003). For example, some do not cover all riparian states. Monitoring, compliance, and conflict resolution mechanisms are often lacking. Many treaties are not flexible or responsive enough to cope with hydrological and socio-economic variations. And most concern rivers—not entire water systems—and none seem to cover river basins.

In line with treaties many transboundary water organizations have been established. Some function well, but many are empty shells because member states lack the political will required for active involvement. Others suffer from the same shortcomings as the treaties—mainly exclusion of some riparian states and a very narrow focus.

Even worse problems for transboundary aquifers

While the situation is bad for transboundary rivers, it is even worse for transboundary aquifers. Aquifers are a huge source of development potential—but they are also extremely vulnerable to overexploitation and pollution (chapter 2). Europe alone has more than a hundred transboundary aquifers. The boundaries and recharge areas of groundwater systems are often unknown. Moreover, the impacts of actions in upstream countries on downstream countries are usually not directly visible and may not even occur until years later. There is a general lack of expertise when it comes to aquifer management, and even less law on transboundary aquifers than on transboundary rivers.

3. Assessing Challenges, Initiating Change

The ultimate goal is integrated water resources management—that is, including land, water, ecosystems, and people—for all transboundary water basins

What needs to be done?

Cooperation on shared water basins is needed to ensure peace and livelihoods for people living in them, to contribute to regional security and economic development, and to protect water resources. But cooperation should go beyond single-purpose action: the ultimate goal is integrated water resources management—that is, including land, water, ecosystems, and people—for all transboundary water basins. Two types of action are needed: First, efforts are needed to prevent conflicts and build joint water management institutions. Better understanding and use of human and political processes are essential here. Second, efforts are needed to expedite integrated management of transboundary water systems, allocating water in the most rational way possible to make the most of its benefits and share them equitably—while taking ecosystem needs into account.

Raising awareness about benefits of cooperation

It is essential to improve governments' understanding of the need to cooperate—first, for the sake of solidarity among countries, and second, for the good of the region. As shown in box 3.2, it should be understood that cooperating on water can yield a wide range of benefits. Sharing best practices is one way to raise awareness.

Providing third-party mechanisms and sharing experience

Dispute settlement can be facilitated at the international level by developing international dispute settlement mechanisms—from strengthening international law to developing third-party mediation. Mediation and conflict resolution can also be efficient at the local level.

International networks and forums can play a preventive role by raising awareness about the need for cooperation and by providing a neutral platform for discussions.

Box 3.2 Sharing the benefits of better water management

The new paradigm for managing shared water systems argues that it is better to allocate the benefits from water rather than the water itself. Benefits can be economic, socio-political, or environmental. Moreover, they can be positive (winning situations) or can involve lower costs (avoided losses). There are several types of water management benefits:

- From water systems—better uses of water for hydropower and agriculture; improved navigation, environmental conservation, water quality, recreation, and flood and drought management.
- For water systems—improved river flows and soil and biodiversity conservation; increased sustainability.
- From stronger joint management—better policies for cooperation and development, increased food and energy security, reduced spending on disputes and the military.
- Beyond water systems—more integrated regional infrastructure, markets, and trade.

Sources: Wolf 1999; Sadoff and Grey 2002.

Transboundary basins 3

> *Every day mutual accusations on the quality and quantity of water are heard from both countries, but practical steps are not taken to build cooperation.*
> —Armenia

Human and political processes should be better understood and better used to improve negotiations

Building institutions

Stronger institutions are needed to oversee shared river and aquifer basins. Efforts are needed to build institutions that:

- Include all riparian states.
- Involve all stakeholders.
- Adapt to changes in socio-economic conditions and basin priorities.
- Reflect treaties based on action plans and targets, with provisions for monitoring, compliance, and dispute settlement.

Successful institutions can emerge from a variety of processes, reflecting regional politics and socio-economic factors. Thus it is hard to provide general guidelines for building institutions. Successful cooperation usually starts at the bottom, often bilaterally, with a single concrete issue—and often also at a personal level. Goodwill and ownership from the states and people involved are essential. Indeed it could be argued that cooperation should be handled solely by states.

But where there are big socio-economic differences among the countries sharing a basin, or where none of the countries has the resources needed to build confidence and negotiate agreements, third parties and donors should get involved. Consider the Rhine and Danube Rivers. The Rhine is an example of successful cooperation that started from the bottom up, decades ago, among riparian countries with similar living standards. On the Danube, where countries' economic situations are more diverse, cooperation started more recently—and was aided by international organizations. In all such efforts, there is a need for greater subsidiarity (see definition in box 3.1) in transboundary management of water systems and for greater involvement of non-state actors.

Improving understanding and use of human and political processes

Water-related cooperation is often driven by a small number of individuals or by the building and fostering of personal relationships. Agreements are reached through negotiations at a political level, and cooperation is driven more by human relationships than by technical considerations. So, while rational and equitable benefits based solutions to water management must be sought, human and political processes should be better understood and better used to improve the needed negotiations. Local knowledge and methods for resolving conflicts can be very helpful. The ability to negotiate sensitive issues and resolve conflicts is often considered a natural gift that some people have and others do not. But there is strong potential for strengthening the capacity of negotiators to understand each other and reach satisfactory agreements.

3 Assessing Challenges, Initiating Change

New transboundary institutions have been created or are being created in more than 10 shared basins

Moving towards integrated water resource management and benefit sharing

Plans should be developed for joint integrated management of shared basins so that water-related benefits (including those for ecosystems) are distributed equitably among riparian states (box 3.2). These plans should be flexible enough to deal with hydrological and political changes, and include provisions for monitoring and evaluating progress.

What is being done?

The Actions Database contains information on about 50 recently developed transboundary water management programmes. Three-quarters of them involve international organizations such as development agencies, non-governmental organizations (NGOs), or development banks. New transboundary institutions have been created or are being created in more than 10 shared basins.

Transboundary activities include scientific cooperation, pollution reduction, ecosystem protection, comprehensive water management, and institutional development. These new arrangements reflect the shift from traditional cooperation on navigation, hydropower, and water allocations to much broader issues such as regional cooperation and ecosystem protection—indicating a clear move towards integrated water resources management at the international level. Such efforts are especially evident among institutions with a history of long-standing cooperation, for example, the Rhine Commission, whose new commitments address flood protection and ecosystem restoration (action 31).

In 2000 there were more than 60 transboundary water management institutions—ranging from regional economic development agencies to joint management bodies—with a variety of responsibilities. Efforts are being made to create new institutions, which generally involve multiple stakeholders and emphasize integrated water resources management. But the creation of management bodies for shared water advances slowly. A management board will soon be organized for Lake Ohrid through a Global Environment Facility programme in Albania and FYR Macedonia (action 37). And for the Irtysh River a joint commission is being created between Kazakhstan and Russia (action 695), and efforts are being made to include China.

Data sharing and scientific cooperation remain the first steps in transboundary cooperation. China, though not a member of the Mekong River Commission, has agreed to share data with the four downstream countries (Cambodia, Lao People's Democratic Republic, Thailand, Vietnam; action 758). The first initiative on the La Plata Basin in South America is scientific cooperation (action 1102). Cooperation between Syria and Turkey's administration of the Southeastern Anatolia Project has started with a joint training programme (action 1179).

Transboundary basins   3

International organizations play an important role in promoting and supporting cooperation on water management

Other cooperative efforts cover a wide range, though most involve just one sector, for example, navigation (action 961 on Mekong), disaster management (action 2463 between Bolivia and Argentina), hydropower (action 2102 between Iran and Turkmenistan), ecosystem protection (action 2333 between Sweden and Norway), management of facilities (action 3001) between Kazakhstan and Kyrgystan). The Senegal River shows the development potential of shared waters. The tripartite commission for the development of the Senegal River Basin (Organisation pour la Mise en Valeur du Fleuve Sénégal) appears to be an active body in Africa, with eight major actions in the Actions Database (actions 221, 226, 894, 1059, 1060, 1061, 1062, and 1291). Noteworthy are attempts to share the benefits of water among riparian states in the case of the Manantali Dam (action 1889). The Senegal River Water Charter of 2002 seeks to optimize competing uses of the water among riparian states—while preserving ecosystems (action 2353).

The Nile Basin Initiative (action 177) is a promising multilateral dialogue established in the late 1990s. A shared vision has been reached between 10 riparian countries to achieve sustainable socio-economic development through the equitable use of and benefit from common water resources. The initiative emphasizes cooperation, transparency, and accountability.

The International Joint Commission between Canada and the United States offers another strong model of cooperation. The 1909 Canada-U.S. Boundary Waters Treaty establishes principles and procedures for preventing and settling disputes, particularly those related to the quantity and quality of boundary waters. In 2001, at Canada's request, the treaty was amended to prohibit bulk removals from Canadian boundary waters, including the Great Lakes, with the aim of preserving the environment for future generations (action 1994). The International Joint Commission is also tackling groundwater contamination (action 2485).

There are also examples of advanced cooperation on transboundary subcatchments. One is in the Meuse River Basin in Europe. A joint river basin action plan has been developed for the Semois/Semoy transboundary catchment (action 632). Joint river basin planning should increase under the EU Water Framework Directive (action 1169). Central America also offers many examples of cooperation on smaller transboundary catchments. An example is the cooperation between NGOs in Belize and Guatemala to tackle pollution on the Mopan River (action 1412).

International organizations play an important role in promoting and supporting cooperation on water management. They offer a platform for debate, help disseminate good practices, and obtain funding. Cooperation is brokered by international organizations such as IUCN–The World Conservation Union, World Wildlife Fund, Green Cross International, Global Environment Facility, and development banks. These organizations make ecosystem protection a driver of transboundary cooperation. Some countries are also deeply involved as third parties in brokering cooperation.

3 Assessing Challenges, Initiating Change

A growing number of transboundary surface water institutions are tackling groundwater issues in their basins

' We propose to start with multiyear planning for water and power resources in the Syr-Daria River Basin. Then long-term economic treaties can be negotiated.
—Uzbekistan '

The Actions Database shows extensive involvement by non-state actors at the international level. A Volta Basin declaration was drafted by a group of civil society organizations (action 2352). South America provides numerous examples of civil society defending social and environmental causes. In Paraguay the Paraná Hidrovia project aims to link Argentina, Bolivia, and Paraguay through a large shipping channel, but the 300-member Ríos Vivos coalition of environmental, human rights, and indigenous groups opposes the project because it passes through an important wetland (action 129). The 2001–05 Joint Actions Programme for the Danube tackles pollution by involving all the stakeholders in the basin, including the private sector (action 606), while recently, 14 NGOs created the Tisza Platform (action 19) to tackle pollution on this Danube affluent. Friends of the Earth Middle East helps communities from Jordan, Israel, and Palestinian Territory work together on water issues through its Good Water Neighbour Project (action 2577).

There are few specific actions on management of transboundary aquifers, though a growing number of transboundary surface water institutions are tackling groundwater issues in their basins. An institutional framework has been strengthened around the Nubian Sandstone Aquifer, and criteria have been set for maximum groundwater extraction (box 3.3). Scientific cooperation is starting on other aquifers through the Internationally Shared (Transboundary) Aquifer Resources Management (ISARM) programme (actions 94, 914, 917, 918, 922). The groundwater management programme for the Southern African Development Community (SADC) supports sound development of groundwater resources in member countries and intensifies traditional links (action 320). In South America shared investigations are under way in various areas, with a major programme having been launched on the Guarani aquifer (actions 391 and 922) that should lead to a joint management programme between Argentina, Brazil, Paraguay and Uruguay.

Box 3.3 Using a decision support system to jointly define more rational use of shared groundwater (action 1315)

The Nubian Sandstone Aquifer System is shared by Chad, Egypt, Libya, and Sudan. Most water is extracted for agriculture, either for large development projects such as the Kufra Production Project in Libya or for traditional oases. In addition, a large project to transport water to the coast is being developed in Libya and is already supplying some 70 cubic metres of water per second (the Great Man-Made River Project in Libya, action 715).

The aquifer, which is located too deep beneath the ground to be replenished by rainfall, is threatened by overexploitation.

Within this context, in 1997 a programme was initiated to develop a regional strategy for the long-term, sustainable use of the Nubian Sandstone Aquifer System. The joint authority on the aquifer previously formed between Egypt, Libya, and Sudan was revitalized, and Chad joined. Two agreements have been signed, for monitoring and data sharing. In addition, a decision support system has been developed. Simulations of the impact of different groundwater extraction scenarios allowed the countries to jointly develop a regional strategy for use of the aquifer through 2060. Both technical and socio-economic issues were taken into account.

The countries have agreed on a maximum drawdown (lowering of the groundwater table) of 1 metre a year. National water development plans should reflect this objective. Egypt, for instance, is preparing a water strategy through 2017 based on the agreement.

Sources: Puri and others 2001; CEDARE/IFAD 2001.

Transboundary basins 3

> *As drought and flood occur at the same time, we should search how to share floodwater between basins and countries.*
> —Philippines

The Permanent Court of Arbitration offers possibilities for mediation

There are debates about whether more or less international law on water is needed, possibly including stronger principles for allocating water and settling disputes. The United Nations Convention on Non-Navigational Uses of International Watercourses (United Nations 1997) and the United Nations Economic Commission for Europe Helsinki Convention on the Protection and Use of Transboundary Watercourses and International Lakes (UN ECE 1992) provide general principles for cooperation but should be supplemented by bilateral or multilateral agreements. The 1997 convention is referred to in the Nile Basin Initiative (action 177) and the Southern African Development Community Protocol (action 792). In addition to these conventions, the body of international law is growing. And because awareness of the importance of cooperation on water is increasing, it will be difficult for anyone to ignore the obligation to cooperate. The Permanent Court of Arbitration in The Hague is getting more involved in water issues and offers possibilities for mediation (action 2415).

Regional instruments such as the EU Water Framework Directive (action 1169) and the conventions arising from the Southern African Development Community Protocol (action 792) show the potential for developing legal agreements and dispute settlement procedures and for defining water management principles and monitoring and compliance mechanisms. The regional scale appears to be appropriate to cooperation, also because economic development is a powerful driver at this level. Moreover, negotiations are easier if cultural differences are slight.

Apart from legal mechanisms, the role of dialogue and negotiations is more widely recognized, and emphasis on conflict prevention and negotiations training is increasing. The United Nations Educational, Scientific, and Cultural Organization (UNESCO) and Green Cross International believe that one of the main goals of water management is to balance the competing interests of water users—including governments, local authorities, and other stakeholders—and thus that managing water-related conflicts and promoting cooperation are essential in water management. They recommend that individual, community, and international behaviour be guided by principles of justice and equity, to be communicated through education. The joint UNESCO–Green Cross programme From Potential Conflict to Co-operation Potential: Water for Peace (action 97) seeks to identify ways of resolving water conflicts and to develop methods for facilitating open discussions and negotiating conflict (UNESCO IHP and Green Cross International 2003).

University networks appear to be successful in building confidence among possible future water managers, as exemplified on the Scheldt River (actions 21, 598). Efforts have also been made to disseminate best practices by twinning river basin organizations led by experienced countries such as France and the Netherlands (actions 21, 47, 74) and by developing general guidelines such as the Guidelines for Constitution of International Commissions for Shared Water Resources (action 1967).

3 Assessing Challenges, Initiating Change

Operational resources for transboundary water management should be financed as much as possible by the riparian countries themselves

Various proposals have been made for a mechanism to oversee transboundary water management at the global level. Such an institution could share experience, broker cooperation, and provide mediation services if requested—for instance, the international shared waters facility proposed by the Swedish Ministry of Foreign Affairs (2001).

In 2000 at the conclusion of the Second World Water Forum, Dr. Mahmoud Abu Zeid, president of the World Water Council, proposed the creation of the World Commission on Water, Peace, and Security to provide an opportunity for third-party mediation of shared water disputes (Secretariat of the Second World Water Forum 2000). The role of the commission would have been to assist nations in current and potential transboundary water issues with an independent opinion to help bridge the gap between concerned parties, to develop and promote common interest for "win-win" solutions. The council recognizes that the lead in some of these areas rests with the United Nations family. It is still examining ways to establish a partnership with the appropriate United Nations organizations. In the long run, through training and education, the need for outside expertise will be considerably reduced. Still recourse to neutral facilitators and mediators will undoubtedly continue.

What remains to be done?

Action is urgently needed to accelerate the development of shared water resources in order to speed up poverty alleviation and accelerate socio-economic development. As noted, transboundary agreements tend to develop from the bottom up. The increasing pressure on water and lack of resources in some countries suggest that more top-level interventions are required to expedite these processes. But the adage "think globally, act locally" is as true as ever here: even if principles should be developed for international water management and international organizations should play a strong role as cooperation brokers, water management should still be as local as possible. Finally, water should be seen as one element only in a more multi-sectoral regional cooperation effort.

Drawing more on third parties, but making action as local as possible

The challenge is to strike a balance between bottom-up approaches to triggering and strengthening cooperation (letting states or other parties start cooperation as needed) and top-down approaches (such as stronger international law and international third parties brokering cooperation). This balance will have to be adapted to the conditions in every country. There is a strong case for building the capacity of international organizations to improve international cooperation—accepting that these activities take time and substantial resources. Resources should be provided for such brokers. At the same time, operational resources for transboundary water management should be financed as much as possible by the countries involved, to ensure ownership and commitment (Swedish Ministry of Foreign Affairs 2001).

Improving institutions

The involvement of non-state actors (local authorities, NGOs, the private sector) should be increased so that "transboundary links" are established at all levels—not just the state level—and subsidiarity can be improved. At all levels, when creating cooperation institutions, it is necessary to ensure mechanisms for financing, executing, and enforcing the decisions made, and to include provisions for monitoring compliance and settling disputes. To improve cooperation at all levels, training on negotiations and conflict resolution should be developed and can start in schools.

Transboundary basins 3

> *Can't we draw up a plan to set in motion the cooperative actions of countries on a global scale?*
> —Japan

Joint integrated water management plans should be aimed at sharing water benefits

Developing and sharing best practices and principles

Best practices should be developed and shared at the international level through informal networks and forums. Training should be offered to all stakeholders involved in managing shared water systems or basins. Experiences should be exchanged directly through twinning arrangements, and university networks should be developed. In addition, principles and good practices for interbasin transfers should be developed at the international level because current legislation omits this increasingly problematic issue.

Creating an international water facility

There is still a need for some form of international institution to facilitate transboundary cooperation and to develop and share best practices and principles in transboundary management. Conceived of as a relatively soft mechanism, this international water facility would intervene only when invited by riparian countries and/or water basin organizations, sharing its expertise and providing mediation services.

Moving towards integrated management of shared basins

Joint integrated water management plans have to be elaborated for all transboundary river basins and aquifers—including the recharge areas of aquifers. These plans should be aimed at sharing water benefits. Decision support techniques (such as scenario building or visioning) and cost-benefit analysis have to be used to assess and choose the most rational water management strategies, taking into account ecosystem needs. Ideally the geographical scope of cooperation should be enlarged from the water system to the entire river basin—and for aquifers, to the entire recharge area, which means also including land. Awareness of the need for cooperation on groundwater should be increased, mainly through more widespread education on groundwater.

Linking water management and sustainable regional development

Water policies should be related to other sectoral policies. Examples can be given in energy and agriculture, when countries optimize water use by transferring or trading hydropower or virtual water (see chapter 10). Broader environmental policies should be harmonized. As is already the case in some regions, water management should be seen as part of a larger framework of overall socio-economic development in the river basin or region.

4. Water and gender

The demands and skills of water users differ, depending on their gender, age, culture, religion, abilities, education, and income. Sustainable water management requires that these differences be taken into account at all levels and for all water activities, from policies to projects. Yet too often, underrepresented users—particularly women, the main users and managers of water—are excluded from decision-making and planning.

The exclusion of women has made water management systems less responsive to demands for water services. Moreover, it has squandered the skills and energy of half the world's population—skills and energy that could be used in developing countries to provide water services and manage natural resources, contributing to social, economic, and personal development.

These shortcomings offer important lessons—and challenges—for the international water community. Women's involvement is crucial to successful water sector reforms. Women's pressing needs for water and sanitation for their households and livelihoods put them at the fore of the community of water users, especially in poor communities. Thus their obvious skills as managers of water resources and water systems must be harnessed more appropriately. What is the best way to do so?

Present situation

There is considerable variation in how men and women provide for the material needs of their families. Men usually meet long-term needs, while women generally provide—and pay for—household goods and food, including water. For example, ecosystems are among the food sources for poor families, and women are usually responsible for exploiting these sources, including fisheries. As a result ecosystem and species losses hit women especially hard.

Although men and women both have water-related responsibilities, gender-based divisions of labour determine who controls the many uses of water. Moreover, water management structures—from the local level to the basin level—tend to be dominated by large water users and by administrative, political, and economic elites. As a result poor families' water needs are often ignored, undermining their welfare and livelihoods. And in some societies men have deeply ingrained insecurities about the notion of women owning property, including land or water rights for farming.

At the international level there is awareness of the gender issues involved in water management, and a range of initiatives have been introduced to improve the situation. Many countries have recognized the benefits of involving women in all

Water and gender 4

Organizations that do not practice gender equality in hiring, capacity-building, and institutional cultures are unlikely to provide services that promote gender equality

aspects of water use. It has been accepted that water policies and programmes that exclude women ignore half of the world's population and are less efficient and effective. Thus most government guidelines, project designs, and programme policies now address gender concerns.

Yet too many projects and programmes focus on the practical rather than the strategic needs of women. An example of this difference in approach is a project that provides water by setting up standpipes rather than seeking water rights for women. Access to water through standpipes can provide women with some immediate income (freeing time in household activities, allowing some short-term economic activities) by building on a gender stereotype. Such a project is non-threatening and does little to change the fundamental economic power relations between men and women. By contrast, water rights would provide women with a permanent means of production —the basis for greater wealth creation, long-term prosperity, and financial security. But such a change challenges long-standing traditions and practices. The issue is not just empowering women; it also involves addressing and altering men's deeply ingrained insecurities about women owning property. Such changes are possible only with fundamental shifts in gender relations.

What needs to be done?

If women are to play a more prominent role in water management, a number of basic concepts must be more widely accepted:

- Efforts to improve the general status of women cannot be seen as separate, isolated undertakings. They must be tackled by taking into account the status of both women and men, recognizing that their life courses differ and that equal treatment will not necessarily produce equal outcomes. And when it comes to water, it must be recognized that women and men have different needs, priorities, and decision-making capabilities, and that institutional structures determine their roles, rights, and responsibilities for access to and control over resources.
- Gender equity in water management requires paying attention to the often-complex relationships between the productive and domestic uses of water, to the importance of participation by both women and men, and to the equitable distribution of benefits from new, decentralized management structures and from improved infrastructure.
- Community institutions for integrated water management must be linked to new basin-level management frameworks. Crucial to the success of such efforts will be informing women about new water management proposals from the local level to the basin level, including them in the design of new institutions, and devising strategies that guarantee their participation while recognizing cultural and social traditions.
- Women often have vital knowledge of local water management. Enhancing their powers enables them to use their knowledge about managing water resources and preventing pollution. Moreover, new government policies and plans, and possibly private investments, can change local arrangements for water management. And by ensuring that women participate in planning, the potential effects on their subsistence and economic development needs can be taken into account and their interests protected.
- The gender sensitivity of services provided by national water management institutions generally reflects internal practices. Organizations that do not practice gender equality in their hiring procedures, capacity-building efforts, and institutional cultures are unlikely to provide services that promote gender equality.

4 Assessing Challenges, Initiating Change

Women-friendly provisions in customary laws must be integrated with any new water sector legislation

> In our culture, we, the men, walk long distances to get water. Outside policies to promote women [without considering such local customs] could ruin [this cultural aspect of] respect between men and women. —Samoa

Many steps need to be taken to achieve gender equity in water management, including affirmative action at various levels, gender budgeting, and actions at the micro level. Meeting these goals requires gender mainstreaming, defined by the United Nations Development Programme (UNDP 1997) as taking into account gender equity concerns in all policies, programmes, administrative and financial activities, and organizational procedures. Such efforts must occur at the national, regional, and international levels, and require high-level political support to succeed.

Promoting affirmative action

Women should be adequately represented in all water management committees and decision-making bodies, accounting for at least one-third of members. Reaching this level may require balancing efforts—that is, providing favourable treatment to the election or inclusion of female representatives in governing bodies—over an agreed period, including provision of data and information, and capacity building and training.

Gender-related water networks should be involved in international consultations, and sufficient numbers of female delegates should participate in international decision-making organizations. Nationally, water policies, institutions, and management structures must reflect the needs, priorities, and representation rights of both women and men for all possible water uses.

A balanced gender strategy will seek equitable water use through integrated water management. Where there is competition for water, exclusion based on gender or ethnicity must be prevented. In some countries customary and formal laws may give women different water rights. Thus women-friendly provisions in customary laws must be integrated with any new water sector legislation.

Supporting gender budgeting

Gender budgeting examines proposed policies and projects to ensure that the resources allocated deliver substantive benefits for women. This approach is increasingly considered critical for gender mainstreaming—a tangible way for women to be involved in the resource allocation decisions most likely to enhance their empowerment, rather than restricted to tinkering around the fringes of social welfare policies, as has generally been the case up to now.

Addressing micro-level issues

Micro-level issues include:

- Facilitating women's participation in community decision-making by taking into account the time and opportunity costs of women's participation, as well as its cultural context.
- Addressing the gender aspects of roles, rights, and responsibilities in households—including men's, and their support for women's participation.
- Ensuring that women's role in providing health and hygiene education does not increase their already heavy workloads.
- Developing a demand-responsive approach to user fees for water and sanitation services and to community contributions for operation and maintenance of water and sanitation infrastructure, taking into account users' unpaid or underpaid contributions and avoiding adding to their workloads. Assessments of willingness and ability to pay must factor in women's contributions to their households as well as their labour contributions. This is particularly important for female-headed households in poor communities, where labour is a critical component of user contributions to water and sanitation infrastructure.

Water and gender

There is growing recognition of women's skills in many aspects of water management—including planning, design, and operation and maintenance

What is being done?

Of the more than 3,000 water actions in the Actions Database, only 3 percent have an explicit gender component (table 4.1). Of these, only half are community-based projects. Still, these actions are but a small sample of the many water-related gender equity efforts under way worldwide.

World Water Vision (Cosgrove and Rijsberman 2000), presented at the Second World Water Forum in 2000, raised awareness of the need to involve women in water management. The global Gender and Water Alliance (action 335) was formed at the forum, and a number of research programmes have been created to better understand women's role in water management. There is growing recognition of women's skills in many aspects of water management—including planning, design, and operation and maintenance—with success stories reported in China, India, Morocco, Pakistan, South Africa, Tonga, Central Europe, and other areas (box 4.1). Most such examples come from developing countries, with Southern Africa and South Asia featuring prominently.

At community level, the actions recorded show that women are typically involved in water supply and sanitation projects, nature conservation and watershed management, and rainwater harvesting. Also encouraging is that women are being empowered through irrigation and agriculture projects or through fishing. Many of these projects have an income-generation component. Rainwater harvesting, for example, can allow women to water small gardens and produce crops, while improved water supply can free up time for income-generating activities.

The Southern Africa Development Community Program (action 365) aims to empower women on water issues in 14 African countries. The programme will review women's participation in water resource development and management across the region, support affirmative action to increase rural women's participation in all levels of water resources development and management, encourage governments to use affirmative action to attract more women to water management careers, strengthen the skills of women dealing with water issues, formulate a regional strategy for integrating gender mainstreaming with integrated water resources management, build the capacity of water professionals to work on gender issues, and improve information dissemination and sharing among women. This programme is linked to the Gender and Water Alliance.

Women's special role in farming, particularly in female-headed households, has received considerable attention in water actions—especially in cases where their spouses have died or migrated to cities to look for work. The Rebeireta Water Management Project in Cape Verde (West Africa) aims to improve water management on the country's islands, with participation from female farmers, to secure sustainable agriculture (action 1578). The project is addressing

Table 4.1 Water actions that promote women's involvement in water management

Type of action	Number
Global gender mainstreaming and networking	10
Research on gender issues	9
Education and awareness raising for women	10
Women's involvement in institutions and planning	5
Community-based projects	34
Total	68

Source: World Water Council, Actions Database (www.worldwatercouncil.org/search_actions.php), February 2003.

4 Assessing Challenges, Initiating Change

Only a few actions to increase women's institutional involvement in water management and planning have been observed

technical, social, and institutional aspects simultaneously. And a project in Syria, assisted by the United Nations Development Programme and implemented in cooperation with the government, has introduced modern irrigation techniques to boost the incomes of farmers—many of whom are women (action 1144).

The Health through Sanitation and Water Project in Tanzania (action 410)—which has provided more than 1 million people with access to clean water, made them less subject to disease, and cut the time required to fetch water—attached great importance to women's participation. In Ukraine a campaign sponsored by a non-governmental organization (NGO) to increase access to safe and affordable drinking water in both urban and rural areas (actions 1478, 1477) has promoted women's leadership in environmental policy-making and sought to improve the health of women and children.

Partnerships have been formed in many countries between international NGOs or donors and local women's associations, as in China (action 1047), Vietnam (action 1058), and Pakistan (action 967). In addition Hungary's Association of Women for Lake Balaton has established an alliance with the Hungarian Water Partnership (action 1321). National NGOs are also targeting women in water management.

Only a few actions to increase women's institutional involvement in water management and planning have been observed, mainly in Asia. These include the Jal-Disha 2010 water resource management plan in Gujarat, India (box 4.1), and the aforementioned actions in Pakistan and Hungary. The Pakistan Water Partnership (action 270) requires that at least one-third of the members of its governing bodies be women. In the Darewadi Watershed Project in India (action 1308), women self-help groups participate in watershed management.

What remains to be done?

Despite progress, much remains to be done to achieve gender equity in water management. Among the outstanding problems:

- The widening socio-economic disparities between men and women, which have caused unequal divisions of burdens, benefits, and decision-making in water management.
- The presence of women in water management committees does not necessarily ensure that their views are reflected in the planning and implementation of water projects.
- Women have not been systematically incorporated into water resources management, because of deficiencies in gender awareness among water organizations and society in general.

Clean, easily accessible water services fulfil many of women's immediate needs, especially in developing countries. But such services will fulfil women's strategic needs only if they are involved in water decision-making, management, and maintenance, and only if the time they save as a result of the services can be used for their advancement—for example, to participate in literacy classes.

Water and gender 4

> *The water brought job opportunities to our province. The women began to work in the textile factories to earn money, increasing their status in society.*
> —Turkey

Gender in Gujarat is proving to be as much about transforming the attitudes and responsibilities of men as about improving the status and access accorded to women

Box 4.1 Gender issues and Gujarat's water and sanitation vision (action 1075)

In drought-prone Gujarat (western India) an action plan is under way to provide every citizen with access to water, sanitation, and hygienic living within the decade. This is Gujarat Jal-Disha 2010, a movement inspired by the global Vision 21 initiative of the Water Supply and Sanitation Collaborative Council (Geneva). Gender issues are central to this effort, in which the key is equitable distribution and access across regions and communities. Gender in Gujarat is proving to be as much about transforming the attitudes and responsibilities of men as about improving the status and access accorded to women. In cooperation with state authorities work has begun on a policy framework that will give women a more equal role in decision-making and build their capacity for self-help.

This movement draws momentum from women activists brought together in Pathan and Dhandhuka districts by Utthan, a local non-governmental organization. They recently took the lead to construct and manage massive rainwater harvesting tanks that despite a disastrous monsoon now hold enough water to meet drinking and other essential domestic needs for two years. A major aspect of this remarkable demonstration has been the ability of unschooled women to master essential technologies and operation and maintenance requirements. Protection of harvested water has been threatened in some areas by traditional caste and male dominance, and women guardians have had to withstand discrimination and even attack. Their promotion of hygiene education and latrine construction is another important signal emerging from even the most conservative and backward communities. A transformation in health is already apparent. The Self-Employed Women's Association (SEWA), a union of self-employed women, has undertaken similar efforts in nearby Santalpur and Banaskantha (action 3541). Although the way before them is a long one, women are proving to be more efficient and effective managers than men. Their needs are now receiving priority attention from a committee of stakeholders set up by the state government to formulate a gender policy for the sector.

Source: Gujarat State Drinking Water Infrastructure Company 2000 (Gujarat Sub-Group on Water and Sanitation Gender Policy).

The first change should come from men. Mindsets need to change: gender is as much about transforming men's attitudes and responsibilities as it is about advancing women's status and access. To respond to all of the concerns identified above, efforts should be made to:

- Ensure that gender mainstreaming address all levels, from national policies to end users.
- Strengthen targeted advocacy at the national, regional, and international levels, and provide additional resources (time, authority, and so on) for people responsible for gender mainstreaming. A key lesson of gender mainstreaming is the importance of high-level political commitment.
- Realign traditional cultural perceptions of male and female roles and responsibilities, to facilitate greater sharing of household responsibilities and so free up the time and talents of both sexes for water management. This is a challenging task—one that cannot be achieved easily or quickly. It will require persistence, perseverance, and support from international agencies, national governments, international and national NGOs, and grass-roots movements.

4 Assessing Challenges, Initiating Change

Promoting equity and gender balance is not just a matter of political correctness. It is about mobilizing all available skills

> While men drink tea and relax, we women fetch water and cook. After a weary day, instead of carrying water, I would like to have time for my children and myself.
> —Turkey

- Promote participatory methodologies that use agreed indicators to measure the effectiveness of women's participation.
- Provide much-needed additional capacity—in training, materials, and financing—to ensure meaningful participation by women.
- Develop gender analysis at the earliest stages of projects and programmes.
- Monitor gender equity in all projects and programmes, including gender budgeting.
- Help project and programme managers by providing frameworks for gender analysis.
- Ensure that water and especially sanitation projects provide women—as well as children and mentally disabled people—with a strong sense of privacy and sexual security.

Like the other issues addressed in this report, water and gender offer cause for cautious optimism. Nationally and internationally, the main challenges are recognized, and there are replicable examples of needed measures. Promoting equity and gender balance is not just a matter of political correctness. It is about mobilizing all available skills—and so increasing natural resilience and empowering people to accelerate poverty alleviation and advance socio-economic development.

5. Water-related risks

Water-related disasters—floods, droughts, tropical storms—are still a large challenge for sustainable human development. Water-related hazards are not completely controllable, and they are leading to large socio-economic losses. Disaster management needs to emphasize risk management initiatives that are far more economic and more humanitarian than emergency relief and post-disaster recovery. And it needs to be integrated into socio-economic development and poverty alleviation strategies, promoting stronger coordination and solidarity among all concerned.

Global warming and associated climate change will further increase the frequency and intensity of water-related disasters, adding to the problems of countries unprepared to face such events. But by taking measures to cope with the effects of the climate variability of today, water and disaster managers can develop resilient institutions and communities better prepared to deal with the effects of the climate change of tomorrow.

Present situation

Natural meteorological and hydrological cycles are characterized by extreme events in both the short and the long term. Humanity has found no means of controlling these extremes and instead seeks to manage the risks that arise as best it can. In the context of this chapter *risks* refers to water-related disasters resulting from climate variability and change. The natural hazards—floods, droughts, landslides, typhoons, and the like—are largely a consequence of climate variability; climate change is likely to increase their occurrence and intensity. There are also human-induced hazards—such as water pollution and adverse effects from inadequate design, operation, and maintenance of infrastructure (key terms are defined in box 5.1). (This chapter does not deal with the risks arising from water-related diseases, which are covered in chapter 9.)

International recognition of water-related risks

Managing water-related risks is a challenge that received little coverage in the *World Water Vision* (Cosgrove and Rijsberman 2000). But it has received much more attention since. At the Second World Water Forum in The Hague in March 2000 the ministerial conference declared "managing risks" to be one of the seven key challenges. And in September 2000 the *United Nations Millennium Declaration* (United Nations 2000, paragraphs 23 and 26) declared two related goals:

- Protecting our common environment: To intensify cooperation to reduce the number and effects of natural and man-made disasters.
- Protecting the vulnerable: To strengthen international cooperation, including burden-sharing in, and the coordination of humanitarian assistance to, countries hosting refugees and to help all refugees and displaced persons to return voluntarily to their homes, in safety and dignity, and to be smoothly reintegrated into their societies.

5 Assessing Challenges, Initiating Change

The effects of water-related hazards are social, economic, and environmental

Box 5.1 Definitions of key terms

The International Strategy for Disaster Reduction, in its *Living with Risk* report, sets out some definitions important for this chapter:

- *Hazard* is a potentially damaging physical event, phenomenon, or human activity that may cause injury or loss of life, property damage, social and economic disruption, or environmental degradation.
- *Disaster* is a serious disruption of the functioning of a community or a society causing widespread human, material, economic, or environmental losses that exceed the ability of the affected community or society to cope using its own resources.
- *Risk* is the probability of harmful consequences, or the expected loss, from interactions between hazards and conditions of vulnerability in relation to capacity, expressed by the equation:

$$\text{Risk} = (\text{hazards} \times \text{vulnerability}) \div \text{capacity}$$

- *Vulnerability* is a set of conditions and processes resulting from physical and other factors that increase the susceptibility of a community to the effects of hazards.
- *Capacity* is the way in which people and organizations use existing resources to achieve various beneficial ends under the unusual, abnormal, and adverse conditions of a disaster.

Source: Based on ISDR 2002c, pp. 24–25.

In 2001 the International Conference on Freshwater in Bonn identified "manage risks to cope with variability and climate change" as one of the actions in governance (Federal Republic of Germany 2001, p. 80). And the *Plan of Implementation* adopted by the World Summit on Sustainable Development in Johannesburg in 2002 recognized that "an integrated, multi-hazard, inclusive approach to address vulnerability, risk assessment and disaster management is an essential element of a safer world in the 21st century" (United Nations 2002, p.16).

Trends in water-related disasters

The effects of water-related hazards are social, economic, and environmental. Social effects are direct—for example, human deaths or the destruction of infrastructure. Economic effects include damage to property and other assets and adverse effects on stock market prices in and around the affected areas because of damage to industry and agriculture.

Environmental effects are relatively direct and sometimes last for decades or even centuries. Water pollution from accidental or deliberate discharges of heavy metals or organic chemicals causes serious long-term damage to all kinds of water bodies and their ecosystems. If the pollutants are trapped in sediments—such as in seaports or riverbeds—they constitute a serious problem that can be costly to remedy.

Water-related disasters result in large socio-economic losses. The world experienced more than 2,400 hydro-meteorological disasters during 1992–2001, accounting for 90 percent of all natural disasters during that period. Of these, 39 percent were caused by floods and 10 percent by droughts. Asia suffered the largest share of these disasters (38 percent), followed by the Americas (27 percent), Africa (16 percent), Europe (14 percent), and Oceania (5 percent) (IFRC 2002, pp. 185–96). Different regions are prone to different types of hazards. In Asia and Central America floods and landslides are the main concerns, while in the Middle East and North Africa droughts are frequent occurrences.

Water-related risks

Hurricane Mitch, which hit Central America in 1998, set the region's development back by 20 years

During the same period hydro-meteorological events (floods, droughts, windstorms) accounted for 85 percent of the deaths resulting from all natural disasters and for 98 percent of the people affected by natural disasters. Floods accounted for 63 percent of the people affected by all natural disasters, and droughts for nearly 22 percent. Still, floods were less deadly; they caused 18 percent of deaths from all natural disasters, compared with 52 percent for droughts. Some 98 percent of deaths from hydro-meteorological disasters have occurred in countries with low and medium human development. These countries have also suffered proportionately larger economic losses than those with high human development.

Hydro-meteorological disasters caused an estimated $446 billion in economic losses in 1992–2001. Floods and windstorms had the greatest economic impact, each accounting for about 40 percent of these losses. The economic impact is much greater for developing than for industrial countries—because of their greater vulnerability and lower capacity to cope. For Ecuador the economic losses from the 1997–98 El Niño event represented 14.6 percent of GDP, while for the United States they represented only 0.03 percent of GDP (ISDR 2002b, p.13). In Mozambique, largely as a result of a flood in 2000, GDP growth that year slipped down to 3.8 percent, compared with 10–12 percent a year in 1997–99 (USAID 2002).

Serious disasters can set back economic development. The United Nations estimated that Hurricane Mitch, which hit Central America in 1998, set the region's development back by 20 years (Abramovitz 2001, p. 26). The cost of rebuilding infrastructure was huge, and most Central American nations were still paying back the development debt of previous decades. Moreover, the impact on livelihoods in developing countries cannot be reflected simply in dollar terms. Losses of just a few hundred dollars may reflect a lifetime of work and savings for a family.

The greater number and severity of hydro-meteorological disasters reflect today's greater climate variability. Moreover, the El Niño and La Niña (Southern Oscillation) events appear to have worsened in combination with this present-day climate variability.

Although hazards are usually seen as having devastating effects, they sometimes have positive ones. Floods bring nutrients to floodplains and are important to certain aquatic species. And climate variability may cause occasional precipitation in drought-prone areas.

Threat of climate change

The climate change that is increasing the frequency and intensity of hydro-meteorological hazards results from internal dynamics in the Earth's natural systems—and the adverse effects of human activities (such as emission of greenhouse gases) on this system. This climate change resulting from human impacts is expected to have additional effects on human lives, societies, and the environment in the future, through changes in the pattern, frequency, and intensity of rainfall; an increase in temperature; and a rise in sea levels due to iceberg melt in the polar regions. According to the Intergovernmental Panel on Climate Change, between 1990 and 2100 average surface temperatures will increase by 1.4–5.8 degrees Celsius, the average sea level will rise by 9–88 centimetres, and the average annual number of people flooded by coastal storm surges will increase several-fold by the year 2080 (IPCC 2001a, pp. 61–64 and 77).

5 Assessing Challenges, Initiating Change

Risk reduction is perceived as a technical problem, a perception that ignores the social factors compelling people to live in hazard-prone areas

These changes will have serious implications for people, for the places they live, and for the environment. Rising temperatures may cause the spread of insect-borne diseases such as malaria. In regions such as Central Asia and the Mediterranean climate change could further reduce river flows as well as the rate at which underground aquifers recharge, worsening the water stress in many countries. Even without climate change, the number of people living in water-stressed countries is expected to triple, from 1.7 billion today to 5 billion by 2025 depending on the rate of population growth (IPCC 2001b, p. 31).

The effects will be much more severe in regions that depend heavily on rainfed agriculture, such as southern Africa. In many coastal areas in South-East Asia the combined effect of more frequent and more intense rainfall and the rise in sea levels will mean greater flooding and erosion, shrinking wetlands and mangroves, and the intrusion of saltwater into freshwater resources. More than a third of the world population living within 100 kilometres of a coast is under threat. It is estimated that as much as 20 percent of the world's coastal wetlands could be lost by 2080 (IPCC 2002, p. 20).

The world faces a period of high climate variability and change, forcing people to live with the reality of higher temperatures, extreme rainfall or rain shortages, and a rise in sea levels that will affect their lives and those of their children, grandchildren, and possibly future generations. This prospect points to great challenges. The world needs to take urgent adaptation measures to cope with climate change and curtail its impacts and to take precautionary actions, such as changing lifestyles and unsustainable patterns of production and consumption.

What needs to be done?

There is a shortage of adequate disaster prevention, preparedness, and mitigation measures worldwide. This shortage stems from several factors. Risk reduction is not always treated as an integral part of water resources management. In addition, it is perceived as a technical problem, a perception that ignores the social factors compelling people to live in hazard-prone areas. And the political will to take adequate risk reduction measures is lacking. This is unfortunate, because investing in appropriate disaster management offers significant benefits. Such measures would reduce the loss of life, improve welfare, and strengthen social stability. Risk reduction would also increase the willingness to make vitally needed investments and would avoid the large opportunity costs faced by countries adapting to the effects of water-induced shocks on their economies.

Water-related risks 5

> *A woman on her own has restored the irrigation canal that had been destroyed by a volcanic eruption. Having seen this achievement, the entire community is now willing to participate in water resources management too.*
> —Indonesia

Conserving and restoring ecosystems are critical to mitigating disasters

Disaster prevention, preparedness, and mitigation need to be integrated into socio-economic development planning, including strategies for environmental conservation and, especially, for poverty alleviation. The impact of hazards varies depending on the socio-economic structure of the region affected—its population density, economic development, and land and urban planning. Moreover, the acceptable design level for disaster mitigation measures is governed by the resources available. Thus industrial countries can pursue a much higher level of protection than can developing countries.

In addition, sound natural ecosystems can provide an effective buffer against disasters. Thus conserving and restoring ecosystems are critical to mitigating the disasters, pointing to the importance of balancing the needs of people and nature.

With floods, the hazard potential relates to the magnitude of the event and the frequency of occurrence. It is becoming increasingly possible to predict floods in real time, though developing countries have less capacity to do this than industrial countries have. Mitigation measures include structural ones (such as dikes, levees, and flood control dams) and non-structural ones (land use planning, flood forecasting, and flood emergency response plans, among many others).

With droughts, the onset is generally slow, but the associated human and socio-economic losses are significant. Some claim that the resulting famines are generally a consequence of a lack of know-how, organizational capacity, distribution arrangements, and human and capital resources in poor regions. A range of short-term responses are available, including relief programmes, crop insurance schemes, changes in land use practices, irrigation from reservoirs or aquifers, and protection of priority water users. Longer-term measures include changing crops, building storage reservoirs, and decreasing risk rates for communities and families. In recent years seasonal and long-term climate prediction has improved markedly, greatly facilitating drought management.

Also needed are effective adaptation measures to cope with climate change, by strengthening the resilience of societies and natural ecosystems. Adaptation measures can be made more effective through accurate prediction of climate change and scenario building and through greater collaboration and dialogue between water managers and the climate community. Just as important as adaptation measures are precautionary measures to change activities that adversely affect the internal dynamics of the Earth's natural systems—measures such as reducing greenhouse gas emissions—and implementation of the Kyoto Protocol. Here, however, water and disaster managers can make only limited contributions.

5 Assessing Challenges, Initiating Change

Disaster mitigation measures lessen damage, but no defence can provide complete security

The major development challenge of the 21st century is the alleviation of poverty, an issue closely linked with risk reduction. Poor people are those most exposed to hazards and thus most at risk of losing their assets and even their lives, and they lack the resources for recovery after a disaster strikes. In the quest for jobs and income, poor people tend to settle in hazard-prone areas—along rivers or on hillsides—close to cities without any precautionary measures, despite government efforts to relocate them. In addition, poor people depend heavily on natural resources for their livelihoods, making them even more vulnerable to hazards—a vulnerability that climate change only increases. All these factors put poor people at great risk of falling into a disaster-poverty spiral. Thus it is no surprise that risk reduction and adaptation to climate change have become key issues in poverty alleviation.

What is being done?

The Actions Database contains a range of actions relating to the challenge of managing water-related risks. These actions can be classified by several themes:

- Enhancing the capabilities of people.
- Establishing and strengthening the framework for risk management.
- Ensuring sound planning and management.
- Developing useful tools.
- Promoting and sharing knowledge.

Additionally, actions show a focus on:

- adapting to climate change
- involving communities in disaster management
- tapping traditional knowledge and practices.

A few countries have recognized the need to strengthen their capacity to manage disasters, having learned the hard way after experiencing major disasters whose effects were exacerbated by inadequate policy and institutional frameworks and insufficient institutional capacity and resources. The recurrent floods in Mozambique provided some practical lessons on the institutional arrangements needed for dealing with disasters (box 5.2).

Enhancing the capabilities of people

Awareness raising. Disaster mitigation measures lessen damage, but no defence can provide complete security. Thus it is important to increase public awareness, across the board, about the measures that can be taken to reduce the occurrence of disasters and the vulnerability of societies and communities to them. The aim is to foster a "culture of prevention". Because the memory of a disaster fades away quickly—the "short memory syndrome"—efforts to raise people's awareness need to be continually maintained and enhanced.

Actions to raise awareness have been most common in Asia, the Pacific, and the Americas, where floods and typhoons or cyclones are particular concerns. One example is Raising Public Awareness for Disaster Reduction in Nepal (action 936), a programme providing awareness raising and training for community leaders. The media play an important role in some actions, such as the Tsunami Disaster Reduction Awareness Programme in Papua New Guinea (action 931), which spreads knowledge through television programmes and school education, and the Radio Soap Opera for Disaster Reduction in Latin

Water-related risks 5

There is a growing appreciation of the importance of regional cooperation in disaster management

Box 5.2 Floods in Mozambique: impacts, consequences, and responses

In 2000 torrential rainfall caused a major flood in Mozambique that directly or indirectly affected about 4.9 million people. The flood displaced more than 350,000 people and claimed 700 lives along the Limpopo River (UNEP UNCHS Joint Mission 2000, pp. 3–4). The next year, with recovery from the 2000 flood still incomplete, heavy rainfall again struck Mozambique, resulting in the flooding of the Zambezi River. Thanks to the lessons of the 2000 flood, preparations in 2001 were largely adequate for dealing with the floods, and less additional help was needed (AFP 2001). Preparations appear to have reduced losses, even if about 230,000 people were displaced and some 115 lives were lost (UN Resident Coordinator 2001).

The floods affecting much of southern Africa in 2000–01 led to greater recognition of the need to prepare for a wider range of sudden threats. The Southern African Development Community (SADC) had already begun to develop disaster management as a regional priority. But the impact of the floods across the region pointed to a need for better institutional arrangements for disaster management in the future. In August 2000 SADC member countries approved the SADC Disaster Management Framework, an integrated regional approach, and in May 2001 they approved the Strategy for Flood and Drought Management (action 1861) for implementation over four years. The SADC countries also signed the SADC Shared Watercourse Systems Protocol (action 792), which provides a framework for transboundary management in the region. Although not all member countries have ratified the protocol yet, there is a growing appreciation of the importance of regional cooperation in disaster management.

In Mozambique a priority has been to improve the provision of public information through the use of professional media equipment, an effort pursued in the Post-Emergency Reconstruction Programme in Mozambique (action 1898). In addition, Mozambique and the Zambezi River Authority have set up the Joint Operations Technical Committee (action 1860) to share data and information on reservoirs. Progress can also be seen in neighbouring countries. Prompted by the devastating impact of the floods, the South African Parliament restarted discussions on a disaster management bill (action 2543).

All these initiatives will help improve disaster management, but several other measures are needed to further strengthen the capacity to prevent damage from future hazards. A key lesson of the floods in Mozambique was that arrangements for coordinating emergency responses were inadequate. Although the Mozambique government had a coordinating body, each emergency assistance agency and non-governmental organization seemed to work independently, based on its own planning or interests.

Another issue relates to the adequacy, timing, and reliability of warning systems. Poor people are often reluctant to evacuate early because they fear that their household belongings will be stolen. Moreover, they tend to mistrust and, far worse, ignore warning messages and related information because of past failures in timely prediction or a false sense of safety.

A third issue is the need to strengthen capacity in a situation of high vulnerability and low preparedness through timely and appropriate use of resources. After the floods the international community gave $100 million in emergency assistance and relief and later pledged more than $450 million for rehabilitation. But before the floods, in 1999, the Mozambique government received less than half of the $3 million international aid it had requested for immediate preparedness and mitigation activities for the upcoming rainy season (ISDR 2002c, pp. 97–99).

5 Assessing Challenges, Initiating Change

Capacity building in disaster management requires education and training from the school to the professional level

America and the Caribbean (action 1945). Local communities and non-governmental organizations (NGOs) also play leading roles, such as in the Floodwater Campaign of the Rhine (action 1908). The Secretariat of the International Strategy for Disaster Reduction conducts the main global awareness raising campaign as a representative United Nations agency, organizing the United Nations World Disaster Reduction Campaigns (action 539), on a different theme every year.

Capacity building. Capacity building in disaster management requires education and training from the school to the professional level. Professional training involves teaching disaster managers and support staff, transferring technical know-how, and strengthening organizational capacity at local, national, and regional levels. The programme Building Capacity in Albania (action 1285) focuses on local authorities and communities, working with them to clarify their roles and improve their collaboration. The Asian Urban Disaster Mitigation Programme (action 796) provides training and education in target countries, among many other activities. And the United Nations Economic and Social Commission for Asia and the Pacific is initiating a programme to strengthen capacity in participatory planning and management in Asian River Basins (action 159).

Emergency response preparation. Disasters require immediate assistance with food, water, shelter, medical care, and other resources. While this assistance tends to be provided by external sources, especially for developing countries, all countries should nevertheless be adequately prepared for emergencies, even those in which hazards are rare.

Several actions have focused on preparing for an emergency response. An action in Vietnam, Disaster Preparedness by the Vietnam Red Cross (action 413), equipped disaster preparedness centres with food and emergency kits for relief operations and established "shock brigades" of citizens. Another action in that country, Disaster Management System in Vietnam (action 907), is installing emergency backup power supply for relief and evacuation efforts. After Hurricane Mitch the Pan-American Disaster Response Unit (action 1369) prepared relief equipment to be shipped anywhere in Latin America and organized volunteers and community brigades for emergencies. The Integrated Community Disaster Planning Programme in the Philippines (action 1297) conducts risk reduction programmes with community members, including preparing hazard maps and constructing health centres and bridges for emergency evacuations. The growing use of mobile phones will be an increasingly valuable means of delivering warning messages in cases of emergency, even for the local poor.

Water-related risks 5

> *Water is the source of life, but it is also a threat and disaster. Protecting and controlling water resources is therefore always on the Nghe An people's minds.*
> —Vietnam

Most cities are destined to become more densely populated and thus more vulnerable to hazards

Establishing and strengthening the framework for risk management

To ensure effective disaster management, all countries need comprehensive policies and strategies, an appropriate legal framework, and relevant institutions. And where these exist, countries must ensure that they are effectively implemented and enforced. Progress in this key area remains insufficient in most developing countries, a serious concern. The poor progress could be due to several factors, including a lack of financial resources, of capacity, or of institutional and political will.

Changing policy and legislation can be politically difficult, and progress in this area has been observed in few countries. Still, there have been several actions seeking policy and legislative changes. Two of these are in Europe, prompted by the flooding across the region in 2002: Flood Prevention and Mitigation Measures in Germany (action 1566), aimed at speeding up and strengthening current programmes, and the European Union Solidarity Fund (action 2346), designed to provide emergency funds rapidly at the request of member countries responding to disasters. In Japan, the Revision of Flood Fighting Law (action 1581) promotes hazard mapping. Legislative actions are also under way in Bolivia (action 1944), St Lucia (action 1988), and Nicaragua (action 1958).

Other actions are focusing on institutional change, with some creating unified management centres or committees to deal with disasters. To take greater advantage of existing synergies and avoid duplication of roles and activities, Switzerland has created the National Platform for Natural Hazards, or PLANAT (action 1901), to foster links among the different sectors involved in dealing with natural hazards. China and India are reforming their disaster management frameworks. China has formulated the National Disaster Reduction Plan (action 1956), covering the years through 2010, and has also established an interministerial coordinating institution, the China National Committee (action 1955). India has set up the High-Powered Committee (action 1953) to strengthen its institutional arrangements for disaster management, is preparing the National Act for Calamity Management, and has reassigned all disaster management issues to a single ministry through the Governmental Shift on Disaster Management (action 1954).

Ensuring sound planning and management

Land use planning. The future population growth that is predicted, especially in developing countries, means that most cities are destined to become more densely populated and thus more vulnerable to hazards. Land use, especially in urban and semi-urban areas, must therefore be planned carefully to minimize the risk due to hazards while maximizing economic development. Overexploitation of land combined with a lack of appropriate mitigation measures increases the severity of flash floods and the vulnerability to drought. Inadequate sanitation and insufficient control of a wide range of wastes and pollutants lead to the degradation of water resources. Actions relating to land use planning for improved disaster management include a regional one in Angola, Bostwana, and Namibia focusing on floodplain planning in the Okavango Delta and Basin (action 905) and one at the country level in Mexico (action 1185).

5 Assessing Challenges, Initiating Change

Disaster mitigation efforts should use nature's own resilience and adaptability as much as possible

> **Flooding and pollution are caused mainly by improper planning and failure to enforce rules and regulations, to please a few people in power. The poor suffer in the end.** —Sri Lanka

Implementation and management. In some parts of the world physical structures to mitigate the effects of hazards have been or are being constructed, but in other parts much remains to be done. To increase the effectiveness of disaster mitigation efforts, the best use needs to be made of existing infrastructure. For example, roads and canals can control floodwater, and natural ponds and lakes make good buffering reservoirs. In narrow basins, however, a retreat from the floodplain might be a solution, as in the United States after the 1993 flood of the Mississippi River (action 1825).

Skilful management of natural resources is important. Poorly managed catchments shed their runoff quickly into rivers and streams, increasing the size of flood peaks. Lack of appropriate soil conservation measures on steep slopes increases their vulnerability to landslides and mudslides. And sustainable sediment management in basins and reservoirs is essential to maintain their capacity for coping with floods and droughts.

Equally important is environmental management. Deforestation in mountainous areas can aggravate floods, droughts, and water pollution. Poverty can worsen the situation by leading to overexploitation of forests and other natural resources. Restoration of the ecosystem can reverse the damage, mitigate the disasters, and lead to other benefits, as in China (action 1325) and Japan (action 1399). For example, healthy wetlands mitigate disasters in many ways—such as through water storage, flood mitigation, shoreline stabilization, and erosion control—and also help maintain biodiversity. The restoration of mangroves in Vietnam (action 2499), intended as a buffer against frequent coastal storms and as a source of local livelihood benefits, helped avert significant damage from the worst typhoon in a decade. Disaster mitigation efforts should use nature's own resilience and adaptability as much as possible.

Efforts to manage water-related disasters require full consideration of the entire hydrological cycle—failure to do so can aggravate the impact of hazards. A systematic approach is needed, since any action will influence the hydrological cycle. Aquifers and soils can both store water and slow the runoff of surface water, lessening the effects of excess water or shortages.

The Actions Database includes a range of management projects, such as the Nagykoru Revitalization Project in Hungary (action 1013) and Flood Mitigation in Milicz Ponds in Poland (action 1275). A project focusing on flood control and groundwater recharge in Beijing (action 1469) aims to recharge groundwater to reduce the impacts of floods in the urban area. The CALFED Storage Program in California (action 1764) and the Efficient Use of Existing Infrastructure in Japan (action 1839) are aimed at improving water management to secure enough water storage capacity to meet demand.

Operation and maintenance. Even when structures are in place to mitigate the disasters, they can become ineffective without proper operation and maintenance and, much worse, can lead to adverse impacts rather than the expected benefits. In developing countries especially, overflow from badly managed urban drainage and sewerage systems threatens human health, leads to water pollution and environmental degradation, and sometimes causes urban flooding. Inadequate operation and maintenance of large infrastructure, such as dams, dikes, and treatment plants, can cause serious problems resulting in huge social and economic losses.

Water-related risks 5

Early warning allows people at risk from a disaster to avoid or reduce the risk and prepare an effective response

Attempts to improve operation and maintenance can be seen in the Lagos Drainage Department Improvement in Nigeria (action 1866) and Drainage Rehabilitation in Quanzhou, China (action 1600), both aimed at securing the capacity of urban drainage systems in the event of floods. The Jamuna-Meghna River Erosion Mitigation Project in Bangladesh (action 2199) aims to tackle riverbank erosion by constructing revetments as well as to strengthen institutional capacity. Ecosystem Management in the Huong River Basin in Vietnam (action 887) focuses on maintaining existing structures, rehabilitating degraded wetlands, and conserving ecosystem services. In the United States an action called Leakage Reduction in New Jersey (action 462) seeks to reduce unaccounted-for water losses in preparation for droughts.

Developing useful tools

Early warning. Early warning means providing timely and effective information, through identified institutions, that allows people at risk from a disaster to avoid or reduce the risk and prepare an effective response. In an action at the local level, the Community Operated Early Warning in Guatemala (action 1370), volunteers monitor rainfall and the water levels in rivers. Cooperation between Hungary and Romania on transboundary pollution in the Crisuri River (action 706) seeks to reinforce the warning system for water pollution. Regional actions include efforts to reduce vulnerability to floods and develop local warning systems in Central America, in the Natural Hazards Project of the Organization of American States (action 909). In Europe a Flood Early Warning System is developed for the Rhine (action 1843), and in Africa the Famine Early Warning System Network (action 1252) covers the drought-prone Sub-Saharan region.

Risk maps and management guides. Risk maps, which identify the places and buildings in a community or geographical zone that might be adversely affected in the event of a hurricane, flood, or other hazard, can help land use planners and decision-makers prevent serious damage from hazards through appropriate development planning and disaster management policies. Actions related to risk maps are particularly evident in industrial countries (action 1644 in France, 307 in Japan, 1715 in Norway, and 920 in the United States). And the Typhoon Committee has just started the Flood Hazard Mapping Project (action 1635) to promote the development of risk maps by sharing experiences and information among eight member countries in Asia.

Risk management guides can provide useful information in preparing for hazards. The Flood Risk Guide in the United Kingdom (action 805) is designed to help land use planners and those who own assets at risk from floods. The Comprehensive Hazard and Risk Management Regional Guidelines in the Pacific (action 1378) can aid in the preparation of national risk management policies. And the Inventory of Potential Accident Risk Spots in the Danube (action 757) provides information on potential sources of water pollutants.

5 Assessing Challenges, Initiating Change

At the heart of effective disaster management are collecting and sharing data and information

Economic tools. Economic tools for disaster management include insurance, micro-credit, and markets for trading water rights. Other tools are also considered effective in reducing risk, such as water prices that encourage efficient use (to mitigate the effects of drought) and water pollution charges.

Areas hit by disasters often lack resources to absorb the losses resulting from hazards, but the risk of such losses can be transferred within or across countries through the insurance system. In the United States insurance covers more than 50 percent of private property losses resulting from natural hazards, while in Asia 2 percent of total losses incurred were reimbursed (Freeman 1999, p. 5). Although transferring risk through insurance is no panacea, the insurance system can reduce the impacts of hazards by providing incentives to adopt cost-effective risk reduction measures and carefully evaluate risks. Under an action in France, Flood Risk Mapping and Insurance (action 1644), a new law has authorized insurance companies to raise their franchise (the fixed amount deducted from what the insurer reimburses) in municipalities at risk from floods. Other actions relating to insurance include the Cambodia Disaster Insurance Project (action 1875) and Weather Risk Management Study in Morocco (action 1876), both aimed at reducing income shocks among farmers and enhancing self-reliance among the rural poor at risk from natural hazards.

Promoting and sharing knowledge

Data and information. At the heart of effective disaster management are collecting and sharing data and information. Providing more precise forecasts of hazards and better predictions of their intensity requires mechanisms for collecting and exchanging meteorological, hydrological, and hydraulic data. Sharing lessons and best practices is also important.

Some actions in this area are transboundary projects. The Tisza Platform (action 19) in Hungary and Romania consolidates the monitoring programmes of NGOs, and Data Sharing in the Mekong River (action 758) has installed two automated hydrologic data stations along the Chinese stretch of the river although China is not a member of the Mekong River Commission. The new World Climate Programme (action 1005) has extended its activities to provide the world water community with current data and information on hydrological and water resources conditions. And in recent years Web sites have begun to disseminate data and information to people affected by natural hazards, such as in the Mozambique Flood Information Project (action 806).

To sustain disaster mitigation efforts and avoid decisions based on inadequate data and information, data monitoring and recording facilities must be regularly maintained and upgraded. The Mekong River Commission has started the Appropriate Hydrological Network Improvement Project (action 1874) to upgrade hydrological data stations.

Networks and partnerships. Creating networks and partnerships aids disaster preparedness by providing platforms for exchanging data and information and sharing lessons and best practices. Regional cooperative schemes increase the benefits of such exchanges by moving them beyond national borders.

Some actions in this area have been initiated by NGOs and by international or regional organizations. Two actions illustrate the leading roles of NGOs: the Community Drought Mitigation Partners' Network in Zimbabwe (action 1934) and the Southern Africa Drought Technology Network (action 1902). These seek to share research results and technical knowledge with local farmers.

Water-related risks | 5

Recent technological innovations, such as satellite monitoring and geographic information systems, have supported more accurate predictions of precipitation and river flow

Actions at the country level include the National Natural Disaster Knowledge Network in India (action 1903) and the Australian Disaster Information Network (action 1904). Each is a "network of networks", or consortium, to support a dialogue among all the organizations involved.

There are several regional actions: the Southern Africa Flood and Drought Information Network (action 808), the Partnerships for Disaster Reduction in Southeast Asia (action 1281), and the Water Level Observation Network for Central America (action 958). Another, PREANDINO—Regional Programme for Risk Prevention and Reduction (action 2156), is a regional coordinating platform in the Andean countries. It aims to promote region-wide risk reduction programmes and to further encourage international organizations to propose and implement projects involving national and regional cooperation to improve the effectiveness of investments.

Global actions include the Global Disaster Information Network (action 1936), which supports provision of the right information in the right form to the right people in time to make the right decisions. Another is the Global Terrestrial Network—Hydrology (action 1012), a network of global data centres and information providers supplying hydrological and meteorological data and information. And the Global Drought Preparedness Network (action 784) allows nations and regions to share experiences and lessons through a virtual network of regional networks around the world.

Research and development. Advanced research helps develop risk management tools and improve the accuracy of hazard prediction. Recent technological innovations, such as satellite monitoring and geographic information systems, have supported more accurate predictions of precipitation and river flow in the short and medium term. Computer and communications technology allows faster analysis and broader and speedier dissemination of data and information to decision-makers and people at risk. In agriculture, advances in molecular biology, functional genomics, and biotechnology offer great potential. New varieties of corn (maize) are more tolerant of drought. And rainfed crops can be developed that provide high yields even with recurrent mild water deficits. These and other developments can do much to increase capacities in disaster management.

Actions relating to research and technology include IHOP2002 (action 608) in the United States, a study that involves tracking water vapour to improve weather forecasting. Other actions are mainly in Europe. The IRMA (International Rhine-Meuse Activities) SPONGE Umbrella Programme in the Rhine and Meuse River Basins (action 419) supports scientific research on floods. Another action is working to set up a European Flood Forecasting System through a consortium of academic and research institutes, based on recent scientific advances (action 1380).

At the international level United Nations agencies, bilateral and multilateral aid agencies, and other international organizations can provide important support to national disaster management strategies and initiatives by developing research and study programmes and sharing professional knowledge and practices. The FRIEND (Flow Regimes from International Experimental and Network Data) Research Programme (action 412) is bringing together research institutes, universities, and operational agencies in an international collaborative study that fosters the exchange of data, knowledge, and techniques.

5 Assessing Challenges, Initiating Change

Developing countries face the greatest potential impacts from climate change but have the weakest capacity to cope with the effects

Another international research initiative is the Prediction in Ungauged Basins Project (action 1863), which promotes the development of the science and technology needed to provide hydrological data where ground observations are missing. By analysing a selection of case studies from around the world, the Associated Programme on Flood Management (action 75) aims to provide a mechanism for coordinating regional flood management activities. The mechanism will be based on a new concept of integrated flood management within the context of integrated water resources management. Actions focusing on technology include the Satellite-Based Monitoring of Large Lake Areas (action 759), which allows simultaneous observation of water quality and such rapidly evolving phenomena as algae blooms and oil spills. The monitoring technology, originated in Europe, can be applied globally.

Climate change abatement policies require a systematic approach, without which any solution will be short term. Actions adopting such an approach include the International Geosphere-Biosphere Programme (action 2340), which is investigating such topics as the characteristic regimes and time scales of Earth's natural variability and the interaction of anthropogenic disturbance regimes with sudden and extreme events.

Adapting to climate change

Few water policy and decision-making frameworks have fully considered the implications of climate change. This is particularly true in developing countries, which face the greatest potential financial, human, and ecological impacts from climate change but have the weakest capacity to cope with the effects. Moreover, these countries may already have highly stressed water resources.

Although few actions relating to climate change appear to have been implemented, some of those under way are significant. One of these is in the Himalayan region, where climate change will lead to the melting of glaciers and glacial lakes, resulting in glacial lake outburst floods (GLOF). After an assessment study, the United Nations Environment Programme created an inventory of glacial lakes and developed the GLOF Monitoring and Early Warning System (action 857) in the Himalayan region. A pilot mitigation project is also under way, the Tsho Rolpa GLOF Risk Reduction Project (action 827) in Nepal. A global initiative is promoting information sharing and dialogue between the water and climate communities (action 71) and is now promoting regional and national dialogues on water and climate as well (actions 1111, 1213, 1214, 1215, 1216, 1217, 1218, 1219, 1584, 1585, 1587, 1589, 1591, 1592, 1593, 1595, and 1596). And efforts are being made to strengthen scientific and technical capacity in the project Assessment of Impacts of and Adaptation to Climate Change in Multiple Regions and Sectors (action 2137) and the Climate Affairs Capacity Building Programme (action 2012). These actions are intended to help reduce vulnerability to the intensified effects of hazards expected to result from climate change and to enhance people's ability to cope with and adapt to climate change.

Water-related risks   5

> *Every year in the monsoon my house is flooded with filthy water from the adjoining canal. I am too poor to move my house to a higher area.*
> —India

Disaster management should directly involve stakeholders in the at-risk communities—because these communities form the front line during disasters

Funding of work related to climate change has been under way since the 1990s. The United Nations Framework Convention on Climate Change (UNFCCC) established a special fund to aid the least developed countries in preparing and implementing national programmes of action for adapting to climate change—the UNFCCC Fund on Climate Change (action 2323), managed under the Global Environment Facility. But the fund has given priority to mitigation strategies for reducing greenhouse gas emissions. Activities to adapt water management strategies have received little attention and often do not meet the funding criteria. Thus water managers need to seek other funding sources for such activities.

Few options exist: the Netherlands Climate Change Studies Assistance Programme (action 2325), or in Canada, the Climate Change Action Fund (action 2324). The latter has already supported several case studies and research projects on risk evaluation, the potential effects of Arctic ice melt and a rise in sea levels, and the potential changes in water quality and quantity due to climate change.

Involving communities in disaster management

Disaster management should directly involve stakeholders in the at-risk communities—because these communities form the front line during disasters. But government programmes are often developed through a top-down process, with too little community involvement. And in developing countries especially, where the state's capacity to protect its citizens may be limited, communities must rely on their own knowledge and coping mechanisms to deal with disasters, just as they have done for generations.

It is just this experience in coping with disasters that makes risk reduction measures more likely to succeed when they are developed with direct community participation in planning, decision-making, and implementation. Community-based approaches are effective for several reasons (IFRC 2002, pp. 22–23):

- Communities define their problems more accurately than outsiders and identify appropriate measures to overcome them by assessing their real needs and priorities.
- Communities draw on local skills and expertise developed by living with disasters.
- Communities deploy low-cost, appropriate technologies effectively, and the technologies are likely to be sustainable because they are owned by the community and build local capacity.

Especially crucial is to involve women at all stages of the decision-making, because women play a central part in managing and safeguarding water. In developing countries women are often the main providers of water for household use, and risk reduction measures such as drought alleviation would reduce the time and effort required to carry water from distant sources. Moreover, in cultures where husbands are often absent, it is women and their children who must respond to disasters.

Some actions involving community participation have already been mentioned. Community-Based Mitigation in Peru (action 906) supports risk mapping and helps expand volunteer brigades specializing in emergency rescue. An effort in the Philippines shows the potential of communities to cope effectively with disasters (box 5.3).

69

5 Assessing Challenges, Initiating Change

Indigenous knowledge and practices can help meet today's requirements in risk management

Tapping traditional knowledge and practices

Indigenous knowledge and practices can help meet today's requirements in risk management. In emergencies the traditional community provides vital support in villages, while urban immigrants often lack networks for cooperation and knowledge about appropriate behaviours to protect themselves. The *Plan of Implementation* adopted by the World Summit on Sustainable Development urges countries to "encourage the dissemination and use of traditional and indigenous knowledge to mitigate the impact of disasters" (United Nations 2002, p. 16).

In many hazard-prone areas, such as in those in Asia, Latin America, and North Africa, land use and other practices are often based on traditional knowledge and customs that have helped deal with natural hazards for centuries. Few actions have been directed at re-evaluating indigenous technology or enhancing cultural networks and relationships in risk management policies. One action, Flood-Resistant Houses in Vietnam (action 908), is using a competition among indigenous organizations to promote the construction of traditional hardwood buildings as protection against floods and typhoons.

Box 5.3 Community disaster response committees in the Philippines

In the Philippines a national network of grass-roots and regional non-governmental organizations has developed strategies to enhance people's capacity to cope with disasters. Working with communities, the network has helped form village disaster response committees, develop early warning systems, organize rescue teams, and diversify sources of livelihood. After a three-day training course on disaster preparedness, community members design a warning system, formulate an evacuation plan, and identify key people and agencies they can tap in case the community needs to evacuate.

One village set up a disaster response organization with five committees. The warning committee recruited volunteers from the village and briefed them on their responsibilities. Three days after the training a typhoon hit the area, but the committee warned the community well in advance and no one was hurt or killed even though the water rose to 1–2 metres in the village. The outcome shows the importance of building people's capacity to monitor hazards and issue warnings to save lives.

Building on the network's experiences, the Philippines Disaster Management Forum was created in 2002 to allow for sharing of experiences and interaction between various stakeholders: non-governmental organizations, local authorities, and national administrations (action 3461).

Source: ISDR 2002a.

What remains to be done?

The problems in disaster management outlined in this chapter are essentially about lost opportunity—to protect and save lives and to attract vital investment. Some countries are addressing these problems and have made apparent progress, though the efforts need to be accelerated and more resources need to be applied.

Among the biggest obstacles to effective disaster management in most developing countries are inadequate institutions. Few countries have established consistent, coordinated programmes that involve government institutions, the private sector, and the population and that prioritize a set of actions (both software and hardware) with clear timelines. Inadequate budgetary resources also stand in the way of effective action.

Water-related risks

Actions must be taken before disasters occur

Much was learned about institutional problems during and after the Mozambique flood. The evidence suggests that several countries have recognized the urgent need to review or establish disaster management policies after having experienced disasters. But many governments still act only after disaster has struck. Actions must be taken before disasters occur. And once all reasonable measures have been taken to reduce risk, care is needed to avoid a false sense of security. People must not assume that nature can be controlled and that they can be completely protected from hazards—constant vigilance is required.

There are clear priorities that need to be addressed at local, national, regional, and global levels:

- Integrating disaster prevention, preparedness, and mitigation into socio-economic development planning, especially strategies for poverty alleviation, an issue closely linked with risk reduction.
- Strengthening the capacity to implement risk reduction measures and immediately establishing legal and institutional frameworks for risk management where they do not now exist.
- Promoting regional or transboundary cooperation in sharing knowledge and information and working on shared challenges. Such cooperation could be aided by initiatives of the United Nations agencies and other international and regional organizations.
- Involving local communities and NGOs in risk management by offering resources and incentives—while ensuring adequate recognition of gender issues.
- Strengthening monitoring, information sharing, and data collection and promoting scientific research and technological innovations by optimizing the development of science and technology (computers, satellites, modelling).
- Replicating useful experiences that could be adapted to other countries and regions, taking into account geographic, climatic, and cultural context.
- Establishing or enlarging funding schemes, such as those under the Global Environment Facility, to improve the coverage of adaptation measures for coping with climate variability and change (not just abatement and mitigation measures) while ensuring links between global policies and national and local actions by water managers.
- Enhancing research on climate change, strengthening adaptation measures for coping with climate change, promoting a systematic approach to climate change abatement policies, and implementing the Kyoto Protocol.

A crucial priority is to increase the investment in risk management. Too little has been invested in practical measures to mitigate disasters and to anticipate them before they strike. Sound, sustainable financing mechanisms need to be developed for risk management and climate change adaptation, drawing on national budgets, bilateral and multilateral aid, and private investment. The costs of prevention and mitigation are usually far less than those of disaster relief and recovery.

Also needed are stronger coordination and solidarity not only among those affected by hazards but also among donor agencies and other organizations concerned, to ensure effective and efficient use of the limited resources. This is important for maximizing the efforts of donor agencies and other organizations, which tend to be driven by "supply side" objectives and interests. Better coordination is also needed in sharing and applying data and information. Abundant information is available locally, nationally, and globally. The question is how to make the best use of it. A strong case can be made for creating a clearing-house—to identify, order, and disseminate the information, ensuring that it gets to those who need it most, at the time and in the form they need it.

5 Assessing Challenges, Initiating Change

A policy approach aimed at climate change abatement must be adopted, an approach that fully takes into account the Earth's natural systems

To avoid increasingly severe disasters, a policy approach aimed at climate change abatement must be adopted, an approach that fully takes into account the Earth's natural systems. Without such a policy approach, no sustainable solution can be reached. Immediate measures are needed to reduce greenhouse gas emissions and encourage carbon sequestration.

6. Financing water infrastructure and services

Investments in water resources are investments not merely in the water sector, but in socio-economic development and poverty alleviation as well. When compared with investments in sectors such as telecommunications and energy, these investments may appear to produce low yields and slow returns. But viewed from a national or regional perspective, they can be enormously productive (as well as enormously damaging if badly designed).

Today investment levels in water institutions and infrastructure are far too low, and, worse, funding from some sources is declining. And water prices are too low to cover costs, putting at risk the financial and physical sustainability of water systems. National governments need to come rapidly to grips with the challenge of meeting financing needs in the water sector—for investment as well as operation and maintenance—taking advantage of the aid community's increasingly favourable attitude towards putting funding into water.

And governments need to translate political decisions into adequate allocations of resources to water. The Millennium Development Goals, especially the goal of reducing poverty by half by 2015, cannot be achieved at current levels of spending for water.

Present situation

As underlined throughout this report, water is central to human development and environmental preservation. But there is a big gap between the high value that society attaches to water—for supporting life, meeting basic needs, safeguarding public health, protecting the environment, and supporting agriculture and industry—and the low profile it is given in national development plans and strategies.

This gap is reflected in underinvestment—and declining investment—in water sector institutions and infrastructure. The current levels of investment fall short of what is needed to meet the Millennium Development Goals for water and sanitation services (see box B.1). It is not clear whether the current rate of investment allows for even simple replacement of worn-out infrastructure.

6 Assessing Challenges, Initiating Change

The main share of the financing for water investments comes from the domestic public sector

> **Rich households pay so little for tap water that they often leave it running all day, while some poor people have to pay high prices for bottled water.**
> —Samoa

A Lehman Brothers study estimates the capital cost of the infrastructure required to achieve the Millennium Development Goal on water supply at 234 billion euros and that on sanitation at 451 billion euros (Averous 2002). So some 50 billion euros a year would be needed just to finance the capital costs of new infrastructure. Adding to the funding problem are water prices too low to support adequate operation and maintenance to prevent deterioration of existing systems.

Increasing investment in water will require tapping all available sources of finance: public funding and users' contributions first and foremost, but also private finance (domestic or international) and development funds. This financing effort must be supported by a more consistent strategy to recover costs from users and to establish incentives to ensure more efficient use of water.

Sources of investment funding

While greater investment is needed throughout the water sector, the financing situation differs across subsectors. In irrigation most investment is funded from public sources (national budgets and aid) and farmers' own resources. In hydropower most investment financing comes from governments, but the private sector, aid agencies, and international financial institutions also contribute. In municipal water, sanitation, and wastewater collection and treatment the funding comes mainly from the public sector, supplemented by utilities' cash flow (from users) and some aid. Investments in flood control, environmental protection, water resources management, and the like are almost entirely the public sector's responsibility.

Public funding. Globally, the main share of the financing for water investments comes from the domestic public sector (figure 6.1). Governments invest in new irrigation schemes, because national food security is an important objective, and in new water supply, but often neglect funding for maintenance and rehabilitation (which is less visible) and investment in sanitation. This results in an incoherent investment strategy.

Figure 6.1 Breakdown of financing in the water sector

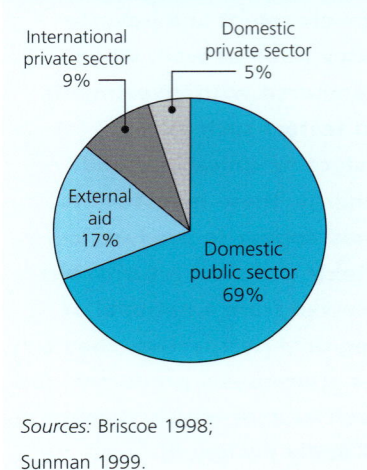

- International private sector: 9%
- Domestic private sector: 5%
- External aid: 17%
- Domestic public sector: 69%

Sources: Briscoe 1998; Sunman 1999.

Forming an accurate picture of public funding for the water sector is extremely difficult. While public funding accounts for the largest share of sector resources, the total amount spent is unknown. One reason is structural: much of the public funding comes from regional and local authorities, and no aggregate data for these sources are available.

Financing water infrastructure and services 6

Projects in the water sector are slightly less targeted to poverty and gender concerns than are those in other sectors

International aid to water. An analysis of water aid by the Development Assistance Committee of the Organisation for Economic Co-operation and Development (OECD) shows that total aid has declined since 1996 (figure 6.2). Moreover, official development assistance still averages only 0.24 percent of donor countries' gross national income, far short of the 0.7 percent target set by the United Nations. But even if official development assistance accounts for a minor share of the funding for water investments, the decline in overall assistance remains a source of concern, particularly for the poorest countries.

Analysis by the OECD of aid for water supply and sanitation yields some interesting results (Benn 2003).

- Most aid-funded water supply and sanitation projects are "large systems", but the number of projects based on low-cost techniques (latrines, hand pumps, rainwater collection, gravity-fed systems, and the like) seems to be growing.

- About 10 percent of aid is directed to water resources policy, planning, and programmes, including technical assistance and capacity building.
- The aid for water supply and sanitation is concentrated in a relatively small number of recipient countries (in 1997–2001 the 10 largest recipients received 48 percent of total aid to the water sector), while many countries in which a large share of the population still lacks access to safe water received little if any aid for this sector.
- In 2000 and 2001 about 57 percent of official development assistance to the water sector came in the form of loans, not grants.
- Projects in the water sector are slightly less targeted to poverty and gender concerns than are those in other sectors.

International private investments. For years international private investors have favoured other infrastructure sectors over water (figure 6.3). Water investments tend to be less attractive because they are capital-intensive and have low yields and long return periods and because their success depends on the institutional and regulatory context. Moreover, private investors have recently become more cautious about investing in developing countries (including emerging market economies such as Argentina and

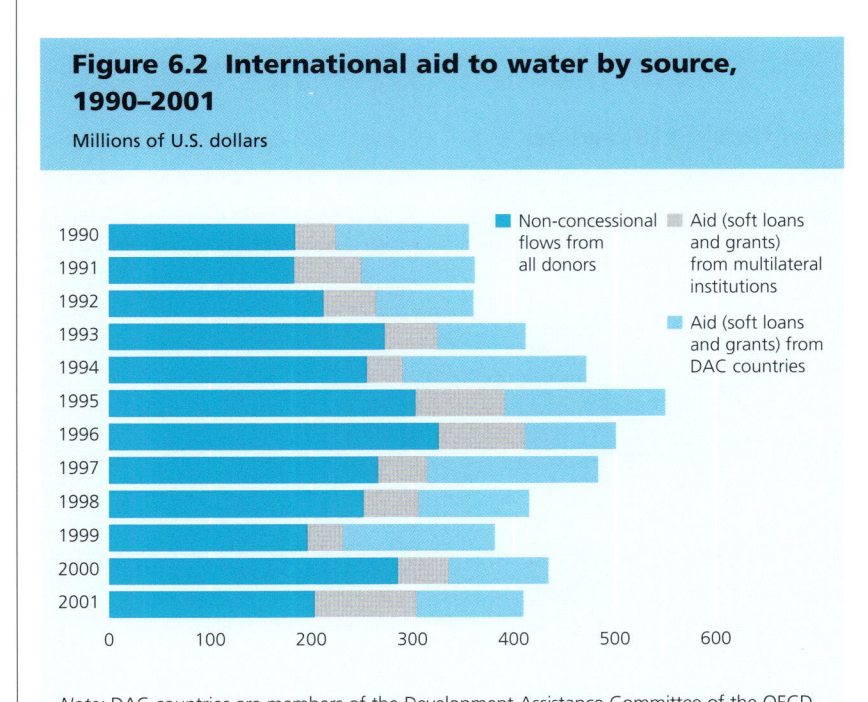

Figure 6.2 International aid to water by source, 1990–2001

Millions of U.S. dollars

Legend: Non-concessional flows from all donors; Aid (soft loans and grants) from multilateral institutions; Aid (soft loans and grants) from DAC countries

Note: DAC countries are members of the Development Assistance Committee of the OECD.
Source: OECD Development Assistance Committee and Creditor Reporting System.

6 Assessing Challenges, Initiating Change

International private companies tend to depart from developing countries or to invest less there, and the water sector suffers

Figure 6.3 Annual investment in infrastructure projects with private participation in developing countries by sector, 1990–2001

Billions of U.S. dollars

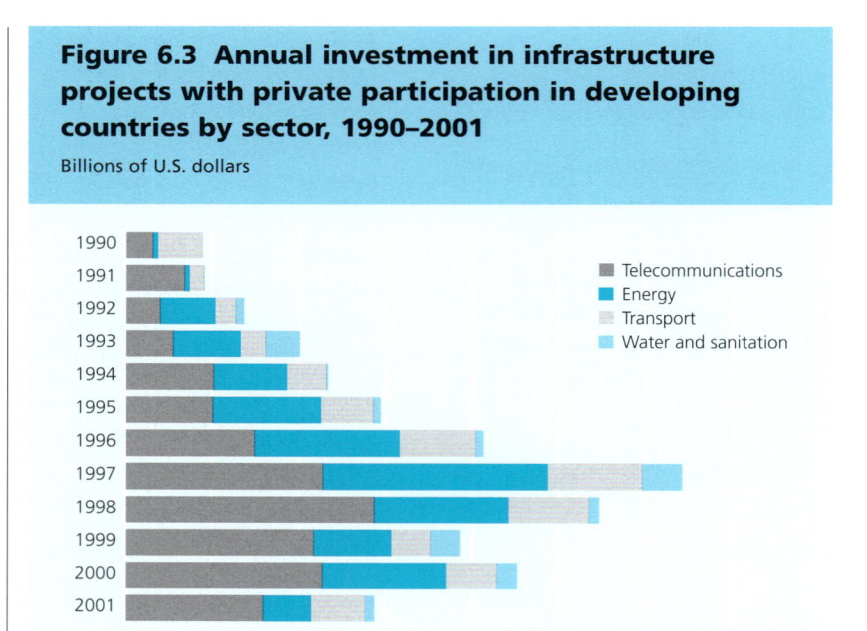

[Stacked bar chart showing investment by sector (Telecommunications, Energy, Transport, Water and sanitation) for each year from 1990 to 2001]

Source: World Bank, Private Participation in Infrastructure Project Database.

Figure 6.4 Net private long-term financial flows to developing countries, 1991–2001

Billions of U.S. dollars

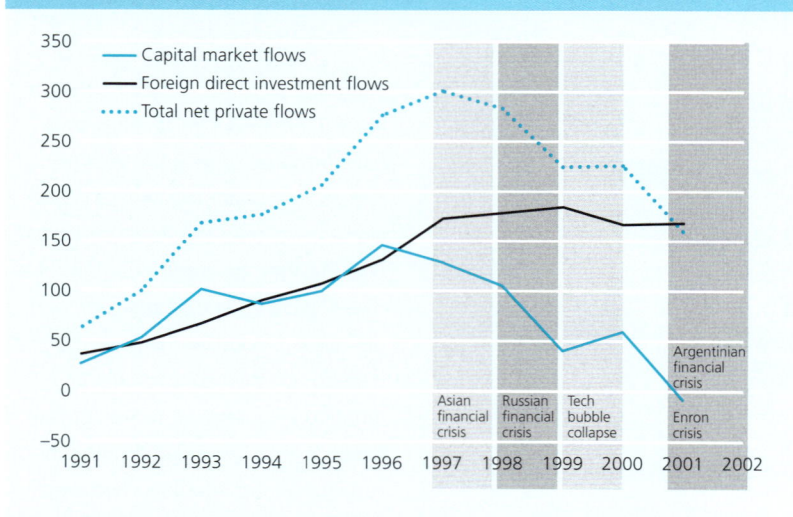

[Line chart showing Capital market flows, Foreign direct investment flows, and Total net private flows from 1991 to 2002, with shaded regions marking the Asian financial crisis, Russian financial crisis, Tech bubble collapse, Enron crisis, and Argentinian financial crisis]

Source: World Bank, Private Participation in Infrastructure Project Database.

Russia) because of the heightened risks associated with the financial crises of the late 1990s, especially those in South-East Asia and Latin America. These crises coincided with a decline in private investment in developing countries generally (figure 6.4). This trend reflects in the investments in water and sanitation with private participation. Unable to consolidate the financial risks in their accounts, international private companies tend to depart from developing countries or to invest less there, and the water sector suffers.

Self-help. Communities generally lack the knowledge to initiate and design water and sanitation projects and are even less likely to know how to finance the project and keep the books. Still, even in a sea of failure there are islands of success. These tend to be based on community participation and use such tools as training, micro-credit, and low-cost technologies.

Financing water infrastructure and services

> *Today only three or four [irrigation farms] remain in the whole country. Without grants to maintain or replace equipment, the system gradually collapsed.*
> —Ghana

Many national governments have delegated the responsibility for water provision to municipal and regional authorities without corresponding powers to raise revenue

Cost recovery

Water is widely underpriced, though the extent to which costs are recovered varies across subsectors. Most municipal drinking water and (especially) sanitation systems do not recover their full costs through user tariffs and other charges. Indeed, most systems probably limit their financial goals to covering the recurrent costs of operation and essential maintenance, and many do not attain even this target. Few systems generate meaningful contributions to capital costs, reflecting the lingering tradition of public funding of water investment.

In irrigation the picture is both clearer and starker. The overwhelming majority of public irrigation agencies recover only a minor share of recurrent costs, with no contributions to capital outlays. In many countries farmers still receive irrigation water at no cost or only a nominal one. Yet studies have shown that they could gain substantial benefits from a more expensive but more reliable service (Pazvakawambwa and Van Der Zaag 2001).

Because of the failure to recover costs, the water sector must depend on subsidies from national governments and international agencies. These subsidies cannot always be relied on, are difficult to predict, may be subject to conditions, and produce a mentality that is the antithesis of the autonomy and consumer accountability needed for long-term sustainability. Moreover, subsidies tend to benefit the better-off people in a community as much as or even more than they do the neediest ones.

Adding to the problem of financing in the water sector, many national governments have delegated the responsibility for water provision to municipal and regional authorities without corresponding powers to raise revenue. And the poor cost recovery makes raising private funds for expanding and modernizing systems more difficult, because lenders and investors look to future cash flows for repayment. Water authorities respond to financial difficulties by delaying spending on items that can be postponed, such as routine maintenance, replacement of defective parts, and periodic upgrading. Assets deteriorate as a result.

Because water is underpriced, users with access to plentiful water have no incentive to use it efficiently. This is particularly the case for those users (the majority) whose consumption is not metered, as an extra unit of consumption costs them nothing. Lack of consumption-based pricing is particularly serious in irrigation, where losses and inefficiency are high.

Pollution control provides an analogous situation. Unless polluters are penalized by legal sanctions or required to pay pollution levies, they have no incentive to stop their polluting, which can be costly to others. By contrast, where pollution levies are used, polluters can choose to continue polluting and thus pay the levy (which can be used to subsidize anti-pollution schemes) or to treat effluents before their release. Unfortunately, pollution levies are rarely set high enough to have much impact on polluters' behaviour.

6 Assessing Challenges, Initiating Change

It should not be assumed that financing a subsidy from general taxation is easier than levying a tariff on water users

What needs to be done?

Responsibility for providing access to water lies with national governments. This principle was reinforced in November 2002 by the United Nations Committee on Economic, Cultural, and Social Rights, which issued a statement declaring that access to water is a human right and that water is a social and cultural good, not merely an economic commodity. The statement also declared that the 145 countries that have ratified the International Covenant on Economic, Social, and Cultural Rights have an obligation to progressively extend access to clean water for all, "without discrimination and equally" (UN CESCR 2002, article 13).

Recognizing the importance of water to human development and the environment

All countries need to recognize the important contribution of water to human development and environmental preservation. Each country needs to develop water laws, strategies, and plans and translate these into budget estimates and financing plans for water in all WEHAB (water and sanitation, energy, health, agriculture, and biodiversity) sectors, in industry, and in disaster management. This requires defining financing needs and sources as well as specifying the level of government responsible for investment. Thus finance strategies are embedded in policy and institutional decisions such as decentralization.

Reducing risk and increasing cost recovery

To encourage investment, measures to reduce risk and improve cost recovery should be taken both nationally and internationally. And to improve the efficiency with which the scarce financing resources are used, low-cost solutions should be promoted. These solutions should include measures to improve daily operation and rehabilitate existing infrastructure.

Improving subsidies

In a financially constrained water sector, cost pricing is a natural way to cover operating costs. And to the extent that it covers reimbursement of investment costs, it also frees up more funds for investment. But full cost recovery can be achieved only in the long term. In the meantime public funds must cover the gap.

The aim of placing the finances of water institutions on a sounder footing does not rule out subsidies for purposes or consumer classes that are particularly deserving, such as poor people, those with large families or specific needs for extra water, and firms investing in effluent treatment. Such subsidies could come from general taxation, social assistance funds, the proceeds of environmental taxes, or cross-subsidies within the water sector. Foreign aid might also be a temporary source (such as for transitional subsidies introduced as part of a reform programme). The important thing is that the subsidies be transparent and well targeted.

In choosing the source of funding for the subsidy, it should not be assumed that financing a subsidy from general taxation is easier than levying a tariff on water users; many countries can ill afford an increase in the tax burden. One option is to use "solidarity" solutions, drawing on

Financing water infrastructure and services   6

National governments and the international community are struggling to fully understand the financial and economic requirements of the water sector

voluntary contributions from non-governmental organizations (NGOs) for defined social programmes.

Analysis of existing subsidy schemes helps identify the obstacles to be overcome and the issues to be addressed in setting up a sound scheme (Gómez-Lobo 2001). Recent studies have shown that subsidies for water provision can be introduced without drastically altering the overall economics of the service (Smets 2002).

Strengthening incentives for efficient water use

Once the vital needs of the population are met, the next challenge is to allocate the remaining resource among competing demands. Where water is becoming scarce and there are potential conflicts over its use, policy-makers should ensure that water is allocated to the sectors and uses with the highest social value. And they should give users incentives (positive and negative) to use their water carefully and efficiently, avoiding waste.

There are different ways to give users behavioural incentives. Consumption-based pricing, where it is feasible, encourages more careful use, since extra consumption always has a cost (unlike with flat-rate charges). Where the legal regime permits, water markets could be introduced to enable holders of water rights to trade those rights, for the short or long term, to others who value the resource more. Trading water rights can be an efficient means of reallocating scarce water as long as the interests of third parties and the environment are safeguarded and monopoly control is avoided (see chapter 2).

Economic incentives have been introduced to encourage more efficient use of water for irrigation and industry, but they often are not set high enough to influence behaviour. Moreover, their effects are often offset by those of subsidies, such as those to encourage productivity.

What is being done?

National governments and the international community are struggling to fully understand the financial and economic requirements of the water sector. What are the funding and investment needs in each country? Where will this money come from? And how can appropriate pricing mechanisms be applied against a background of resistance to higher prices from a range of sources?

Developing national strategies

Improving the enabling environment—through appropriate laws, regulations, and national policies—is the first and most important step towards ensuring adequate financing for the water sector. In the general effort to revise the legal and regulatory framework for the water sector (see chapter 2), a few governments have passed laws dealing with aspects of pricing and financing (such as the state government of Queensland, Australia, in action 1066). But only South Africa has recently worked out a comprehensive approach that integrates laws, policies, and financing strategies for the water sector down to the planning and budgeting processes (Box 6.1).

6 Assessing Challenges, Initiating Change

Either in cash or in kind, citizens' contributions are an essential component in any progress towards improving not only water and sanitation services but also irrigation

Box 6.1 Financing water management in South Africa

In South Africa, a country with tremendous income inequality, much of the population remains unserved by water supply and sanitation services, although the constitution guarantees the right of access to water for all. The country has been putting in place a comprehensive water policy framework since 1994 (see, for example, actions 1221 and 1476), defining priorities for water management, and developing local and national financing solutions.

The government has set a target of providing all households 6 cubic metres of water a month at no charge (action 340), financed by progressive tariffs. Water services have been decentralized, and local authorities have tackled the challenge of expanding service coverage, often by contracting private companies and with user participation (actions 342, 344, 1109, 1224, 1225, and 1239). But local authorities often lack the financial and technical capacity to properly manage water services. The government has tried to help by providing capacity building, providing grants for infrastructure development (action 1223), and devising financial pooling mechanisms to boost cost recovery.

The country has also undertaken extensive infrastructure development, relying on the user-pays principle. Water use is licensed, and the licenses are widely traded. To ensure recovery of the costs of infrastructure development and a return on assets, the proposed water pricing strategy includes resource management and economic scarcity charges (action 2488). The private sector is involved in funding infrastructure (action 2479), but the government can also provide initial funding (actions 315 and 371).

The government funds activities with "public good" characteristics, such as provision of water to poor farmers and households, monitoring and measurement of water quality and quantity, planning, and protection of the environment. Although environmental protection remains a big challenge, a recent charge system for waste discharges introduces the polluter-pays principle (action 2182).

This comprehensive water policy has already improved water supply services and water resources development, while enabling the country to finance its water needs. In part these successes reflect factors specific to South Africa—a strong economy, long history of public spending on water, use of much water for activities with high economic returns—and so may not be entirely replicable.

Much remains to be done to provide water to all, to protect the environment, and to respond to climate change. But South Africa continues to improve its water institutions—it recently introduced an active gender policy (action 1417)—and to build its water management capacity (actions 1482 and 1540).

Sources: Muller 2002; World Water Council, Actions Database (www.worldwatercouncil.org/search_actions.php).

Increasing financing and ensuring its efficient use

Enhancing citizens' contributions. Either in cash or in kind, citizens' contributions are an essential component in any progress towards improving not only water and sanitation services but also irrigation. NGOs are advocating support to communities in the form of micro-credit, revolving funds, and other similar schemes, especially for water supply and sanitation investments (action 3106 in Sri Lanka). Such approaches can be very effective (see box 6.2) and there is clearly a need for wider dissemination. Citizens' contributions alone will not be able to bridge the funding gap, but it should be recognized that the gap will not be bridged without tapping this resource.

Increasing official development assistance. Some countries have made commitments to increase funding to the water sector, such as the Netherlands (action 1979) and the countries of the European Union (action 1678). Such commitments were made, for example, at the Second World Water Forum in The Hague in 2000 and the World Summit on Sustainable Development in Johannesburg in 2002. And during the International Conference on Financing for Development in Monterrey, Mexico in 2002, other commitments were made to increase official development assistance, with

Financing water infrastructure and services   6

> *If it's water for basic needs, it is a right. If it's water for comfort, for luxury, you should have to pay.*
> —Bangladesh

Even if recent commitments are fully realized, official development assistance would still fall far short of the United Nations target of 0.7 percent of donor countries' gross national income

---

Box 6.2 The Soozhal initiative (action 3093)

The Indian government has launched a series of Total Sanitation Campaigns in rural areas. One of the chosen districts is Cuddalore in Tamil Nadu. At the outset of the programme, sanitation coverage was less than 6 percent, well below the national rural average. Soozhal, a group of local non-governmental organizations, succeeded in increasing this to 25 percent in their target area within two years. The key elements of Soozhal's strategy were:

- *Establishing effective financial arrangements:*

Two financial instruments complement government subsidies of 500 rupees (approximately $11) available to households for latrine construction: bridging loan funds to cover working capital requirements and a revolving loan fund. Women's microfinance schemes have raised more than 1,100,000 rupees (approximately $24,000) for the revolving loan fund. It is notable that local banks which in the past would only fund micro-finance for traditional income-generating activities are now lending for sanitation because of the low default rate and high turnover of the Soozhal micro-finance scheme. The NABARD government bank, for example, is now offering households credit at annual interest rates as low as 4 percent for sanitation.

- *Community capacity building:*

The programme provides a model of how to optimize the use of limited resources from both domestic governments and external development aid in order to benefit large numbers of low-income households. Small government subsidies and non-governmental organization seed funding have levered considerable private household contributions that would not be sufficient in themselves to gain access to improved sanitation. The initiative also shows that low-income rural communities, if mobilized and well organized, can become empowered to take charge of improving their water supply and sanitation.

Source: Sakthivel and Fitzgerald 2002, cited in Terry and Calaguas 2003, p. 20.

---

the United States, for example, pledging to increase its annual assistance by $5 billion (action 3639). But even if these commitments are fully realized, official development assistance would still fall far short of the United Nations target of 0.7 percent of donor countries' gross national income. Moreover, some commitments are presented in a way that makes it difficult to differentiate new financing from previously committed funds.

Mobilizing private investment from water companies. Facing a decline in official development assistance and insufficient domestic resources, some countries have tried to mobilize private investment. This goal has been one of the factors driving legislation to allow private participation in infrastructure, such as in Bolivia (action 2542) and the Philippines (action 577). In support of such efforts, development organizations such as Agence Française de Développement, the Inter-American Development Bank, and the World Bank Group are developing financial tools to reduce risk for private investors, such as guarantees and other risk mitigation instruments (World Bank 1998).

When private operators enter the water sector, however, ensuring efficient use of public funds allocated to the operators becomes an issue (it is also an issue with public operators, of course). A programme in Brazil addresses this concern by linking funding to operational results—or output— giving private operators an incentive to improve daily operation (box 6.2).

The World Bank is developing such output-based funding approaches for use in water concession schemes while recognizing the difficulties they may raise in terms of defining the output to be used as a trigger for payments and of assessing the

6 Assessing Challenges, Initiating Change

Whatever the origin of funding, more of it should go to rehabilitation than to new infrastructure until existing infrastructure is properly maintained and operated

---

Box 6.3 Output-based payments for catchment restoration in Brazil (action 1008)

In Brazil's Catchment Restoration Programme (PRODES), the federal government, through the national water agency, provides subsidies to private firms that construct and operate new sewage treatment facilities in highly polluted catchments (action 1008). To ensure that the funding is used efficiently, the government applies the output-based funding principle, linking subsidy payments to an operator to its achievement of predetermined performance targets. The 2001 programme is assisting 1.9 million inhabitants, and it is expected to reduce biochemical oxygen demand (an indirect measure of biodegradable organic compounds in water used to evaluate the efficiency of treatment processes) by 81 tons a day.

---

achievement of the objectives (Marin 2002). In contrast to the traditional approach of financing inputs with no control over performance, output-based funding schemes tie much of the compensation for private operators to their delivery of outputs or results specified by the public authority. The targeted results could include, for example, pollution abatement or improvements in service delivery in specified areas (such as poor communities). Thus the public authority retains responsibility for defining goals while relying on private companies for efficiency. Such schemes should give donors comfort, because they allow the donors to fund tangible results.

Experience with output-based funding schemes can be traced to the early 1990s in Guinea, where the approach was used for urban water services. But the Guinean experience was not entirely successful, and the scheme ended with the departure of the private operator (action 244). An analysis of the Guinean scheme argues that the case "illustrates the challenges of creating effective performance incentives for private operators when regulations and monitoring are weak and the operator is not fully subject to commercial risk" (Brook and Locussol 2001, p. 36).

Mobilizing private investment through capital markets. While local authorities may be more willing to invest in water projects than is the central government, they have less access to lending. But in a unique scheme in South Africa a private company, Infrastructure Finance Corporation Limited, helps municipalities gain access to capital markets by taking the financial risk and pooling it among beneficiaries (action 2479).

Another capital market approach to increasing funding has centred on investment funds. Several actions involving investment funds have been recorded since 2000 (actions 2183, 2192, 2193, 2194, and 2195), though the funds have not been particularly attractive to investors.

Targeting resources effectively. Whatever the origin of funding (international, domestic, private), more of it should go to rehabilitation than to new infrastructure until existing infrastructure is properly maintained and operated. The European Bank for Reconstruction and Development financed such upgrading projects by Polish public utilities (actions 3083, 3084, 3085 and 3090). This approach is easier when long-term support is provided, as Finland is doing with a 15-year programme to support reform in Haiphong, Vietnam (action 2293).

Small and medium-size cities should receive at least as much support as large ones. This is not unrealistic: to improve water supply in Romania, the Netherlands set up a scheme that helps secure private funding for water supply companies in medium-size cities, building on the substantial savings that rehabilitation can bring to daily operating costs (action 2150).

Financing water infrastructure and services 6

Facilities that already exist should be used as financial vehicles, replenished and empowered as necessary

Box 6.4 Main recommendations from the World Panel on Financing Water Infrastructures

The first priority is for host governments to be clear on their strategies and priorities for the water sector—and to plan accordingly. Donors, non-governmental organizations, multilateral financial institutions, companies, and others can assist, but there has to be real political "ownership" of the effort from host governments as a precondition.

Examples:

- Preparation of water sector strategies.
- Detailed action programmes for meeting Millennium Development Goals.
- Inclusion of water policies in Poverty Reduction Strategy Papers.

Second, facilities that already exist should be used as financial vehicles, replenished and empowered as necessary. Unnecessary constraints on their operations should be removed. Organizations with viable plans and projects, but a shortage of finance, should be targeted.

Examples:

- Donors to refocus aid for water and coordinate through the Development Assistance Committee of the Organisation for Economic Co-operation and Development, and others.
- Donors to give priority to strengthening core public capabilities.
- Multilateral financial institutions to reconsider attitude to capital provisioning.
- Greater use of guarantees.
- Export credit rules modified.
- Multilateral financial institutions and donors to resume qualified lending for water storage.
- Non-governmental organizations with good project pipeline to be targeted for assistance.
- Private companies (local and international) to be used as contractors and managers.

Third, proposals for new agencies, funds, and schemes should urgently be studied for their detailed feasibility, and their implementation mapped out, with sponsors identified.

Examples:

- Decentralized Fund for Local Initiatives.
- Revolving Fund for tender preparation and contract award.
- Devaluation Liquidity Backstopping Facility.

Fourth, policy changes and reforms to institutions likely to have longer lead times should be set in motion.

Examples:

- Tariff reform
- Reforms to public water agencies.
- Measures to strengthen financial powers of sub-sovereigns.

Source: World Panel on Financing Water Infrastructure 2003.

Developing an international strategy. To help increase funding for the water sector, the World Water Council, the Global Water Partnership, and the Secretariat of the Third World Water Forum established a task force of high-level experts, the Panel on Financing Water Infrastructure (action 571). Chaired by Michel Camdessus, the former managing director of the International Monetary Fund, the panel includes financial sector experts and representatives of countries and NGOs. The panel has undertaken a study with a 25-year perspective, conducting regional consultations in all parts of the

6 Assessing Challenges, Initiating Change

The ability of poor people to pay higher water prices is an issue that must be addressed

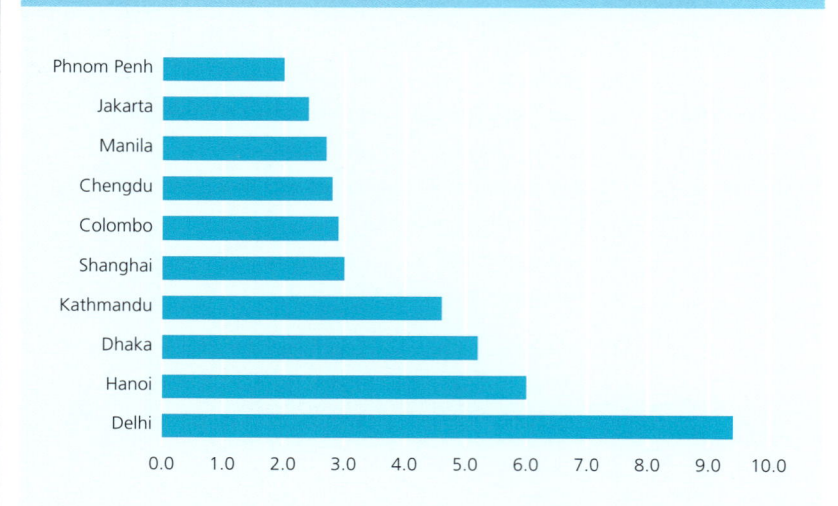

Figure 6.5 Ratio of potential to actual water service revenues in selected developing country cities, 2001

City	Ratio
Phnom Penh	~2.0
Jakarta	~2.3
Manila	~2.7
Chengdu	~2.8
Colombo	~3.0
Shanghai	~3.0
Kathmandu	~4.5
Dhaka	~5.2
Hanoi	~6.0
Delhi	~9.3

Note: Potential revenue is calculated based on an assumption that each household pays an annual charge for water equal to 5 percent of its income, with income being up to $5,000 a year.

Source: McIntosh 2003.

world. Its final report, presented at the Third World Water Forum, recommends measures to improve financing (box 6.4).

Regular monitoring is required to identify financial needs in the water sector relative to goals (such as coverage in water supply and in sanitation, reliability of service, and water quality). Recent efforts in this area, triggered by the Millennium Development Goals, have been led mainly by the United Nations system (Millennium Project, action 2361) and the World Bank (action 2482). These actions will help improve the understanding of financial needs and spending in the water sector.

Improving cost recovery

The Actions Database provides examples of what can be achieved through water sector reform that ensures sufficient revenues for the operator. Consider the results attained by the water supply authority in Phnom Penh, Cambodia, between 1993 and 2002 (action 2486):

- Service coverage rose from 50 percent of households in the inner city to 100 percent, and from zero in the suburbs to 40 percent.
- Some 750 kilometres of new distribution network were added to the existing 280 kilometres.
- Supply became more reliable (previously water had been available for an average of only 10 hours a day).
- The share of unaccounted-for water fell from 72 percent to 22 percent.

These results were supported by a tariff increase introduced over seven years. They show that users will accept price increases if they are gradual, transparent, and justified by better service. A similar approach is being taken in Zhanjiakou, China, where progressive tariff increases allow improvements in water service over eight years (action 2487).

But the ability of poor people to pay higher water prices is an issue that must be addressed. One of the barriers to improved cost recovery is a belief that large parts of the population, especially poor people, cannot afford tariffs that fully cover costs (see chapter 7). A study of the issue in Asia shows the potential revenue to be gained by water service providers. If water charges were raised to the ceiling rate of 5 percent of household income, a reasonable benchmark of affordability in Asia, revenues would be anywhere from two to nine times greater (figure 6.5).

Financing water infrastructure and services · 6

Few countries have initiated a comprehensive national approach to the water sector— all countries should do so

If subsidies are to be introduced to achieve affordability for all, the ground must be carefully prepared, starting with a general agreement on which users or purposes are to be subsidized, how the subsidy will be financed (from general taxation, from other users through cross-subsidies, or from another source), and how much subsidy can be provided.

Several actions offer guidelines for provision of the minimum amount of water to which everyone should be entitled. These actions include the Solidarity Bill in the United Kingdom (action 59), the Convention Solidarité Eau in France (action 440), a national programme with subsidy studies in Brazil (action 1519), and the policy commitment to providing a free basic amount of water in South Africa (action 340).

In irrigation, cost recovery is always going to be more difficult. Delegating responsibility for cost recovery to user associations can help, because it creates a closer link between the revenues collected and the quality of service provided. Another possibility is to give farmers an incentive to conserve water by introducing penalties for consuming more than the norms agreed on with the authorities. But these reforms take time: irrigation reform in Tunisia is expected to take 16 years (1990–2006) to reach targets for user participation and economic balance (action 1823).

What remains to be done?

The Panel on Financing Water Infrastructure has spent many hours consulting experts, analysing, and debating how to increase funding for water infrastructure, and this report has not attempted to duplicate its work. Governments and the international community should give serious consideration to the panel's recommendations and implement those that are most promising as quickly as possible.

Few countries have initiated a comprehensive national approach to the water sector—developing water laws, strategies, and plans; defining financing needs and sources; specifying the level of government responsible for investment; and translating all this into budget estimates and financing plans. All countries should do so.

Donor countries and multilateral aid agencies can support progress by acting quickly to provide financing to countries that take measures to develop such approaches. This will encourage the countries that are taking action and provide an incentive for those that are slow to do so.

Even if such assistance accounts for only a small share of water investments, an increase can only help. The decline in overall official development assistance should be stopped and reversed, and the share allocated to the water sector increased.

85

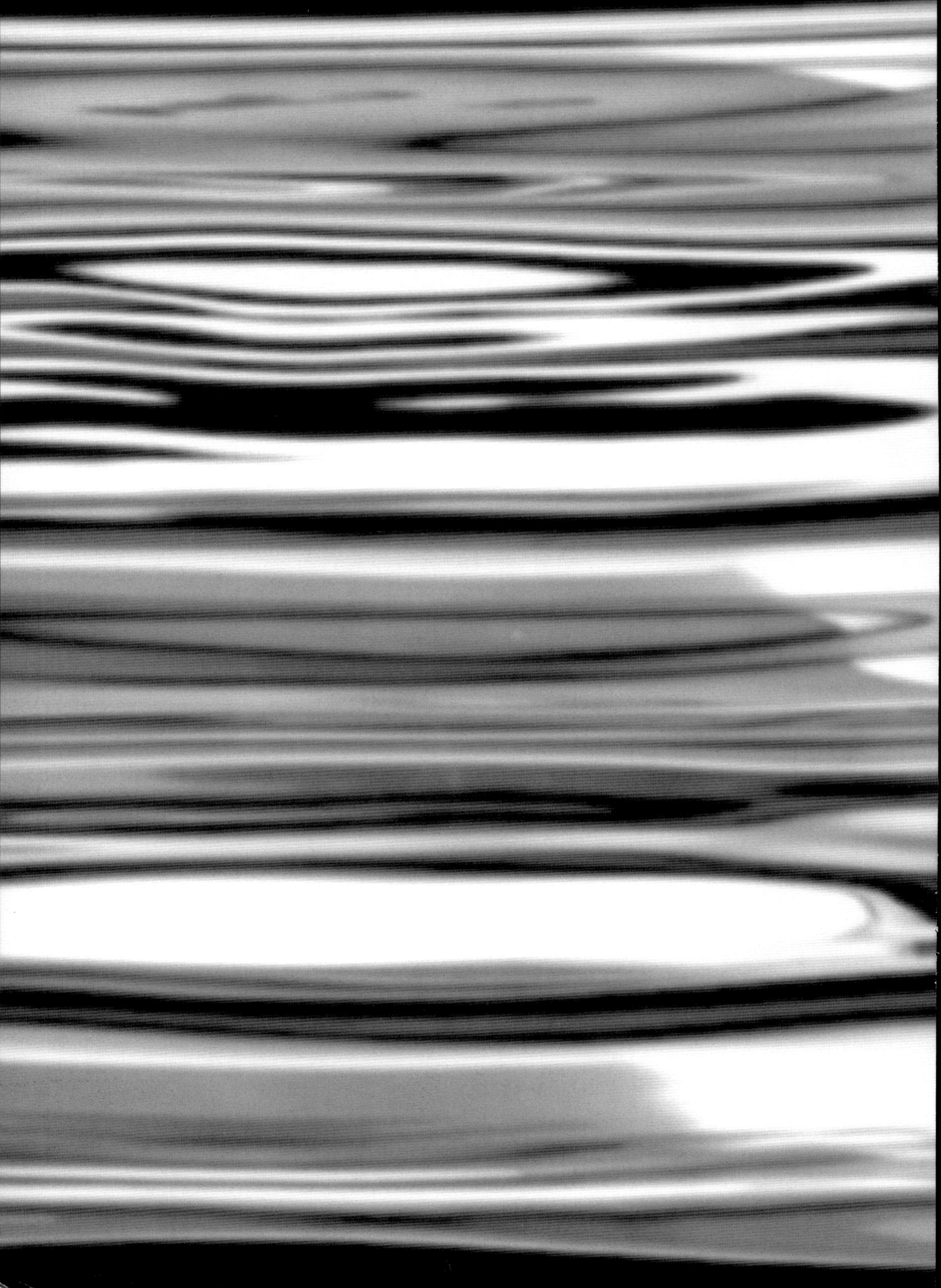

2

**Focusing on Key Areas,
Promoting Change**

7. Water supply and sanitation

Safe, adequate, reliable water supplies, good sanitation, and sound hygiene are essential to the development of communities and the well-being of people. Yet one in six of the world's people lack acceptable water supplies, and two in five are without proper sanitation. People who lack basic water and sanitation services remain trapped in poverty and depressed development. And unless sufficient attention is paid to water and sanitation, none of the Millennium Development Goals will be achieved.

Yet remedies are readily available: around the world, many developing countries offer thousands of examples of how to provide water and sanitation services. Moreover, many developing countries are reforming policies and institutions to help expand these services. But current efforts are nowhere near sufficient to fill the backlog in service provision—much less keep pace with growing populations and increasing urbanization—and many governments refuse to make water supply and sanitation a priority. To increase services, slums and periurban areas should be connected to urban water and sanitation infrastructure, and self-help should be facilitated in both urban and rural communities.

Governments and the international community can accelerate these efforts—as long as there is political and bureaucratic will to implement institutional reforms. National strategies and programmes—complemented by international support—are needed to fill the gaps in water and sanitation services. These programmes must use the full range of service providers and empower communities (including women) to develop and manage water and sanitation infrastructure, prioritizing local and affordable solutions. Local, national, public, and private resources should be mobilized more effectively to enable these efforts.

Present situation

At least 1.1 billion people lack access to an improved water supply, and at least 2.4 billion lack acceptable sanitation. Every year these shortfalls sicken and kill hundreds of millions of people, many of them children under five. Moreover, many analysts claim that these official data seriously underestimate the extent of the problem. In parts of South Africa, for example, local research raises serious doubts about official data (WWAP 2003). Moreover, the number of people lacking education on personal and household hygiene is probably much higher. Yet there are few reliable statistics in this area—a serious problem given its importance to people's health.

Though safe water is increasingly recognized as a human right, many governments fail to ensure its availability. The most difficult challenge is changing the preoccupation of most authorities with capital-intensive, high-tech solutions and moving them towards demand-based solutions using decentralized institutional arrangements. Most governments continue to think like service providers or project implementers, but they should be thinking like facilitators. Their inability or reluctance to transfer power—to genuinely empower people and communities to act for

Water supply and sanitation 7

This report describes many experiences with a range of political, institutional, and technical options—and shows that problems with water, sanitation, and hygiene can be solved

themselves—is at the root of many water problems. Corruption has a lot to do with this. Moreover, many governments that give high priority to water neglect sanitation and hygiene. Lack of secure land tenure is often among the reasons given for not providing these services.

Lessons for decision-makers

This situation creates both challenges and opportunities for national and local decision-makers:

- A lack of safe water is now universally recognized as politically dangerous. Less well known is how essential proper sanitation and hygiene are to good health. Thus there is an urgent need to move sanitation and hygiene to the top of the political agenda.
- Though providing water and sanitation involves complex challenges, experiences from around the world show what can be done and how to do it. Over the past 30 years countries in every region have tested and demonstrated a range of political, institutional, and technical options from which urban planners and rural communities can choose. This report describes many of these experiences—and shows that problems with water, sanitation, and hygiene can be solved.

- Empowering people and local authorities through decentralized policies works.

The challenges of achieving the Millennium Development Goals

In 2000 the United Nations Millennium Development Summit set a target for safe water supply. The 2002 World Summit on Sustainable Development endorsed this target and set a corresponding target for sanitation. Together the targets seek to halve, by 2015, the proportion of people without adequate safe water and sanitation (see box B.1).

These targets raise serious questions (including about the official data on people who currently lack reliable water supply and sanitation) and formidable challenges:

- During the 1990s an average of 224,000 people a day gained access to improved water supplies and 205,000 people a day to improved sanitation. But during this period the world's population grew by 216,000 people a day—so the number of the world's people with safe water grew only slightly, and the number with decent sanitation actually fell.
- To reach the targets for 2015, the number of people gaining access to improved water supplies will have to increase to 292,000 a day (30 percent more than in the 1990s) and the number gaining access to improved sanitation will have to increase to 400,000 a day (nearly 100 percent more than in the 1990s).

7 Focusing on Key Areas, Promoting Change

Despite the obstacles they face, many poor urban residents have shown enormous resourcefulness in meeting their needs for jobs, housing, and utility services

The main obstacles to achieving the Millennium Development Goals are inadequate institutional and managerial capacity, insufficient financial resources, and (more rarely) hydrological and geographical limitations. Underlying the first two of these are lack of political will and failure to mobilize the self-help potential of poor communities. With increased political will, community mobilization, and empowerment of women, service provision could sharply accelerate—easily surpassing the rather modest Millennium Development Goals.

Many urban areas are facing crises partly because poor communities have not been integrated into formal planning. Poor communities account for more than a quarter of the population in new urban settlements in many developing countries. Moreover, the homes and settlements that poor people develop, in many cases without legal rights, are often the main sources of new housing in urban areas. Such communities have demonstrated that they can mobilize significant human and financial resources to solve problems and advance development. Despite the obstacles they face, many poor urban residents have shown enormous resourcefulness in meeting their needs for jobs, housing, and utility services.

There is a misperception that sanitation is less important than water supply. Sanitation may be in lower demand by men. But women, who are responsible for addressing most household water and sanitation challenges, place a very high value on sanitation and hygiene education. If women are involved in water supply, sanitation, and hygiene education efforts, there is no shortage of demand. The target for sanitation set at the World Summit on Sustainable Development takes a comprehensive view, defining basic sanitation as including hygiene education, latrines and hand-washing in households and schools, enhanced service delivery arrangements, and wastewater management. Achieving this target will require marketing sanitation to policy-makers, decision-makers, and men.

Problems of service delivery

Low-income countries have far less water supply and sanitation infrastructure than do middle- and high-income countries. Moreover, the utilities that operate such infrastructure are often inefficient, with widespread illegal connections, poor billing, and weak cost recovery. Most utilities are not focused on serving customers or providing quality services. Services are often interrupted, and leakage rates are high. Though some countries have an active cadre of small, independent water providers—such as street vendors—the quality of their services and water is generally low and their prices often high. Rarely do utilities, regulators, and informal service providers maintain the formal relationships needed for successful service provision.

Water supply and sanitation 7

> *Access to clean drinking water is a right of all citizens worldwide. It is a shame that governments allow investors into the drinking water business.*
> —Uganda

> *Communities—including women—must be empowered to participate in service provision. Also needed are appropriate payment systems, so that service providers can cover their costs*

Rising water pollution

Communities worldwide, large and small, discharge untreated wastewater and animal waste into streams, rivers, lakes, and groundwater, often polluting the water they need for drinking and destroying the ecosystems they depend on for their existence. Many urban areas generate effluents that, along with polluted river discharges, enter coastal seas and estuaries.

Although accurate global data on water pollution are hard to come by, the problem is widespread, insidious, and growing. Municipalities, industry, and agriculture generate an estimated 1,500 cubic kilometres of wastewater each year (WWAP 2003). Less than 10 percent of this wastewater is treated. This serious problem requires urgent attention. The good news is that appropriate treatment technologies are available, if political will and resources are applied to use them.

What needs to be done?

It is a formidable challenge to extend water and sanitation services to the millions of people who lack them while also maintaining existing systems and coping with growing populations and increasing urbanization (chapter 2 deals with some of these same recommendations on the need to reform water management). National strategies and programmes are needed to fill the gaps. Service delivery is the most pressing issue, and to address it the full range of service providers and approaches must be used. In addition, communities—including women—must be empowered to participate in service provision. Also needed are appropriate payment systems, so that service providers can cover their costs, and technical solutions. Finally, efforts are needed to control water pollution and improve hygiene education. In all these areas, international support—financial resources, technical know-how, capacity building—is essential.

Defining needs

Because the water and sanitation debate centres on the numbers of people unserved and the target numbers to be served by 2015, service delivery is clearly the critical issue. But what services should be delivered, and how? All people, rural and urban, want:

- A safe and reliable water supply in or close to their homes. For drinking, safe hygiene, and food preparation, each person requires up to 50 litres a day, available 24 hours a day.
- Places to bathe and wash clothes, and somewhere hygienic to defecate.
- Paved pathways and drains to remove wastewater and unwanted rainwater.
- Collection and suitable disposal of solid waste.
- Water not just for household purposes, but also for all kinds of livelihood activities. Water is also needed to fight fires and clean cities.
- Systems to provide all of this that are reliable, understandable, cheap to install and maintain, and suited to the needs and capacity of the community as well as capable of being extended as it grows.

7 Focusing on Key Areas, Promoting Change

Private companies can bring a wealth of engineering and managerial know-how

‘ As long as the government rigorously evaluates private companies before they may engage in water works, I do not see [private provision] as a problem.
—Japan ’

Setting the scene for better service delivery

To move forward, efforts are needed to:

- Decentralize and encourage subsidiarity of service provision.
- Reorient service providers, encouraging a service and customer orientation.
- Encourage growth in the number and range of service providers.
- Empower communities to help themselves.
- Move governments away from being service providers to becoming enablers, monitors, and regulators.

Forming partnerships. No single authority or stakeholder can resolve water and sanitation shortfalls. Far more partnerships are needed among governments (national and local), communities, private organizations, and non-governmental organizations (NGOs). NGOs can be extremely valuable as moderators between community groups and governments. And private companies can bring a wealth of engineering and managerial know-how—for example, as part of public–private partnerships.

Fostering an enabling environment. Achieving these goals requires creating an enabling environment through policy, legislative, and regulatory reforms. Reformed institutional structures must be accountable, transparent, and participatory. And as government's role moves from provider to facilitator, regulation becomes a crucial responsibility (see chapter 2).

Strengthening local governments. Local governments must be much more involved in water and sanitation. But some lack the resources to do what is required and the skills and experience to work with community groups. Local governments and communities need capacity building and training to cope with these problems.

Empowering stakeholders and harnessing the enormous power of self-help. When empowered to do so, communities exhibit immense capacity to improve their environments. Communities have a proven ability to take actions to help themselves, and even socially marginalized groups—including women and poor people—can mobilize enormous resources. But they need encouragement—not indifference and discouragement, which is what they often encounter. As noted, for example, women's participation in decision-making is essential to successful water supply and sanitation. But in many cases men must be convinced to share responsibilities so that women can contribute their best experiences and skills.

Building incentives into financial structures. Financial policies and arrangements should encourage communities to contribute the most they can to the costs of operation and maintenance (see chapter 6). If required, targeted subsidies should be considered to defray the initial costs of connecting to water and sanitation networks for the poor who are unserved.

Combating corruption. Widespread corruption undermines the delivery of water and sanitation services, and strong action is needed to overcome it. Contracts and bidding procedures should be structured to eliminate the potential for corrupt behaviour.

Water supply and sanitation   7

For corporatizing utilities to be effective, clear roles are needed for governments, regulators, utilities, and customers

Promoting the essentials of good service delivery

In recent years a great deal has been learned about how to provide water and sanitation to all people. This knowledge has come from practical experience with what works and what does not. Progress is possible—and there are many examples to prove it.

Taking into account the overall framework for water management. To address people's priorities while protecting ecosystems, the water management aspects of water supply and sanitation have to be considered within the larger context of integrated water resources management.

Responding to demand. Services must be responsive to the demand for them. Communities should be able to choose the service standards they can afford and are willing to pay for, including delivery and management arrangements. They should also have the right to choose who should provide services and how, and they need to be empowered to make informed choices.

Matching problems with solutions. Given the range and complexity of water and sanitation problems, locally suitable solutions should be identified at the planning stage—before services start. Sustainability, equity, and efficiency concerns should be identified and analysed, and the solutions chosen should address them. Though there are no universal solutions, a variety of tried and tested options is available which are within the capacity and competence of all kinds of communities and authorities.

Highlighting the importance of operation and maintenance. Sound operation and maintenance and proper repair and renewal of water supply and sanitation systems are crucial to people's well-being. Their deficiency lies at the heart of many utility failures in both industrial and developing countries.

Making utilities more efficient. As noted, providers of water and sanitation services can range from centralized utilities to small independent suppliers. Most utilities are public and will continue to be for some time. But being public does not—and should not—mean being inefficient. Indeed, efficiency matters far more than whether utilities are public or private.

Many governments are moving to corporatize utilities, giving them more autonomy. For this move to be effective, it must be accompanied by:

- Adequate long-term planning for development and management of assets.
- Clear roles for governments, regulators, utilities, and customers.
- Predictable, efficient, stable regulation.
- A strong customer focus and service ethic, with service contracts and well-defined goals for all utilities.

Using various service providers— including the private sector. Services should be delivered by a range of organizations, including public and private utilities and small private operators—whether entrepreneurial companies, NGOs, or communities. There is no preferred approach, but communities should be able to choose the delivery mechanism based on their demand and ability to pay.

Private participation in water and sanitation utilities can take many forms, from concessions for full-scale management and operation to contracts for building and operating infrastructure or managing customer billing. Private participation is no panacea, but it does perform several vital functions. For example, efficient private utilities provide essential benchmarks against which other utilities can be measured—in terms of overall management, billing and cost recovery,

7 Focusing on Key Areas, Promoting Change

Distributing water of adequate quality is essential for people's health

> It is common here to prepare for sudden water reductions by keeping buckets of water at home.
> —Honduras

infrastructure maintenance and repair, and technical innovations in treatment systems and service networks. Moreover, introducing private participation tends to expedite regulation and increase accountability throughout the sector. In addition, competition among service providers, including conventional utilities and others, helps poor families gain access to water supply and sanitation at affordable costs. Contracts, legislation, and regulatory incentives should be structured to facilitate extending and upgrading services in poor communities.

Recognizing the role of small independent providers. The importance of privately financed, profit-making small service providers has only recently been acknowledged. To be effective, small providers must be protected from the legal monopolies of local utilities (which may have service provision plans that duplicate their coverage) and from unfair competition from subsidized operations—though the activities of small providers must also be regulated. Small independent providers can also perform better if they are given help in developing technical and service standards and in forming partnerships and contractual arrangements with other organizations involved in service delivery, including utilities, local authorities, NGOs, and community groups.

Changing the culture of service delivery

Clearing up misconceptions. A common misperception among politicians is that poor people are unwilling to pay for water and sanitation services. At the same time, many international analysts argue that poor people pay exorbitant prices for water from street vendors—yet also claim that poor people cannot afford to pay for water. These misconceptions and contradictions are among the main barriers to expanding water and sanitation services.

Poor people are willing and able to pay for reliable water and sanitation services delivered by accountable organizations that operate in a transparent, well-regulated environment. True, some households cannot afford network connections and find it hard to make regular payments for services. But there are many ways to overcome such problems, including by amortizing connection costs, designing innovative tariff structures (such as water stamps and differential water tariffs), and developing local payment arrangements. Special attention should be given to the wants and needs of women, as they often pay for water and sanitation services from their shares of household budgets.

Securing low-cost small loans. Poor households seeking water and sanitation services should have easy access to low-cost small loans (microfinance). But such financing should not be limited to households. Bulk credit (for example, from a national fund or a revolving fund) for groups of consumers is also required to extend community water and sanitation services. External assistance (such as donor funding) should be used sparingly, to reduce dependence on a potentially unsustainable source.

Improving water quality

To ensure that water delivered to people is of appropriate quality, investments are needed in water treatment systems, and people need to be taught about the dangers of drinking unsafe water and how to avoid it. But most important is reducing overall pollution of water systems, as exposed in many other chapters of this book—including pollution through domestic waste. And decoupling pollution from sanitation is important for the quality of ecosystems.

Improve water quality for health. Distributing water of adequate quality is essential for people's health. A wide range of solutions for water treatment are available. But the answer remains controlling pollution at the source—industrial, agricultural, or domestic—especially

Water supply and sanitation 7

Many countries have reformulated policies to recognize all people's right to water and sanitation services

because some organic and mineral pollutants are almost impossible to remove from water.

Reduce pollution from sanitation. Household demands for clean water supplies and private, convenient places to defecate pose major challenges for wastewater disposal. Household wastewater includes human waste as well as wastewater from washing (of people and clothes), and food preparation. In some cases "grey" water (from washing) can be reused in urban agriculture. But in general, people want wastewater to be directed away from their homes.

For large cities sanitation systems generally concentrate large volumes of polluted water and discharge them at a single point on a river. Major improvements in infrastructure management are often needed to ensure that treatment plants function properly. More sustainable solutions have to be designed to dispose of sludge that is left over after treatment. Community-level solutions, if well managed, may have fewer harmful effects on the environment. Developing more environmentally friendly solutions for larger urban areas as well remains a considerable challenge.

What is being done?

Around the world, policy and institutional reforms are helping to extend water and sanitation services to unserved populations. The Actions Database shows that in many countries, national strategies and programmes are being implemented, utilities are being reoriented, communities are becoming more involved, payment mechanisms are being adjusted, new technologies are being introduced, and international support is increasing. Still, current efforts are nowhere near sufficient to fill the gaps in service coverage.

Implementing national strategies and programmes

Water management reforms are playing a major role in extending water and sanitation services. Many countries have reformulated policies to recognize all people's right to these services. Moreover, new laws and institutional structures have helped create an environment that allows water of sufficient quantity and quality to be delivered to everyone.

National policies that support water supply and sanitation have been created in Bangladesh (action 1458), Benin (action 660), Ethiopia (action 655), Sri Lanka (action 286), and Tanzania (action 1697). In addition, rights to safe water and sanitation are recognized in the national strategies of Chad (action 697), Kiribati (action 1426), and Lao People's Democratic Republic (action 303). Uganda's new water strategy (action 576) delegates responsibility for urban water services to private companies, authorizes the creation of autonomous rural water supply and sanitation authorities, and decentralizes service provision to the district level.

In 1999 China began its fourth rural water supply and sanitation project (action 372), to run through 2005. The second phase of Ghana's Programme for Community Water and Sanitation (action 561) began in 2000 and will run until 2009. The programme encourages decentralization and targets district assemblies as implementers. Nepal's Community-Based Water Supply and Sanitation Project (action 791) will rehabilitate old systems, build new ones, and provide hygiene education. Guinea's Latrine Dissemination Programme (action 248) focuses on sanitation. And in the Indian state of Gujarat, the Jal-Disha 2010 Programme (action1075) is a model for complete overhauls of community water, hygiene, and sanitation services through local action.

7 Focusing on Key Areas, Promoting Change

The provision and improvement of safe water and sanitation have become central components of many government- and donor-sponsored poverty alleviation and economic development programmes

Efforts to improve water and sanitation in industrial countries are more focused on ensuring people's health and well-being than on expanding services. Australia's government will help water suppliers ensure the quality and safety of drinking water (action 2484). Similarly, Canada's Water Quality Task Group (action 2483) has prepared a document dealing with water quality from source to consumption. And the U.S. Environmental Protection Agency has set a target that by 2005, 95 percent of community water systems will meet health standards for drinking water (action 880).

Reforming utilities

According to the Actions Database, water and sanitation utilities have undergone reform in at least 35 countries. Of particular note, given the country's size and influence, is the reform of Russia's *vodokanals*—municipal water supply and wastewater enterprises. They are being transformed into independent, corporate, self-sufficient utilities subject to regulation, published service standards, and service contracts with consumers (action 51). Countries in Latin America—including Argentina (action 929), Bolivia (action 946), the Dominican Republic (actions 1521 and 2035), and Nicaragua (action 1514)—and Eastern Europe (action 3080) are adopting similar reforms. And in West Africa utility reforms involve national enterprises that provide both water and power, with an increase in private sector involvement (actions 244, 253, 542, 651, and 658).

Using water and sanitation as an entry point for poverty alleviation

Inadequate water and sanitation services are among the most visible signs of poverty, causing widespread ill health that lowers poor people's productive capacity (see chapter 9). There is a close relationship between the state of a country's economy, the living standards of its people, and the availability of basic water and sanitation services. Progress depends on whether governments and communities can break the vicious cycle in which poor people cannot afford the basic services essential to escaping poverty. As a result the provision and improvement of safe water and sanitation have become central components of many government- and donor-sponsored poverty alleviation and economic development programmes.

Many countries' water and sanitation projects include poverty alleviation activities. In India the Restructured Central Rural Sanitation Programme (action 458), launched in 1999, is a community-led and people-centred project. Sanitation in rural schools was a major component of the project and was used as an entry point to tackle poverty. Better sanitation and health care have lifted many people in project areas from poverty.

Water supply and sanitation 7

Providing poor people with services may be crucial to ensuring the operators' financial sustainability and to avoiding civil disorder

Kenya launched a national water campaign aimed not only at providing adequate water supplies but also at alleviating poverty (action 602). Kenya also showed a close relationship between water availability and income-generating activities such as keeping small livestock and vegetable gardens (action 280). And in Kutum, Sudan, water use preferences changed in response to improved and increased supplies and related changes in household finances and livelihoods (action 283).

Around the world, urbanization is occurring faster than ever. In most developing countries new urban residents often have to settle illegally because of insufficient financing to expand housing. Meeting the water and sanitation needs of rapidly growing cities is difficult, but professional operators—public and private—are coming up with ways to provide poor people with these services, tailoring solutions to their needs, as in Bolivia (action 135), the Philippines (action 566), Gabon (action 720), and South Africa (actions 1108 and 1235). These operators have realized that poor people are an enormous consumer group and that providing them with services may be crucial to ensuring the operators' financial sustainability and to avoiding civil disorder.

Box 7.1 Voluntary Action for Development, Uganda (action 3512, one of three winners of the Water Action Contest)

Since its establishment in 1996, Voluntary Action for Development (VAD), a Ugandan NGO, has successfully implemented several community-based water supply and sanitation programmes and sustainable agriculture programmes. Under the programmes, 60 water sources have been completed in Wakiso District, Wakiso and Kakiri sub-counties, helping the people with clean and safe water supply. Sixty water user administration committees were set up to empower people's participation.

The long-term results of the programme are positive change in behaviour to promote the safe water chain and improve the hygiene and sanitation of the community. The VAD-trained community mason was given job opportunities during the course of the programme and for post-construction maintenance. The reduction of water-related diseases has increased household savings through reduced expenses for treatment of such diseases.

The community was involved right from the baseline survey and designing their own action plans as well as mobilizing the locally available resources. The communities also designed their own safe water chain monitoring tools and chart. VAD provided the other materials and the technical labour for construction of the 60 water sources in the 5 parishes. Nevertheless, the difficulty was that people sometimes had to attend to their own gardens yet VAD wanted to achieve its target in the 5 parishes within 24 months of programme commencement.

After completion, the systems were handed over to the local government for continued supervision of operation and maintenance. VAD designed a monitoring model to ensure close monitoring at the household level. In this model, school children or women took up the responsibility to report by writing the monitoring chart for all actions taken towards safe water chain sanitation. The Parish Development Committee then collected that information from the households to complete their monitoring chart at parish level. At sub-county level the water, environment, and sanitation committee synthesized the information from the parishes. This has ensured documentation of progress and of the actual impact of the programme in the target area.

7 Focusing on Key Areas, Promoting Change

Ending the world's water crisis will require new strategies that put people at the centre of decision-making

> On World Water Day this year, sewerage got mixed in with the domestic water supply. So to fix the pipelines, the Water Supply Corporation in Kathmandu gave us a "water holiday".
> —Nepal

Box 7.2 Connecting slums to water and sanitation networks: India's experiences

An experiment in linking deprived communities through "slum networking" has begun in some cities in the Indian states of Gujarat and Madhya Pradesh. India's efforts to connect urban slums to water and sanitation networks show how living standards can be raised in poor areas through shared experiences and resources. Sanitation is at the top of the agenda in such efforts, reflecting the country's goal of achieving complete sanitation coverage by 2010. The natural drainage paths in slums are considered ideal routes for infrastructure such as sewerage, roads, and storm drainage and water supply systems.

Source: Gujarat State Drinking Water Infrastructure Company 2000.

Promoting participation by communities

The *World Water Vision* presented at the Second World Water Forum in 2000 argues that ending the world's water crisis will require new strategies that put people at the centre of decision-making (Cosgrove and Rijsberman 2000). The Actions Database supports this view. Recent development goals for water and sanitation cannot be achieved without genuine decentralization and widespread participation. Real change has occurred where people have actively participated in project planning and implementation. But community participation cannot proceed unless a country's institutional framework allows it.

With intelligent, creative approaches (including basic technical assistance, but also financial support such as access to small loans, as described in chapter 6) and encouragement from the relevant authorities, communities can work wonders in solving their problems. Self-help initiatives are proven techniques, offering further evidence that water supply and sanitation challenges can be tackled. These initiatives also show how city managers can make their jobs easier by helping poor communities solve their own problems—at a fraction of what it would cost the city to do the work. Uganda's new water strategy (action 576) allows people to participate in decision-making at the district level. European Commission rural water supply programmes in Papua New Guinea (action 1227) emphasize the importance of decentralization and micro-project approaches. And in Benin a municipal development project (action 1668) decentralized water distribution responsibilities to local governments.

The Actions Database suggests a great deal of grass-roots NGO and community involvement in low-cost water and sanitation provision, including work by NGOs and community-based organizations in Honduras (action 714), Kenya (action 2155), Kiribati (1355), and Morocco (action 1816). Some such programmes are led by governments, as in Nepal (action 1679). Building the capacity of local entities to work with communities is key to increasing local people's participation, as illustrated by the Ugandan NGO Voluntary Action for Development's approach to rural water supply and hygiene (see box 7.1).

Although most water actions rely on rural communities where solidarity is a long-standing tradition, urban communities can also be mobilized to take charge of schemes adapted to their needs. India, for example, shows that slums can transform cities when empowered to act (box 7.2).

Furthermore, success stories shared during the Second World Water Forum are being replicated. For example, India's Orangi Pilot Project (action 2359) is a condominial sewerage project, a low-cost, small diameter system of sewers which are largely built and operated by peri-urban communities themselves. It is used as a model by 50 settlements in Karachi and several cities in Pakistan (such as Lodhran (action 1827). The

Water supply and sanitation

Technological progress makes desalination viable in a growing number of situations

project's influence is also evident in South Africa, Central Asia, and South Asia. Still, given today's water challenges, success stories need to be replicated even more.

Making services affordable and recovering costs

A number of water actions show financial issues being dealt with openly—involving users in decision-making and recovering costs. Some are community-based projects, others are partnerships between stakeholders. Most show that it is difficult to fully recover service costs in poor communities, but that community contributions to operation and maintenance costs are widespread.

In the Dominican Republic (action 2065) community water management committees have been created, and men and women are trained in routine maintenance, plumbing, and repairs. Water investments are externally funded, with communities contributing their labour. Local residents set water tariffs based on the estimated costs of routine maintenance and emergency repairs. Communities also decide on payment mechanisms, concessions for poor people, and sanctions for non-payment.

Network-based services have been improved through partnerships between a utility and communities in South Africa, with meter-based billing (action 1685), and between a private operator and community organizations in the Philippines, with specific arrangements for billing (action 566). Household connections are not always the preferred solution. For example, in Lambarene, Gabon (action 1372), Mueda, Mozambique (action 1360), and Ndiawdoune, Senegal (action 671), communities have established and managed water posts. In all cases a large percentage of users pay for services.

Exploring alternative technical options

Technology can play a major role in addressing the water crisis. Though water and sanitation pose complex challenges, experience shows what can be done using a variety of options and approaches. Alternative technical options are needed not just for wastewater but also for water supply and for latrines.

Since 2000 experiments with and applications of innovative approaches have expanded. New technologies for water treatment have been invented and disseminated—some of which are simple, affordable, easy to operate and maintain, and adaptable to local cultures and behaviours. One of the winners of the Water Action Contest, Bombas de Mecate, illustrates this very effectively (see box 7.3). Moreover, attitudes towards waste reduction and recycling in Asia, Africa, and Latin America offer lessons for the rest of the world. The following sections describe a few of these technical alternatives.

Desalination. Technological progress makes desalination viable in a growing number of situations. Given the enormous number of coastal cities, especially in arid and semiarid areas, desalination can ease pressures on freshwater, save water for other users, and decrease use of non-renewable groundwater. National water policies rely more and more on desalination, as in Algeria (action 2765), China (action 3061) and Israel (action 612). Most recent desalination installations are in countries with easy access to energy, but the increasing efficiency of the technique—and the alternative to distillation provided by reverse osmosis—should soon make this less necessary. Another constraint is the limited technical capacity of local staff to manage desalination plants. Thus increased use of desalination will require capacity building.

Desalination is also expanding on islands. Recent examples include Fernando de Noronha, Brazil (action 388), and a mobile seasonal installation in Corsica, France (action 1031); it is also being considered on the Pacific Islands (action 994). The environmental impacts of desalination include disposal of brine. However, this is just one component of the impacts, to be compared to those of other water supply options.

7 Focusing on Key Areas, Promoting Change

Many local governments have failed to recognize the potential of rainwater harvesting and give it the necessary support

Box 7.3 Technology Transfer Division, Bombas de Mecate (action 3047, one of three winners of the Water Action Contest)

The action describes the South–South technology transfer process of the rope hand pump. This hand pump has been developed and actively promoted by the private sector in Nicaragua and already reaches 23.6 percent of the rural population.

A low-cost rope hand pump for boreholes and hand-dug wells up to 70 metres deep has been developed, marketed, and subsequently mass-produced in Nicaragua by local, small, privately owned workshops since the early 1990s. It is easy to maintain, and highly efficient at the family level as well as the community level. The pump has met with high social acceptance amongst rural users ever since the early rudimentary models were first made available.

By 1995 the technology became an integral part of rural water programmes implemented by non-governmental organizations and government agencies. Rural water supply coverage since then has doubled from approximately 27.5 percent to 54.8 percent. Of this 27.3 percentage point rise, rope pumps account for 23.6 percent (or 85 percent of the total increase).

The income-generating capacity of the rope pump has been an important reason for its acceptance and successful introduction. In addition, credit schemes linked to the introduction of the pumps have proven successful, whilst comparative studies of farm income show that families with a rope pump generate an average $225 of additional annual income which can represent up to 50 percent of the total income for the lower income groups. The pump is now produced by about a dozen independent workshops and has made Nicaragua the country with the highest hand pump density per rural capita.

Bombas de Mecate is actively networking to replicate this success story by disseminating the technology in other countries. By the time of the Third World Water Forum in March 2003, such rope pumps were being produced by independent local manufacturers in a dozen countries.

Most recent projects have been in South Asia, including India (actions 777, 1304, 1305, 1322, 1435) and Sri Lanka (action 755). But there has also been activity in China, East Africa, and Asia and the Pacific. The Global Rainwater Harvesting Collective was created in 2002 (action 1306) to promote rainwater harvesting worldwide by establishing pilot projects in countries where the approach seems useful and NGOs agree to start such initiatives. Assisted by the Australian Centre for Sustainability, the Desert Rainwater Harvesting Initiative was conducted in India (action 1435) to train volunteers in water technologies and serve as an information hub for rainwater harvesting projects. In northern Gujarat, India (action 2356), even during a drought year there is enough water stored to cover two years of household needs. In Tonga household rainwater catchment projects have been implemented through out the entire kingdom to improve household and community water supplies (action 1427).

Rainwater harvesting. Rainwater harvesting is beginning to be widely practiced around the world. Still, many local governments have failed to recognize its potential and give it the necessary support. The same criticism can be made of many international donors.

Water supply and sanitation   7

It is unsustainable for the world to continue using a third of its treated water to flush toilets

Ethiopia's Rainwater Harvesting Association was founded in 2000 (action 1307) and established 400 systems during its first stage. And as a result of efforts by the Kenya Rainwater Association (action 277), women's groups in several districts have adopted catchment systems. Rainwater harvesting tanks are so valued in Kenya that they are sometimes given as wedding presents.

Rainwater harvesting has also blossomed in industrial countries such as Germany, Japan, and the United States. It is especially appropriate in areas subject to floods, water shortages, and land subsidence (the lowering of land levels from excessive use of groundwater). For example, Sumida District, in the Tokyo metropolitan area, has some of the world's highest rainfall. As a result it often suffers from floods—but paradoxically, adequate water supply remains a problem. The introduction of rainwater use systems, or "mini dams" (action 1815), has helped the district store rain during flood seasons. Hays County, in central Texas, is the first county in the United States to provide rebates on taxes and city water bills for rainwater harvesting (action 108). Germany has also provided tax incentives (action 57) that encourage residents to store and recharge rainwater, which saves the government money on storm drainage.

Ecological sanitation. It is unsustainable for the world to continue using a third of its treated water to flush toilets, passing the waste along to "downstream" areas. Ecological sanitation offers an alternative to such practices and promotes human health, respects ecological integrity, and recycles nutrients from human waste for use in agriculture. It also allows for local operation and maintenance. The most widely used ecological sanitation technologies are urine-diverting toilets, composting or dehydrating toilets, and biogas toilets.

Pilot ecological sanitation projects have been and are being carried out in both developing and industrial countries, including China, El Salvador, Ethiopia, Mexico, Norway, South Africa, Switzerland, Uganda, and Vietnam. The Swedish International Development Authority is one of the main international supporters of such efforts in developing countries, along with the United Nations Children's Fund, United Nations Development Programme, German Agency for Technical Cooperation, World Bank, World Health Organization, and Austrian and Swiss bilateral agencies.

The largest ecological sanitation programme is in China (action 396), where results are particularly encouraging in terms of acceptance and effectiveness. The Ministry of Health introduced a pilot project using urine-diverting toilets in 1998. Once the technology had been tested, a campaign to improve the rural environment was launched—and by the end of 2002, 200,000 urine-diverting toilets had been built. Ecological sanitation has also been promoted in India and Sri Lanka (action 721) in locations ranging from urban to coastal to rural. Many urine-diverting toilets have been built attached to and inside homes. In sanitation projects initiated by Water Aid and local NGOs in rural northern Mozambique (action 411), different technological options were offered, but the demand for ecological sanitation toilets increased.

Ecological sanitation is not only for poor people. Thousands of units are used in houses in Germany, Sweden, and the United States. The water and sanitation policy approved in 2002 by the Swedish municipality of Tanum (action 1471) makes urine separation compulsory for new and renovated houses. In addition, homeowners who voluntarily install urine-diverting toilets pay lower sewage fees. Japan launched a research project to provide guidance on ecological sanitation (action 2187).

7 Focusing on Key Areas, Promoting Change

Water supply and sanitation have achieved greater visibility on the international stage

Increasing international support

As chapter 1 also shows, water supply and sanitation have achieved greater visibility on the international stage. The 2001 Bonn International Conference on Freshwater emphasized the importance of water supply, sanitation, and hygiene education. The 2002 World Summit on Sustainable Development put water supply and sanitation at the top of the development agenda in its WEHAB (*w*ater supply and sanitation, *e*nergy, *h*ealth, *a*griculture, *b*iodiversity) structure for alleviating poverty through sustainable development. And the Millennium Project Task Force on Water and Sanitation, one of several task forces created by the United Nations Millennium Project, is supposed to identify the best strategies for achieving Millennium Development Goals related to water and sanitation (action 2361). In doing so, it has been using data from *Global Water Supply and Sanitation Assessment 2000*, a report by the World Health Organization and United Nations Children's Fund's Joint Monitoring Programme for Water Supply and Sanitation (action 88).

Cooperation between industrial and developing countries and among developing countries has been strengthened in terms of sharing water resources and exchanging information. The Water and Poverty Initiative (action 409), led by the Asian Development Bank, advocates further actions and financing to address poverty alleviation. In addition, the EU Water Initiative (action 1170), Africa 2000 Initiative for Water Supply and Sanitation (action 151), and West Africa Water Initiative (action 1358) aim to improve water services.

The Water for African Cities Program (action 154) is being sponsored by the United Nations Centre for Human Settlements in response to the growing urban water crisis and to protect Africa's water resources from increasing urban pollution. The Water Utility Partnership Program (action 1638), to be implemented in nine countries—Côte d'Ivoire, Ethiopia, Ghana, Malawi, Mali, Nigeria, Senegal, Tanzania, and Zambia—aims to make water and sanitation more accessible and affordable for poor urban communities by exchanging experience, producing guidelines, and developing best practices. (See chapter 9 for other international programmes involving water, sanitation, and hygiene.)

A number of international projects and programmes are designed to build the capacity of water and sanitation utilities. The International Water Association is testing a framework for benchmarking the operations of water utilities (action 2412). This will be followed by similar benchmarks for sanitation operations. The research centre for public utilities at the University of Florida (in the United States) offers international training on utility regulations and strategies (action 2413). Finally, a Web-based database called Sanitation Connection (www.sanicon.net/), operated by a consortium of agencies and organizations, offers knowledge and experience on sanitation and hygiene (action 2414).

Water supply and sanitation 7

The world is not making the best use of available expertise, particularly the lessons that developing countries offer one another

What remains to be done?

Much of what needs to be done to improve the world's water and sanitation services has already begun. This chapter has been able to report on only a small portion of these efforts—partly because of space constraints, but also because many such activities go unreported. Still, some communities have figured out what to do and have done it successfully. Despite often limited resources, solutions are being implemented.

Moreover, progress is not limited to large developing countries with extensive resources. Although Brazil, China, India, Pakistan, and South Africa have success stories, so do many smaller, landlocked countries. Often little is known about success stories outside the countries or communities where they occur. As a result the encouragement and examples that could be drawn from the successes are not available to motivate others that still face challenges.

Working with the Millennium Development Goals

Will current progress be sufficient to achieve the Millennium Development Goals for water and sanitation? In some countries, probably. On a global basis, no. Resources need to be dedicated to monitoring progress on them, defining the various terms, and assessing whether official data are credible. But just as crucial is engaging countries and communities in setting their own targets, in terms of what they want and what is within their capacity.

Cataloguing successes and scaling them up

There is no central catalogue of what has worked administratively, politically, financially, and technologically in providing sustainable water and sanitation services around the world. Such a catalogue could be of enormous assistance in helping poor communities make the best choices given their circumstances. Although success stories are reported at conferences, featured in consultant reports, and contained in all kinds of publications, these stories present only part of the picture because many efforts go unreported. Also needed is a register of best practices for delivering, managing, maintaining, upgrading, expanding, and regulating water and sanitation services. With proper organization and resources, such a register could be derived from the central catalogue just discussed—possibly using as its basis the Toolbox (action 64) recently developed by the Global Water Partnership. The world is not making the best use of available expertise, particularly the lessons that developing countries offer one another.

Engaging all allies

Sustainable water supply and sanitation services can be provided to all communities, poor and otherwise. The political risk of securing such services is falling given the many successful experiences around the world—while the political risk of not doing so is growing. Many resources are available to help, the most important being communities themselves. But vital assistance also comes from members of the media, water professionals (though they need some retraining and guidance on working with communities), and donors (though they need to do a much better job of working together within countries). In addition, women should be involved in decision-making and management, and men must be encouraged to accept and support their involvement. The private sector, large and small, should join in all aspects of service provision—not just delivering services but also managing billing systems, contributing to system designs, and providing materials. Finally, regulators should be willing and able, with adequate resources, to monitor the activities of private participants.

8. Water for energy

Water and energy are inextricably linked in several ways, and both are central to poverty alleviation and socio-economic development. Yet the way that much of the world's energy is produced is detrimental to planetary climate cycles, with negative effects on water supplies. Unless carefully managed, the extraction and combustion of fossil fuels and the use of power production infrastructure all have harmful effects on ecosystems.

A huge expansion in energy production is vital to support development in lower income countries and to realize lifestyle preferences worldwide. Yet energy inefficiency is widespread, and big savings in energy use are possible worldwide. Modern technologies for electric power generation offer ample opportunities to move away from the combustion of carbon-rich fossil fuels, such as coal and oil (which generate large amounts of carbon dioxide), to combinations of renewable energy sources. The overhaul of rundown infrastructure in both power and water systems offers further significant opportunities to enhance the efficiency of energy use while minimizing harmful environmental impacts.

The water sector is a big user of electric power, for irrigation and municipal water supply systems. Since much of this water is used wastefully or lost through leakage, large power efficiency gains are possible through improved design and overhaul of management systems and infrastructure.

Given the central importance of energy and water in development, and the links with health, climate-related risks, and ecosystem protection, governments need to ensure that water and energy are fully integrated into the national planning and development process.

Present situation

The development of water and energy services is inextricably linked. Water plays a crucial role in many aspects of energy production, and energy has a vital role in moving water from its source to the places where it is needed. It is a close and symbiotic relationship that reflects the critical importance of safe and reliable supplies of both water and energy to poverty alleviation and socio-economic development. In a rapidly urbanizing world, reliable water and power supplies are essential to the proper functioning of communities, whether large or small, urban, peri-urban, or rural. These services are vital not only for day to day living, but also for support of livelihoods and business in general. Despite the many benefits of energy, there are significant downsides in its production and use, including water pollution and the perturbation of natural climate cycles, leading to more extremes of climate, such as floods and droughts.

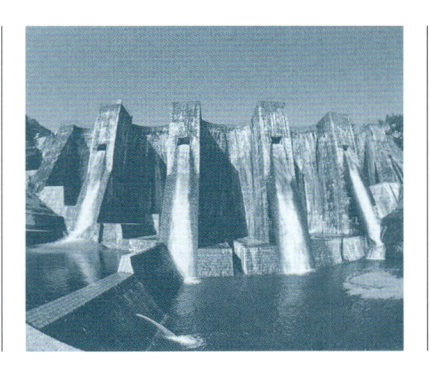

Water for energy | 8

As the world population grows and seeks higher standards of living, more water and energy will be required

Shortage of energy impedes development and reduces well-being

The main sources of energy for humans are fossil fuels (coal and oil) used in thermal power generation, transport and industry, and households; biomass (trees and, in many poor countries, animal wastes); thermal and hydropower generation plants both large and small; solar energy used to heat water and, through photovoltaic equipment, to produce electricity; and a range of renewable sources including wind power, river flows (to produce mechanical energy), tidal flows, and geothermal energy. Electricity is the fastest growing form of energy, with world electricity consumption predicted to grow by 73 percent between 1999 and 2020 (WWAP 2003), most of it in developing countries.

An estimated 2 billion people in developing countries lack access to electric power (World Energy Council 2001). For the poorer parts of the world, this means no labour-saving devices, no refrigeration for improved vaccine storage and food preservation, no light to prolong the working day, and no energy to power industrial development and more transport. Instead of being pumped, water must be carried to the home, usually by women, with negative consequences for health, livelihood activities, childcare, literacy, gender equality, and other elements of human resources development. Hygiene suffers because the quantities of water carried from distant sources are too limited. And the same people who suffer the health impacts of insufficient water supply, get injured carrying wood and charcoal and get sick breathing polluted air in their homes (from domestic heating and lighting generated by the use of fossil fuels in small, poorly ventilated houses). And harvesting fuel wood destroys forests which are crucial for regulating rainwater runoff to rivers and streams and controlling flooding and soil erosion, and also affects the global carbon cycle, to the potential detriment of global climate cycles.

As the world population grows and seeks higher standards of living, more water and energy will be required. But how much more? And where will the additional supplies come from? If this issue is not addressed, demand for water and energy will rise in line with population growth, perhaps by as much as 50 percent over the next century—or even more as countries seek higher per capita consumption rates approaching the water and energy consumption levels of, say, the United States. Such outcomes will be grossly unsustainable.

Energy production has detrimental effects on water

The use of fossil fuels has serious effects on water. Oil and coal extraction can pollute nearby surface and groundwater; the acidification of water from mining wastes is a particular problem. Oil and petroleum spills pollute surface water, and leaking underground fuel storage tanks can seriously pollute groundwater. The gaseous emissions from fossil fuel combustion contribute to the acidification of surface waters, both marine and freshwater, and to global warming. The climate perturbations arising from global warming are increasing the number of extreme climate-related events such as floods and droughts, as well as the threat to islands and coastal communities from rising sea levels (see chapter 5). Water used to cool fossil fuel-burning thermal power plants can lead to localized thermal pollution of the watercourses into which the water is discharged.

Hydropower is widely regarded as a relatively benign source of energy. To a large extent this is true. It avoids most of the problems of thermal electric power generation. However, the dams built along rivers to produce hydropower can have a number of negative effects. They disrupt natural flows, which has a negative knock-on effect on the functioning of associated

8 Focusing on Key Areas, Promoting Change

All energy sources can have deleterious environmental and other impacts

Box 8.1 All energy sources affect the environment and human health

Although considerable attention is given to the various sources of energy, consumers do not demand energy itself. Rather, they demand the services that energy provides, the choices it allows, and the flexibility and comfort it brings—that is, the things that make electricity useful. Some energy sources are converted into useful energy more efficiently than others. And some have fewer environmental impacts, whether at the local, regional, or global level.

Fossil fuels have adverse effects on the environment and human health, though technologies exist to mitigate most of them. But non-fossil fuels also have detrimental effects. For example, the operational safety and potential proliferation of nuclear power are public concerns, as are the treatment and storage of hazardous nuclear waste. Again, technology mitigates these problems; and possibilities exist for reducing the size of plants and for arranging serial production of power units to cut costs.

Large hydropower schemes also raise concerns. Although dams have contributed to human development and generated considerable benefits, "in too many cases an unacceptable and often unnecessary and high price has been paid to secure those benefits, especially in social and environmental terms, by people displaced, by communities downstream, by taxpayers and by the natural environment" (World Commission on Dams 2000, p. 28).

Large-scale biomass use creates worries about sylvan monocultures and biodiversity losses, competition for agricultural land and water, and the adverse impacts of biomass harvesting and burning. Meanwhile, wind and solar power are criticized for their intermittency, and wind power as well for the visual intrusion of windmills and their impact on bird mortality in some locations. Similarly, the manufacture and disposal of solar photovoltaic cells create environmental hazards. Tidal power (from estuarine barrages) causes mud flats to be covered by water, preventing wading birds from reaching food. And ocean energy can disturb salt gradients.

In short, all energy sources can have deleterious environmental and other impacts. If people are to receive the energy services they require in a sustainable way, these impacts must be understood and addressed.

Source: Based on World Energy Council 2001, pp. 47–49.

ecosystems. Dam infrastructure can interfere with the migration of fish. And the flooding of large areas for reservoirs can displace communities, taking away long established ways of life and destroying livelihoods. In addition, the decomposition of submerged biomass can create toxic pollution and the release of greenhouse gases. Despite these problems the potential benefits of hydropower are huge. While the industrialized world has developed 80 percent of its hydroelectric potential, the developing world has harnessed only 10–20 percent of its potential. It will need to harness much more to support its development.

Other renewable sources thought to have great potential include wind power and the conversion of solar energy to electricity via photo-voltaic cells. Today, however, these renewable energy sources account for less than 2.5 percent of the world's primary energy consumption (UNDP 2000). Moreover, all energy sources—including renewable ones—have environmental impacts (box 8.1).

Water for energy 8

> *Although it is highly uneconomical to pump water in this way, farmers can afford it because of government energy subsidies.*
> —India

Inefficiencies arise from the amount of run-down infrastructure in use

Problems are compounded by inefficiency in energy uses

One of the great problems of energy consumption, which has a knock-on effect on water, is the low efficiency of use of electricity and other forms of energy. This extends from the low conversion efficiency of many thermal power plants to the inefficient use of electricity for industrial, agricultural, municipal, and domestic purposes.

This problem of inefficiency compounds the problems for the water sector. Vast amounts of electricity are used to pump water for irrigation and for municipal and industrial use. Water use efficiency in irrigation is low, and losses in municipal water supply systems through leakage can reach well above 50 percent. Poorly designed delivery and distribution systems, which cause large water head losses, also contribute to inefficient use. This is a serious problem for the water sector. In municipal water utilities, for example, energy costs, mainly for pumping, are the third highest of the main cost centres, after depreciation and personnel costs.

Other inefficiencies arise from the amount of run-down infrastructure in use, particularly in lower income countries. The infrastructure for generation and distribution is frequently barely maintained, including silted-up dams for hydropower generation. And run-down water delivery systems also contribute to inefficiencies. Government subsidies can also encourage inefficient and wasteful use of both energy and water. In India, for example, government subsidies for diesel fuel and electricity for water pumps encourage overpumping and wasteful use, leading to serious depletion of groundwater. Agriculture takes more than 90 percent of freshwater withdrawals, and something like one fifth of the country's total electricity production is used to pump water from wells.

Box 8.2 Karnataka, India—generating benefits by combining efficiency gains and greater reliance on renewable energy

A study on water and energy in the state of Karnataka, India, showed that a combination of simple efficiency improvements, small hydroelectric power plants, cogeneration of electric power from sugarcane waste, and use of methane gas from other wastes or small amounts of natural gas and solar water heaters would achieve far greater and more rapid development progress than the fossil fuel generation plan of the main state electric utility. The study found that the combined energy plan could require 40 percent less electricity, cost some 65 percent less, and reduce carbon dioxide emissions by 95 percent compared with the planned fossil fuel generation plant. This points the way clearly to the potential for meeting developing countries' electricity needs at much lower cost and carbon emissions through such combined approaches than through traditional fossil fuel generation.

Source: Hawken, Lovins, and Lovins 1999, p. 250.

What needs to be done?

The great challenge is to achieve the required huge expansion in energy use of all kinds, while minimizing the environmental impacts and the negative effects on various parts of the water sector. There is evidence to suggest that this can be done through a combination of greater efficiency in energy generation and use and more use of renewable sources of energy. The potential for extending the approach is enormous. The state of Karnataka in India shows the gains that are possible from such an approach (see box 8.2).

8 Focusing on Key Areas, Promoting Change

Rehabilitating existing infrastructure and improving infrastructure operation and capacity would add additional generating capacity without constructing new infrastructure

Promoting energy savings

The gains from investing in greater energy use efficiency are even more substantial for the developing world than for the advanced economies, since lower income countries are, on average, three times less energy efficient than developed countries. Advanced economies can support greater efficiency in developing countries by stopping the negative technology transfers of exports of obsolete equipment to lower income countries. For example, Denmark has banned the export of technologies that are considered unfit for domestic use on economic and environmental grounds, such as obsolete coal-fired electrical generation equipment.

Vast savings in energy consumption are possible by conducting energy audits, replacing inefficient machinery and transmission systems, and designing buildings to conserve heat and energy. The assumption that the cost to replace inefficient equipment outweighs the energy savings is often not borne out. The electricity costs of a large industrial motor, for example, of which there are hundreds of millions worldwide, surpass the motor's capital cost every few weeks, so switching to more efficient motors can result in very rapid payback.

The required energy use efficiency gains will come from across the board of energy use. But the water sector, as a major user of electric energy, has a very significant part to play by reducing wasteful use of water, including inefficient irrigation practices and water losses in municipal water distribution systems. Improvements in rundown infrastructure in the energy and water sectors will offer further efficiency gains. Ending perverse subsidies that encourage overexploitation of surface water and groundwater will also contribute to greater energy use efficiency.

Reversing the decline in the stock of infrastructure

Some 80 percent of the world's hydropower potential has yet to be developed, from large-scale schemes to small-scale, stand-alone plants that generate less than 10 megawatts. Certainly, as noted, there are potential problems with large dam projects. However, since the report of the World Commission on Dams in 2000, which commented on many of the negative aspects of large dam development, considerable debate has taken place. It is now recognized that many of the negative impacts can be avoided by careful planning and design and thorough consultation with all stakeholders. It is also recognized that poverty alleviation and socio-economic development will suffer unless there is a large increase in water storage, particularly in multiuse reservoirs, where water is used for electricity generation then for irrigation, drinking water, and industrial purposes.

Getting the most out of existing infrastructure

There is also considerable unused hydropower capacity on many existing dams. Only about 20 percent of the world's large dams are dedicated to electricity production (Lecornu 1998). A recent study in the United States concluded that some 20,000 megawatts of hydropower could be gained by adding generating units at 2,500 existing dams (Conner, Francfort, and Rinehart 1998). Rehabilitating existing infrastructure and improving infrastructure operation and capacity (for example, by reducing siltation) would add additional generating capacity without constructing new infrastructure. Some dam infrastructure is beyond rehabilitation, however, and needs to be replaced. Infrastructure replacement is a routine feature of any production operation and must be factored into the operating and managing systems and the costs must be included in price structures and tariffs.

All aspects of energy production that have a direct impact on water must be designed and operated to minimize any negative environmental or social effects. Thus dams need to be designed to minimize the loss of water to aquatic ecosystem. Designers should try to avoid the worst impacts of interrupting river flows and to preserve a passage for migrating aquatic species. Tighter control needs

Water for energy

> *Two directions should be explored: the development of energy production techniques that contribute less to global warming, and wiser behaviour to save energy.*
> —Japan

Community-based projects have helped preserve aquifers by developing alternative water supplies through rainwater harvesting and water conservation

to be exercised over the water pollution associated with oil extraction and coal mining. Where thermal power plants continue to be used, they should extract the maximum amount of usable energy from fossil fuel consumed, by combined heat and power generation, for example. And water used for cooling should be reused, through tower cooling processes.

There is considerable potential to produce more water supplies for coastal areas through desalination, especially where there is a plentiful supply of low cost energy. Energy costs are falling worldwide, and desalination technology is becoming more efficient. In other areas there are deposits of brackish groundwater that can be converted to usable water supplies, including to potable standards, at costs that are increasingly competitive with more conventional water supply approaches thanks to lower energy costs, improved desalination technology, and relatively lower salinity (compared with seawater).

What is being done?

Attempts are being made to improve decision-making on water and energy—for example, through multistakeholder processes, demand management initiatives, and a few national processes. And around the world, examples abound of efforts in the areas identified above. Moreover, awareness of these issues is growing.

Integrating water and energy issues

Although the links between water and energy have become more widely recognized, especially for irrigation and hydropower, there is little reason for pride. The fact is, these links have been obvious for more than 4,500 years of human history. However, today there are institutions, like in Nepal (action 953), that deal with both water and energy, which should make it easier to integrate the issues.

The desirability of delivering water and electricity to rural villages to foster their development is exemplified by a programme to answer energy and water needs in rural Western Africa (action 1534). Similarly, local projects such as those in Baharbari, India (action 2163), show how energy supply development leads to water resources development and better livelihoods.

At the same time, the need for demand management in energy is especially evident in the links between energy and irrigation. As noted, in India energy subsidies have led to uncontrolled overpumping of aquifers. The problem is well known, and several studies have concluded that energy tariffs should be raised (IWMI 2001). Although such decisions are politically difficult, the future of agriculture in large rural areas will be compromised unless energy policies force prudent water management.

Community-based projects, especially in South Asia, have helped preserve aquifers by developing alternative water supplies through rainwater harvesting, water conservation, and other efforts (actions 978, 1322, and 1627). Such projects make it possible to better manage water and consume less energy.

Getting the most out of existing infrastructure

Some national energy programmes include infrastructure rehabilitation—for example, in Chad (action 1950), in a context where the same utility manages electricity and water, and in Georgia (action 2056). The Actions Database also identifies a handful of individual efforts to rehabilitate energy infrastructure. Attempts have also been made to prevent siltation, for example, in the Niger Basin (action 420) and in China (action 2082).

8 Focusing on Key Areas, Promoting Change

Proponents and opponents of projects in energy production need to take care that sound schemes are not blocked

Reversing the decline in the stock of infrastructure

International business partnerships exist for projects that combine large hydropower development, "new" renewable energy, and water supply and sanitation. Deregulation has created opportunities for investments in energy—including hydropower in Algeria (action 2068), Brazil (actions 2055 and 2058), and Guinea (action 2071)—as well as water supply and treatment. But there is still considerable hostility towards private sector involvement in these activities and much misunderstanding. Both proponents and opponents of such projects need to take care that sound schemes are not blocked.

In many developing countries there is a strong belief that large hydropower schemes offer an important means of moving away from fossil fuel use, providing needed energy services, and supporting economic and social development (actions 2072 in Kenya, 2079 in Tanzania, 2084 and 2085 in China, 2087 in India, 2096 in Pakistan, 2097 in the Philippines, 2101 in Turkey, 2103 in Uzbekistan, 2105 in Vietnam, and 2121 in Nicaragua). Meanwhile, other countries (such as Thailand, action 2100) prefer thermal and pumped-storage plants to avoid the controversies of new hydropower projects.

Comparing the effects of energy production approaches

Integrated planning that involves various users and takes into account entire river basins is increasingly considered necessary for dam projects. Such planning makes it possible to address potential conflicts at an early stage. Proponents must proceed with caution because of environmental and social concerns, while opponents should be aware that tighter regulations and guidelines can add costs that make projects unattractive or infeasible.

The complexities, benefits, and costs of dams have been carefully examined by the World Commission on Dams (action 73), which in 2000 concluded that although dams have made a significant contribution to human development, their negative impacts have not always been anticipated and well managed. National policies are starting to reflect this view, with compromises between the need for more infrastructure and local development and the need for ecosystem protection—as in Pakistan (action 2160), South Africa (action 886), and the United Kingdom (action 2162). Such policies are also emerging in countries that have hosted workshops on dams in recent years in partnership with the Dams and Development Project (action 826). And India has created a committee to develop guidelines for better dam projects (action 2057). National programmes can favour a single approach—such as in Nepal, where small-scale hydropower schemes are preferred because the country is well-suited to such schemes and because they can be managed locally (action 1554).

The Mekong River Commission—a joint initiative of countries that share the river—is formulating a hydropower development strategy that explicitly considers environmental and social impacts (action 903). The commission will coordinate its strategy with other international activities—such as the Water Utilization Program; Environment Program; Fisheries Program; Agriculture, Irrigation, and Forestry Program; and Navigation Program—and with its own efforts to mitigate and manage floods. Power trade in the Greater Mekong subregion is another topic that it will take into account.

Issues overlooked when the Lake Victoria Dam was built in Australia have to be addressed now. In response to concerns about significant damage to cultural heritage and Aboriginal burial plots that have been exposed on the lake's shores, a management plan is being developed for the reservoir that aims to reconcile water storage needs, environmental concerns, and cultural values (action 1137).

Water for energy

More and more countries are making environmental assessments of dams compulsory

In addition, payments can be made to compensate for the harm dams have caused. For example, after a dam was built on Australia's Mitta Mitta River, local farmers were compensated for the cost of irrigating pastures that dried out because of the dam (action 450). And in Quebec, Canada, Cree tribes were given money as well as jobs at the hydropower company to compensate for the ecological, cultural, and social impacts of the installation of a hydropower dam (action 107).

Assessing environmental impacts

Environmental impact assessments can be performed during the planning of dam projects to take into account the different uses of water. More and more countries are making environmental assessments of dams compulsory—as in Nepal (action 760). Romania is also developing environmentally sound management practices for hydropower projects (action 921). In addition, the World Bank requires environmental impact assessments for big dam projects, though its loans for large dam construction have declined drastically.

Operational rules for the Najar Dam in Orissa, India—which will store water for irrigation—have been developed with due consideration for the flow requirements of Chilika Lake, a major threatened lagoon downstream (action 584). In Japan, improved operations of dams are worked out as a means to avoid building new infrastructure (actions 1839 and 1840). Globally, IUCN–The World Conservation Union is contributing to the elaboration of specific tools for optimizing dam design and management (action 1603).

Various actions also show replacement of carbon-based energy sources with more sustainable, less polluting sources. Uganda has designed a plan within the framework of the Prototype Carbon Fund mechanism for reducing greenhouse gas emissions (action 2080). A large-scale hydropower programme in Western China is intended to reduce pollution from carbon-based energy sources (action 2085).

Using cleaner technologies

Renewable energy sources are increasingly being used for water supply and treatment. For example, solar and wind power are being used to supply water mainly, but not exclusively, in arid and semiarid areas (for solar power, see actions 480, 489, 963, 1138, and 1576; for wind power, see actions 482 and 671; and for uses of both technologies, see actions 664 and 2168). Such projects have been initiated by governments, non-governmental organizations (NGOs), and international organizations. Governments can provide economic incentives that encourage such technology, as Mexico has (action 1009).

Still, the need to save energy when transferring and treating water cannot be overemphasized. Such improvements are difficult to identify in the daily operations of water providers. The success of three Swiss towns and one French town in identifying ways to supply water at much lower electricity costs (actions 1703 and 3354) are isolated examples in the Actions Database. For the future, the energy impact of large-scale water transfers remains a source of concern (see actions 34, 186, 189, 315, 361, 382, 838, 972, 1200, 1395, 1849, 1931).

It is worth noting that the energy efficiency of advanced water treatment technology is constantly improving. Progress has been made on desalination technology, and the Actions Database shows that the technology is being used to generate water supplies on a growing number of islands (actions 388, 994, 1031). Distillation, which has been used for decades in energy-rich countries, is expanding in the Middle East. And where energy is costly, inverse osmosis (which consumes much less energy than distillation) is increasingly used to treat brackish water and to provide clean water.

8 Focusing on Key Areas, Promoting Change

The water sector, as a major user of electric energy, must play its part in improving energy use efficiency

> We are supplied with clean and safe water from the taps. However, when the electric utility cuts power, the water supply stops or is interrupted.
> —Tanzania

What remains to be done?

Water and energy have a central role in poverty alleviation and socio-economic development. They also play key roles in improving health. And the energy sector, through its impact on climate, has strong knock-on effects on the water sector. Thus water and energy development need to be incorporated explicitly in the national planning process, recognizing the connections between them and optimizing the beneficial aspects of their relationship while minimizing the negative ones.

Pursuing optimization of energy production and use

The analysis here has pointed the way towards better management of energy. A combination of increasing the efficiency of energy use, switching to forms of electricity generation that minimize the production of carbon dioxide, and increasing the reliance on renewable energy sources would allow a substantial expansion of energy production without a corresponding increase in harmful emissions. Where high carbon fossil fuels are used, means to extract the maximum amount of energy from their combustion must be pursued, such as combined heat and power stations, where appropriate. All forms of power production, both existing and planned installations, should be reviewed to minimize the harm they cause to vital natural ecosystems.

Promoting efficiency in water sector energy consumption

The water sector, as a major user of electric energy, must play its part in improving energy use efficiency. Reducing waste in irrigation water use and leakages in municipal water supply systems can lead to considerable energy savings from reduced pumping. So can rainwater harvesting. Further energy savings are possible from designing water distribution systems to minimize head losses and reviewing the machinery used in pumping. Energy audits of existing systems and the design of new systems to achieve higher energy efficiency will also make positive contributions. There is also substantial scope to increase the contribution that renewable energy sources can make to water supply and treatment. And governments should avoid, where possible, subsidies that encourage overpumping of water and wasteful use.

Consulting a wide range of stakeholders when developing energy projects

Decision-making about water and energy activities is a complex, multidimensional undertaking. Too many people inside the business community oppose or ignore the social and environmental aspects of these activities. People outside the business community often know little about how much such activities cost until they are asked to pay for them. And while many people are willing to speak up for the social aspects (though not all are in a position to make their voices heard), too few people are prepared to speak for the environment, the final arbiter of sustainable development. And in both cases, an excess of focus on social and environmental issues could hurt long-term sustainable development.

The work initiated by the World Commission on Dams and followed up by the Dams and Development Project is not over. But even if the guidelines proposed by the commission have not been fully endorsed, the multistakeholder process that has emerged allows for better decision-making—where it is adapted to local situations. Though this process is occurring in a handful of countries, much remains to be done in other countries. Still, the unexploited potential of hydropower and the growing demand for economic development in most developing countries make good energy project management an urgent need—especially when multiuse reservoirs, offering a range of benefits, are proposed.

9. Water for health

Water sufficient in quantity and quality to meet basic human needs is a prerequisite for both better health and sustainable development. But because of ever expanding development activities that often overexploit and pollute the world's finite water resources, water scarcity and water contamination have become major global concerns. Water-related diseases and excess levels of harmful substances in water supplies threaten human health and constrain socio-economic development.

What is needed are measures to prevent, control, and reduce water-related diseases and hazards within integrated water management systems. Most important are ensuring safe drinking water and sanitary disposal of human waste, changing hygiene behaviour, and improving water management practices. Although successful experiences with integrated approaches to managing water-related health risks are limited in number, many single practices have proved effective under specific conditions. The record shows that preventive measures are more cost-effective than remedial ones.

Present situation

The link between health and poverty is clear and unequivocal: the biggest enemy of health in developing countries is poverty, and better health is pivotal in poverty alleviation. The biggest single cause of ill health among poor people is water-related disease. In Brazil's public hospitals patients with water-related diseases occupy 90 percent of the beds—a situation common in developing countries.

So, better health, especially among poor people, is critical to socio-economic development. And the strong links between health and water quality mean that huge improvements in health management and water management must go hand in hand to alleviate poverty.

The main water-related diseases and hazards—and their causes

Drinking water can convey viruses, bacteria, parasites, and chemical contaminants that threaten human health through their ingestion. The two most common water-borne illnesses caused by drinking contaminated water are cholera and diarrhoeal disease. Annually, there are close to 4 billion diarrhoeal episodes and more than 2.2 million deaths from diarrhoeal disease, 90 percent of them among children under five (WHO and UNICEF 2000, p. 3).

Water contamination by human activity is one of the main causes of water-related diseases. Improper sanitation leads to faecal water pollution and spreads bacterial and viral diseases. Water can also be polluted by livestock excreta and the use of pesticides and excess fertilizer in agriculture. Industry is a source of pollutants in groundwater and surface water ranging from bacteria to metallic and organic pollutants. Improper waste management can lead to the dissemination in the environment of contaminants that threaten human health. And groundwater can naturally contain chemicals at threatening levels, such as lead, arsenic, and fluoride, and can show high levels of radioactivity.

Contamination of groundwater by arsenic threatens tens of millions of people in Bangladesh with cancer and skin diseases. Contaminated water can also lead to the contamination of food, as when organic pollutants accumulate in fish or animal flesh or when contaminated groundwater or improperly treated wastewater is used for irrigation.

9 Focusing on Key Areas, Promoting Change

Reaching the Millennium Development Goal target on water supply and sanitation is an important step in improving human health

Lack of sufficient water for sanitation and hygiene is also a large source of health problems. The most important category of diseases relating to personal hygiene that affect school-age children is intestinal helminth infections. Other "water-washed diseases" are scabies, trachoma, and impetigo. Annually, some 6–9 million people become blind as a result of trachoma, and another 500 million people are at risk (WHO and UNICEF 2000, p. 3).

Reaching the Millennium Development Goal target on water supply and sanitation is therefore an important step in improving human health. Also critical is to increase awareness and education about water and hygiene. Lack of knowledge about water quality leads to the use of water unsuitable for drinking, a problem that can occur at both the household level (where water may not be boiled or chlorinated before drinking) and the national level (where groundwater quality may not be monitored).

Water-related vectors—such as insects or snails living in wetlands or aquatic ecosystems—carry diseases with which they contaminate human beings. Bilharziasis, filariasis, malaria, and onchocerciasis are the most rampant of these vector-borne diseases. Malaria alone causes almost 300 million infections and kills more than 2 million people (more than half of them children under five) a year—and more than 2 billion people are at risk of infection. Bilharziasis infects around 200 million people annually, causing more than 200,000 deaths, and another 600 million are at risk of infection.

Poor water management practices increase the risk of such diseases. In irrigation and energy schemes poor water management leads to stagnant or slow-moving water and the proliferation of insects. Stagnant (and often polluted) water in communities and households also acts as a breeding ground for health-threatening insects.

Water can also cause accidental injury or death, most commonly through drowning. Floods not only cause drowning and economic losses, but they also often lead to widespread pollution by carrying and spreading waste, garbage, and contaminated substances stored under the flood level, such as fuel from low-lying tanks or chemicals from industries bordering the water. Lack of water also poses dangers, by preventing correct fire-fighting. And the need to fetch and carry water over great distances can lead to injuries and fatigue.

Water-related health problems worsen during war, drought, and the displacement of populations. Climate change could also exacerbate such problems, through changes in temperatures and precipitation (box 9.1).

Box 9.1 Water, health, and climate change

Climate change could adversely affect human health in many ways. Some examples:

- Water-borne diseases are likely to increase. Recent models suggest that by 2100 climate change could lead to a substantial increase in the share of the world population living in potential malaria-transmission zones.

- The sea level could rise, affecting the health of vulnerable populations through heightened storm surges and through damage to coastal infrastructure (roads, housing, and water and sanitation systems).

- Extreme weather events, such as floods, storms, and heat waves, may become more frequent, leading to direct and indirect effects on human health.

Source: UN ECE and WHO 1999.

Water for health 9

> *I am worried that the rice grown with contaminated water from the canal will be harmful to our health.*
> —Jordan

Despite the proven efficacy of preventive health approaches, health services are focused on cure rather than prevention

The consequences of water-related health challenges

For poor families water-related diseases and hazards can have devastating consequences:

- Illness or death of the family breadwinner can bring the supply of both food and income to a sudden stop.
- A previously able breadwinner can suddenly become a dependent, straining food supplies and the meagre family income.
- Paying for medical treatment can impoverish the family, which may have to use all its savings and sell off precious assets. A downward spiral into severe poverty usually follows.
- If a working parent becomes sick or dies, children may be withdrawn from school and sent to work instead.
- Transporting a sick family member for treatment is often costly in terms of both direct transport expenses and lost income earning opportunities.

Water scarcity is linked to significant nutrition issues:

- Where water must be fetched and carried over long distances, people must expend large numbers of calories to meet their basic needs for water.
- Where water is costly, malnutrition levels are high, a problem associated with diarrhoeal disease.

Strong correlations have been found between improved water supply and better sanitation and hygiene practices, on the one hand, and better nutritional status, on the other. Most episodes of diarrhoea can be prevented through improved childcare practices, most of which are related to personal and domestic hygiene practices and improvements in water supply and sanitation. The most important practices are:

- Ensuring sanitary disposal of faeces.
- Washing hands (including fingernails) with soap or ash.
- Providing safe drinking water (by boiling or otherwise disinfecting it).
- Ensuring sufficient quantity and quality of water.

The problem of public health services

The problems of water-related disease are exacerbated by the situation in the health sector. There are no effective vaccines for the most prevalent and virulent water-related diseases. Antibiotics and other medical treatments are becoming increasingly less effective as the pathogens develop greater resistance to them. Insects have developed resistance to the commonly available insecticides. And, particularly critical, the public health services in many countries are in disarray.

In most developing countries the public health service is regarded as having only marginal importance relative to the delivery of health care. Public health services are typically underfunded and poorly staffed. Yet poor people constantly identify poor nutrition, dirty water, poor sanitation, and pollution among their greatest concerns—all problems that should be addressed by the public health services in coordination with the water sector.

These deficiencies create an intolerable situation. The drugs available for curative health care are often too expensive for poor people. And many of the medical interventions that are available are ineffective for water-related diseases.

Yet despite this situation and the proven efficacy of preventive health approaches, health services are focused on cure rather than prevention.

9 Focusing on Key Areas, Promoting Change

"Halving the number of people without access to water and sanitation by 2015—two prerequisites for health"

—Gro Harlem Brundtland

Water-related diseases and international agreements

The international community has agreed on goals for reducing water-related diseases and hazards. Adopted in London on 17 June 1999 by the members of the United Nations Economic Commission for Europe and the Regional Commission for Europe of the World Health Organization (UN ECE and WHO 1999), the Protocol on Water and Health (action 1387) has as its basic objective to protect health and well-being by improving water management (including the protection of ecosystems) and preventing, controlling, and reducing water-related diseases.

The Millennium Development Goals have clear links with these issues. The ability to achieve the goals for poverty, major diseases, child mortality, and maternal mortality is directly and heavily influenced by water-related diseases and hazards. So is the ability to achieve the education and gender equality goals, though to a lesser degree. Together, these represent a large share of the Millennium Development Goals. As Gro Harlem Brundtland (2002), director general of the World Health Organization commented in November 2002 on the release of the United Nations Committee on Economic, Cultural, and Social Rights statement on access to water as a human right, "The declaration of water as a human right is a major boost in efforts to achieve the Millennium Development Goals of halving the number of people without access to water and sanitation by 2015—two prerequisites for health". When this factor is combined with the problems of water-related disease, it becomes abundantly clear how crucial it is that the world meet these challenges.

Why things must change

All the evidence shows that better health translates into greater and more equitably distributed resources. A healthy workforce produces more. Healthy families are better educated. Healthy families also save more, increasing the resources available for community and national investment. And they have fewer children and more widely spaced births.

Earlier, investing in health was often regarded as a luxury, something a country did after it tackled energy, defence, transport, and the like. Now we know that the health of a nation's people is a major determinant of not only its own development but also that of the entire global community. The bad news is that it has taken so long to accept the obvious. The good news is that there are solutions that are both achievable and affordable.

What needs to be done?

Increasing education and raising awareness are essential—because at the centre of the effort must be a massive change in attitudes and behaviour, shifting the focus towards prevention rather than cure. This change must extend from the highest levels of government down through communities of all sizes to families and individuals, young and old.

Also critical is *adopting policies that place health at the centre of the development process*. Policies at the national level should involve the education, finance, labour, trade, agricultural, and environmental sectors. Ministers and senior officials must be made aware of the threats relating to water-related diseases and hazards in their sector and the needed preventive measures. The earlier underinvestment in public health services must be reversed, with the revived services giving priority to the poor. Policies and guidelines for pollution control and drinking water quality need to be developed and put into place (see chapter 2).

Linking health and integrated water resources management is essential. The management of water-related diseases and hazards must be a key element of policies for integrated water resources management. The cost-effectiveness of preventive interventions needs to be evaluated,

Water for health

Health must become an issue in integrated water resources management

not only to demonstrate the cost savings relative to curative interventions but also to point to the broader returns for socio-economic development. And preventive actions and scientific research need to be developed for chemicals that disrupt the endocrine system, before they lead to serious public health effects—in industrial or developing countries.

Health must become an issue in integrated water resources management at both river basin and city levels. Governments must regulate to ensure that designers and developers of water projects (water supply, irrigation, hydropower, and the like) are aware of water-related diseases and hazards—and are made responsible for developing projects that minimize the threats. River basin managers and city planners need to be similarly sensitized, and they need to be shown how better planning and zoning regulations can mitigate the threats. City managers must attend to garbage collection and the maintenance of storm drainage systems, and industries to the health effects of their effluents.

Farmers and water project managers too have to be alerted to the threats of water-based and vector-borne disease and trained in the improved water management techniques that can mitigate these threats. The solutions are widely known but not nearly as widely practised. Incentives for implementing such solutions need to be created.

Water reuse is an expanding solution in integrated water resources management. But because it can affect health, research is needed to explore its full implications.

Emphasizing local management is critical. Water supply and sanitation services need radical improvement, including shortening the distance between water supply and households and increasing the per capita water supply for households. Drinking water sources—whether community sources or household water storage—must be protected against pollution. Improved human waste disposal is essential, whether by dry latrines, flush latrines, or low-cost community sewerage systems. Sites that are seriously polluted or associated with water-based and vector-borne disease must be clearly identified, and nearby communities and families at risk notified of the threat.

Family preventive health training is a must, even for preschool and school-age children. Men must not be neglected. Not only must they improve their personal hygiene practices, but they must share in the training of their children.

With suitable help communities can do much of the work. Poor communities have excellent coping mechanisms and can muster substantial collective resources. But if progress is to be made, national governments must support district-level governments and local public health services.

9 Focusing on Key Areas, Promoting Change

While only a small number of initiatives are directly aimed at producing health benefits, many lead indirectly to improvements in health

> **'We are reaping the consequences of our actions that led to the degradation of swamps and mangroves: an outbreak of sickness and limited water supply for domestic use. —Ghana'**

What is being done?

Successful experiences with integrated approaches to managing water-related health risks are limited in number, but many single practices have proved effective under specific conditions. And while only a small number of initiatives are directly aimed at producing health benefits, many lead indirectly to improvements in health, such as those focusing on increasing the water supply, improving sanitation, or reducing pollution.

Increasing education and raising awareness

Initiatives to increase education and raise awareness about water-related disease and preventive measures are under way—from the local to the international level. At the local level in China the Barefoot Doctor Training Project (action 1047) is training village representatives in the basics of public health management—safe water collection and storage, sanitation and waste disposal, and personal and domestic hygiene. In Turkey an innovative malaria control programme relies on volunteer female community health leaders to help increase community resources for malaria control (action 1968). The Water and Sanitation Project in the Mekong Delta (action 505) is improving school sanitation through efforts linked to wider improvements in town water and sanitation and promotion of public health awareness.

In India the Restructured Central Rural Sanitation Programme (action 458) has been promoting rural school sanitation as both an entry point for and a major part of improving sanitation and public health services. Another school sanitation project, in the Indian state of Gujarat, has installed latrines in thousands of schools (action 2416). The facilities help ensure practical hygiene education and help spread better sanitation practices to parents and households. Also in Gujarat, the Self-Employed Women's Association (SEWA) has embraced hygiene education as a cornerstone of its "Know Your Body" Programme for its 300,000 women members (action 2285). SEWA has also promoted hygiene education among childcare workers.

Several significant initiatives are under way at the international level. The Water Supply and Sanitation Collaborative Council (WSSCC) has initiated the Water Sanitation and Hygiene for All (WASH) Campaign (action 737), a global advocacy effort aimed at placing sanitation, better hygiene practices, and improved water supply firmly on the political agenda. The campaign is working with its members, strategic partners, and allies in more than 140 countries (actions 738, 740, 741, and 742). The Global Hand Washing Initiative (action 239), is a public–private partnership involving several major soap producers, that works in cooperation with national governments. It builds on a previous experience in Central America. A hand-washing campaign has been launched in Ghana in 2003 (action 3472), and consumer studies in Nepal, Peru, and Senegal. Exploratory work is being undertaken in China; the global steering committee is very active in facilitating cross-country knowledge exchanges and developing a framework for conducting hand-washing behavioural studies. The Iguaçu Action Programme (action 1188), developed by WSSCC, promotes people-centred approaches and focuses on hygiene behaviour, environmental sanitation, institutional management reforms, community-based approaches, and monitoring. The School Sanitation and Hygiene Education Programme (action 240), a joint effort of the United Nations Children's Fund (UNICEF) and the International Water and Sanitation Centre (IRC), pursues a similar goal through school education.

Water for health

Adopting policies that place health at the centre of the development process

Policy initiatives have been both national and regional. At the national level the South African Department of Water Affairs and Forestry has launched the Dense Settlements Project (action 1336) to reduce water pollution and improve community health in densely populated settlements where sanitation and waste collection are inadequate.

Spanning the period 2002–06, the Children and Women's Environment Programme (action 1679), a joint effort of UNICEF and the government of Nepal, aims to reduce illness and death, and to improve nutrition among Nepalese children. It focuses on four public health interventions: school sanitation, safe drinking water, hygiene awareness campaigns, and community-based hygiene and sanitation. The Integrated Development of Basic Urban Services in Provincial Towns (action 787) is a comprehensive project in Mongolia with a focus on public health improvement. In addition to improving water supply and sanitation systems, it will rehabilitate public bathhouses and construct new ones, refurbish and replace centralized heating and hot water supply systems, and improve solid waste management. The Environmental Technology Verification–Arsenic Mitigation Project (action 1785) in Bangladesh is addressing the problem of arsenic-contaminated groundwater. This project will develop a process for assessing and verifying arsenic mitigation technologies and a programme for certifying viable ones.

At the regional level a European Union (EU) programme is dealing with one of the modern water quality problems—pharmaceutical residues in water and wastewater. A cluster of projects under the PHARMA Programme (action 1858) will work to develop advanced monitoring and removal technologies for water and wastewater (including wastewater for reuse) and investigate the environmental risk of veterinary medicines in sludge used for agriculture. Another EU project, CatchWater (action 1203), has been investigating water reuse, including the development of best-practice guidelines.

In Mexico and Central America applications of DDT for malaria control have been reduced, but malaria poses a serious and growing threat. A project has been strengthening national and local institutional capacity to control malaria, replacing the use of DDT or other persistent pesticides with cost-effective and environmentally sustainable systems that are replicable worldwide (action 744).

Linking health and integrated water resources management

The International Water Management Institute is conducting research on how to use local approaches to malaria control (actions 402 and 640). The aim is to understand the links between vector breeding and agricultural practices and to develop environmental management techniques to control malaria vectors.

In Turkey the Southeastern Anatolia Project (action 380), which has created large dam reservoirs for irrigation and other regional development activities, includes a number of public health components. The Solid Waste Management Project in Anatolia (action 2007) is working to develop systematic and sustainable solid waste management in the rapidly urbanizing areas of the region. Another project, being carried out in cooperation with the Turkish Association for Parasitic Diseases, is assessing the increased risk of vector-borne disease posed by the reservoirs and will develop an appropriate public health action plan (action 1969).

9 Focusing on Key Areas, Promoting Change

Further research on the implications of wastewater reuse for water quality, public health, and the environment is critical

The mounting stress of water scarcity has forced countries to include the use of wastewater—in agriculture and in urban water systems—in their development plans. The reuse of treated wastewater involves significant trade-offs. It is widely practised in agricultural production, especially in developing countries. The problem is that most farmers lack awareness of the potential health consequences, and in most cases the wastewater is applied to fields before being properly treated. Further research on the implications of wastewater reuse for water quality, public health, and the environment is critical. Failure to properly evaluate the risks linked with wastewater reuse and to put into place and enforce standard hygiene regulations will lead to adverse effects on both human health and the environment.

Started in 2001, the Urban Reuse of Treated Wastewater Programme (action 2048) began to tackle serious water pollution problems in several big cities in China and to provide opportunities for incorporating reuse into new urban wastewater schemes. In southeastern Turkey where municipal wastewater discharge is growing, a project aims to develop safe technologies for reusing municipal wastewater in irrigation (action 1982). In Singapore a project blends wastewater, after high-technology treatment, in a reservoir to be used for purposes other than potable water (action 1914). The Melbourne Water Recycling Strategy (action 732) has adopted a target of recycling 20 percent of the treated effluent in its major sewage treatment plant by 2010. Similar strategies are beginning to be pursued in Bahrain (action 1896), Jordan (action 1817), and many cities around the world.

Regional multipurpose research programmes are also needed. One such programme is the Northern Rivers Ecosystem Initiative (action 1343), which deals with drinking water quality as well as with endocrine disruption in fish populations.

Emphasizing local management

Dozens of actions are aimed at improving rural water supply. They help women save time and energy fetching water and avoid the health defects and injuries sustained carrying heavy water containers. For example, in China underground water storage tanks are being installed in remote mountainous areas (action 1047). These tanks enable women to avoid the 8- to 12-kilometre walk once needed to collect water.

The Safe Water System (action 1279) is a household-based water quality management system, developed jointly by the U.S. Centers for Disease Control and Prevention and the Pan-American Health Organization. Field tests in Africa, Asia, and Latin America show that it can reduce the risk of diarrhoea by 44–85 percent. Large-scale implementation is now under way in many countries.

Mali, Mauritania, and Senegal have established a major programme to combat bilharziasis and malaria in the Senegal Basin (action 1059). Elsewhere in Mali, the non-governmental organization Mande Ja Kele Ton is helping to establish village management committees that will construct latrines, promote health education, protect wells from contamination, and organize garbage collection and disposal (action 1263). South Africa responded to a cholera outbreak in Eastern Cape Province in 2001 with a public health education programme involving close to 100 villages (action 1689). The programme included constructing latrines, developing new drinking water sources from groundwater and rainwater harvesting, and conducting health and hygiene awareness campaigns.

Water for health 9

> **There is a need to promote water purification technologies to rural communities.**
> **—South Africa**

The efficacy of sound public health and hygiene practices is now being rediscovered, but what needs to be done is summed up in the old adage: an ounce of prevention is worth a pound of cure

What remains to be done?

The actions described here are but a tiny share of a large and growing worldwide programme to improve public health. Clearly this effort must continue—and both expand and accelerate. The biggest need is to reinforce and accelerate changes in attitude and behaviour—in water supply and in sanitation and hygiene practices—at all levels, from government ministers to individuals. That means that education and awareness programmes are still required.

The efficacy of sound public health and hygiene practices, allied with public health engineering for water supply and sewerage, has been known for more than a century, yet has been largely ignored in lower income countries. It is now being rediscovered, but the previous period of neglect resulted in horrendous illness and death among poor people, especially children. What needs to be done is summed up in the old adage that an ounce of prevention is worth a pound of cure. Increase the investment and resources in public health services and public health engineering projects (whether public, private, community, or non-governmental), and the results in health, poverty reduction, and socio-economic development will be dramatic.

10. Water for agriculture

Even though current global food is sufficient for global needs, 800 million people suffer from hunger and malnutrition, and many more live in poverty. Innovative water and food actions are needed to achieve food security, alleviate poverty, and improve livelihoods, especially in developing countries.

These actions must consider the environmental sustainability of food production systems—a major oversight in many of today's agricultural practices, when 70–80 percent of the world's freshwater withdrawals are used to irrigate crops. Reforms to improve incentives in the agricultural and irrigation sector should revitalize productivity and attract new investments.

The *World Water Vision* (Cosgrove and Rijsberman 2000) suggests ways to meet the growing demand for agricultural water, taking into account the water needs of ecosystems. Approaches include increasing water productivity, enhancing water availability, reducing agricultural pollution, and improving management of water resources, irrigation, and drainage.

More than 300 water actions address water and agriculture. They mark a tangible shift towards reform but also indicate a need for greater effort. With growing awareness of water issues, many governments are adjusting policies for water and agriculture, and in some cases for the entire water sector. And some countries have done remarkable work to develop water user associations and river basin authorities.

But many of these initiatives need to be accompanied by reformulated roles for government agencies. Some hesitant starts have been made on the institutional reforms required to support effective management of water resources and irrigation infrastructure.

Most of these innovations are still in the form of research and pilot projects to investigate new arrangements for developing, managing, and funding water infrastructure and for disseminating new technologies and practices—especially simple, affordable ones. In addition, reforms and capacity building for both irrigated and rainfed agriculture should be intensified, giving stakeholders a say in their own future. And international agreements should be established on trade, tariffs, and quality standards to give developing countries access to protected markets while respecting their rights to food sovereignty.

Finally, the transaction costs involved in structural adjustment of agriculture need to be accounted for in a framework that addresses water management for sustainable agriculture.

Water for agriculture

Alternative approaches have to be found to provide the water needed to produce the world's food

Present situation

As populations and incomes increase, the global demand for food rises. Using almost the same water and land resources, more food must be grown for the 800 million people malnourished today and the 2 billion more people expected around the world by 2025. The water needs of households and industry will also jump.

More than 1.3 billion of the world's people are absolutely poor, living on less than $1 a day. Another 2 billion people are only marginally better off. The foundation of livelihoods is food security, which at the national and household levels can be achieved through a combination of domestic production, secured imports, and effective food distribution. But in some severely water-scarce countries that are not self-sufficient and do not earn enough foreign exchange (through exports) to purchase the required food, large portions of the population often suffer from hunger—and sometimes famine. And people in all countries suffer from hunger if they cannot afford to buy available food.

The looming water crisis is already apparent. Overexploitation of water resources—mainly for agriculture—has created environmental disasters. Alternative approaches have to be found to provide the water needed to produce the world's food.

In addition, global warming is likely to make precipitation patterns more variable, reducing water availability in some regions and increasing it in others. This shift would have a huge impact on both irrigated and non-irrigated agriculture. Changes in precipitation would make extreme weather events more common, leading to more severe and frequent flooding and to lower dry-season water flows in rivers. More intense rainfall would increase erosion and sedimentation in reservoirs and canals. Past investments in water control will lose their value if reservoirs no longer fill and irrigation canals do not run full.

Today's water and food situation is recognized as a serious global issue, and the international community has prepared many initiatives in response to it. The Ministerial Declaration signed at the Second World Water Forum identified "securing the food supply" as a key global challenge for the 21st century. Similarly, the first Millennium Development Goal from the United Nations Millennium Summit (United Nations 2000) seeks to halve extreme poverty and hunger by 2015. The 2002 World Food Summit calculated that more than 22 million people a year would have to escape hunger to achieve that goal (FAO 2002). The 2002 World Summit on Sustainable Development (WSSD) took this thinking a step further and included agriculture in its WEHAB (water supply and sanitation, energy, health, agriculture, and biodiversity) framework for tackling the world's most pressing development challenges.

Although agriculture consumes more freshwater than does any other use, it also significantly contributes to national economies, employment, and food supplies. Thus in most developing countries it remains an important way for poor people to sustain and improve their livelihoods. Rainfed and irrigated agriculture depend on the secure, adequate quantity and quality of water. But increasing demands for limited freshwater resources, without putting in place the right incentives for agricultural production, may be a serious hindrance to meeting the future demand for food.

10 Focusing on Key Areas, Promoting Change

The enormous pressure on freshwater resources makes it more necessary than ever to increase communication between farmers and environmentalists

What needs to be done?

The *World Water Vision* addresses food supply concerns in light of current water availability, taking into account social, economic, environmental, and cultural factors that could affect the future of water. It is estimated that with more efficient irrigation 40 percent more food could be produced using just 15–20 percent more water. The Vision projects that by 2025 such an increase in water productivity, combined with better water management, could meet about half of the demand for agricultural water. But the other half cannot be covered unless new water resources are developed.

Increasing water productivity

Efforts to improve food security and rural livelihoods must focus on raising water productivity in both rainfed and irrigated agriculture and on increasing the availability of affordable, environmentally acceptable water that generates maximum socio-economic returns. Better agronomic practices and crop selection can save water and reduce waste. Biotechnology can provide seeds with higher yields, better resistance to pests and diseases, and higher tolerance for inundation, drought, and saline water. Yield-increasing water-saving technology—advanced or simple—can also raise water productivity. In addition, better communication systems can provide market, weather, and other information that enhances production decisions. And all these technologies will improve the management abilities of irrigation and drainage agencies, leading to better, cheaper services.

Harnessing new water supplies

Whatever agricultural advances are made, the fact remains that growing more food requires more water, whether production is rainfed or irrigated. Even under favourable assumptions about improvements in irrigation efficiency and agronomic potential, water supplies for agriculture will have to increase 15–20 percent over the next 25 years to meet the world's food requirements.

Some of this additional water can come from harvesting rainwater in arid and semiarid regions and from developing small-scale water sources such as shallow aquifers. These are preferred solutions because they can be used in areas with extensive poverty, little water, and rapid population growth. Reducing waste in return flows from agricultural, municipal, and industrial users can also improve water supplies. On the other hand, preliminary research results indicate that water requirements for environmental and ecological needs amount to at least 30 percent of the total run-off in river basins. It is obvious that where demands for both requirements exceed the amount available, choices and compromises have to be made. The enormous pressure on freshwater resources makes it more necessary than ever to increase communication between farmers and environmentalists. Importing food will also reduce the stress on the water systems but its impact on local poverty, socio-economic, cultural, and environmental situations has to be better understood.

Water for agriculture 10

> *Farmers sell their water and land rights . . . because they don't have money. Later, there will be no agriculture in developing countries. Then who will feed these countries?*
> —Thailand

Reservoirs perform functions that are hard to replace by other means

Expanding storage capacity

New storage capacity will be required to replace capacity lost to sedimentation and to save water lost during floods for use during times of scarcity. New storage can be surface storage in reservoirs or groundwater storage and will generally serve a variety of users. The challenge is to increase groundwater storage to make new water available during dry seasons and to reverse the drawdown of groundwater tables. New techniques and institutional mechanisms are urgently needed to enhance, recharge, and improve management of groundwater aquifers.

New surface reservoirs are a subject of considerable controversy because of their potential effects on local communities and the environment, including inundation of land, resettlement of people, and disturbance of river ecosystems and fish migrations. In addition, such reservoirs are subject to sedimentation and evaporation. But reservoirs perform functions that are hard to replace by other means and so will remain a necessary option in water resources development.

Empowering communities and user groups

Individuals and groups must be empowered to make decisions so that local populations can control a share of development resources. Many government agencies have pulled back from day-to-day water management, creating new roles for civil society organizations. User associations are being formed to run irrigation systems, and new multistakeholder catchment committees influence water allocations and management practices. Such organizations can protect the interests of poor farmers and engage them in other collective actions that improve their livelihoods. The central role of female farmers in many of these activities must be better recognized, with their rights (to water, for example) and representation redefined.

Ensuring access to food

Access to food at the individual, local, regional, and global levels should be ensured. Infrastructure for storing and distributing food should be developed, as should the ability to generate foreign exchange in countries that must pay for food imports. Domestic development policies (including subsidies and implicit taxes), international assistance programmes, and international trade agreements will have to acknowledge and support the centrality of agriculture-based development in these circumstances.

Reforming water management institutions

Reforms should reorient water management institutions towards people, making them more service-oriented, user-controlled, and self-financed, with transparent decision-making and accountability. These institutions should be embedded in a system of integrated water management with empowered multistakeholder basin organizations managing surface and groundwater. This approach should enhance water access for poor people and disadvantaged groups, and allow minimum flows for basic needs and the environment.

10 Focusing on Key Areas, Promoting Change

The envisaged shift to a service orientation may require changes in attitudes, skills, and management practices

Qualified, skilled people are needed to develop and run these institutions. Moreover, the envisaged shift to a service orientation may require changes in attitudes, skills, and management practices. The motivation, knowledge, and skills of staff have to be developed through education, training, and human resources management. These processes require increasing the capacity of local professionals and researchers to provide education and training on water and food production; facilitating the exchange of knowledge between local users, technicians, and professional water managers; and establishing or strengthening links between water users, water managers, education institutions, and water research organizations.

Making needed investments

Investments are needed to meet the demand for food, to increase the productivity and development of water, and to improve the livelihoods of rural people. Investment programmes should respond to the key principles of subsidiarity, participation, accountability, and transparency and should foster representative institutions in an integrated water resources development and management context.

Investments should develop water resources to enable community-based irrigation, modernize existing irrigation and drainage systems, and replace and augment storage capacity in reservoirs and groundwater basins—particularly in water-scarce countries. Groundwater recharge programmes should be initiated to help restore groundwater tables. Moreover, investments are needed in drainage and reclamation of degraded irrigated land, restoration of eroded lands, and provision of flood protection and drainage in frequently inundated areas. And environmental regulations and parallel investments in municipal and industrial waste treatment are needed to improve the quality of river water, reducing dilution requirements and increasing supplies.

Both funding for investment and for operations are to be the result of a negotiation process between the authorities, the service provider, and the users on the level of services and the associated costs of service provision. All costs must be recovered, partly through contribution from users and partly from the government representing the interests of the society at large.

What is being done?

In the Actions Database, initiatives dealing primarily with water for agriculture involve efforts in one or more of the following categories: formulating long-term water policies and related strategies, increasing water productivity, promoting water availability, controlling agricultural pollution, reforming institutions and management, enhancing stakeholder participation, raising awareness and developing information systems, developing human resources, supporting action-oriented research, and adopting innovative technology.

Water for agriculture   10

> *I know what the irrigation [water] has brought to my family: my son and all other members of my family no longer need to go to other regions as seasonal workers.*
> —Turkey

Many countries have only subsectoral water policies, which are often inconsistent

Formulating long-term water policies and related strategies

Every country has unique legal, institutional, economic, social, physical, and environmental conditions that influence its water management policies and strategies. The formulation of national strategies for integrated water management depends on many factors, including a country's size and political organization, its hydrological conditions, its regional context, and the diversity of its stakeholders. Many countries have only subsectoral water policies (for irrigation, water supply, and so on), which are often inconsistent. But some governments—such as the Netherlands (action 2539) and Jamaica (action 2118)—have adopted agricultural water policies that integrate the management of natural resources, including water, soil, and biological resources.

The actions show that water strategies in arid and semiarid regions (the Middle East, Africa, Central Asia, parts of the Americas), where water is the key element in food production, are mainly concerned with achieving water security for irrigation, with an increasing focus on conservation-oriented agriculture. Examples include actions in Egypt (action 191), Morocco (action 1178), Pakistan (action 1177), Tunisia (action 723), and Yemen (action 1142).

National policies, especially agricultural policies, make the link between globalized food markets and local water markets. Subsidies paid by industrial countries, particularly to their farmers as in the United States (action 1510), are seen by developing countries as one of the main causes of the food crisis in many African countries. Agricultural subsidies in Europe and North America, estimated at $350 billion a year, are six times foreign aid to developing countries. Combined with trade barriers imposed by industrial countries, subsidies prevent developing countries from competing in global markets. According to Oxfam (2002), abolishing these subsidies would increase cash flows from industrial to developing countries by $100 billion.

Subsidies also exist in developing countries. Removing them requires a prudent transition—as illustrated by Nepal (action 2063), where too quick a move had negative consequences for the country's agriculture.

Increasing water productivity

In planning and implementing agriculture projects, countries try to bridge the gap between population growth and large urban populations on the one hand, and food production and rural development on the other. These projects are carried out in conjunction with efforts to provide sufficient water supplies while protecting the environment and ensuring economic and financial support—essential elements for sustainable projects.

Some agriculture projects have adopted innovative measures in their efforts to reclaim land and add it to the productive land base. Egypt's El-Salam Canal Project (action 189) is designed to boost local food production to satisfy growing demand, and to develop rural areas to attract populations from the densely populated Nile valley and delta. To ensure its success, the project reused agricultural drainage water (within accepted hygienic and environmental norms), secured funds using cost recovery measures, and attracted foreign investments to finance the development, operation, and maintenance of project infrastructure. Similar measures for sustainable land reclamation were used in Pakistan's low-cost, water-saving salinity reclamation project (action 1154), which showed that where water

10 Focusing on Key Areas, Promoting Change

Some 90 percent of the increase in global food production will have to come from existing cultivated land, with just 10 percent coming from newly reclaimed land

> When agriculture water is taken from the river, opinion is often divided between farmers and fishers. We agreed on securing adequate river flow for the survival of the fish. —Japan

tables are 1 metre or deeper, abandoned saline soils can be reclaimed for agricultural production within a few years.

Despite the success of such land reclamation projects, several predictions indicate that 90 percent of the increase in global food production will have to come from existing cultivated land, with just 10 percent coming from newly reclaimed land (Schultz 2001). Thus efforts to produce enough food for growing populations will increasingly have to involve installing modern irrigation and drainage systems to boost the productivity of existing cultivated land, as in Egypt's second national drainage project (action 722). And in rainfed areas without water management systems, improvements in agricultural growth can be achieved through watershed management that increases farm productivity, as in India (action 1308) or China (action 2608).

In addition to large-scale installations of modern irrigation and drainage systems, small-scale measures can improve the livelihoods of poor individuals and families. For example, introducing treadle pumps, first developed in Bangladesh, for irrigation in Kenya, Niger, Zambia, and Zimbabwe (action 438) makes use of simple, affordable technology to help small farmers lift water for irrigation. Family drip irrigation systems in China (action 580) use the latest technology but do not require special infrastructure (such as pumps and electricity), making them ideal for small plots and fields. A mix of such small-scale measures is promoted by Kafuku Farm Institute (action 3142). Although small-scale operations are the only feasible approach in areas experiencing pressure on irrigable space, a mix of large and small systems is best when access to large-scale expertise, technology, and economies is needed, as with Egypt's Toshka Project (action 186).

Enhancing water availability

Water stress situations results mainly from limited supplies (as in arid regions) or poor reticulation and inequitable distribution through supply networks, or both. Accordingly, actions focused on promoting water availability try to tackle both problems—by augmenting water supplies and controlling the demand for water.

To supply more irrigation water, desalination is still too costly a process, and weather modification and cloud seeding techniques raise environmental and social concerns, so that increased storage capacity remains the favoured option. The Actions Database indicates that two main approaches are used: building dams or reservoirs and artificially recharging aquifers with water for future use. Dam issues are considered in chapter 8, but dams also fit into any discussion of water for irrigation. The growing practice of artificially recharging ground aquifers is illustrated by the U.S. East Bay injection and extraction groundwater pilot project in Oakland, California (action 1672). Promoting groundwater storage is important because of its many advantages—including the potential removal of some contaminants and minimal evaporation losses—and because of the continuing opposition to dams.

Efforts to control the demand for irrigation water represent an alternative to conventional supply-driven water management, which has long responded to "shortages" by relying on capital investment in new supply and distribution networks. Demand management focuses on reducing water consumption, and thus improving water use efficiency. Demand management measures include:

- Introducing short-age crop varieties, as with efforts to mitigate water stress in rice cultivation in Sri Lanka (action 1714).
- Introducing pricing mechanisms to reduce irrigation water demand, like in India (action 977) and cover operational costs, like in FYR Macedonia (action 2585).

Water for agriculture 10

Water conservation measures include introducing short-age crop varieties, introducing water pricing, developing water-saving irrigation techniques, modernizing irrigation systems, introducing salt-tolerant crops, and reallocating irrigation water to crops that consume less water

- Developing water-saving irrigation techniques, as in China (action 676).
- Modernizing irrigation systems, as in Vietnam (action 2049) or the United Arab Emirates (action 2613).
- Introducing salt-tolerant crops in areas that are arid, saline, or served by brackish water, as in the Middle East (action 1780 and 2282), in the Aral Sea basin (action 3105).
- Reallocating irrigation water to crops that consume less water, as in Egypt (action 1166) or to other users, as in Australia (action 1769).

Some projects use several such measures, such as China's water conservation project (action 368).

Demand can also be controlled by harvesting and reusing water. For example, new techniques that optimize rainwater harvesting and make rainfed agriculture sustainable, as applied in Tunisia (action 1645), offer promise where freshwater supplies are limited. In the drought-prone Tarija Valley of Bolivia (action 1793) a local non-governmental organization (NGO) helped eight rural communities dig hundreds of rainwater harvesting ponds that allow each local family to regularly irrigate a third of a hectare, thus helping to alleviate poverty. Such concepts can be applied on a large scale, as in Gansu, China: see box 10.1.

Box 10.1 "121" project (action 2604, one of three winners of the Water Action Contest)

The Gansu Research Institute for Water Conservancy (GRIWAC), China, is a government-organized non-governmental organization (GONGO) carrying out research, demonstration, extension, and training on the rational utilization of water resources and water saving technology mainly in the rural areas in Gansu Province.

Gansu is one of the poorest and driest provinces of China. Most of the river runoff during normal flow is salty and unfit for domestic or agricultural purposes, while groundwater is very rare and also of bad quality. Agriculture has relied entirely on unfavourably distributed rain, with frequent droughts during which people have to rely on relief water transported hundreds of kilometres by trucks. Aridity has caused serious soil erosion.

From 1988 to 1992, a GRIWAC team carried out an experiment, demonstration, and extension project on rainwater collection and utilization in four counties located in the middle part of Gansu, and conducted training courses to replicate these experiences in more than 2,000 households. Under the support of the provincial government, by the end of 1994 the team had helped farmers in the area to build 22,280 systems which solved drinking problems for about 110,000 people and supplied irrigation water for 0.14 square kilometres of land and 16 green houses.

The team has compiled the "Technical Code of Practice for Rainwater Collection, Storage, and Utilization", which was issued by the relevant government agencies in 1997. The successful experiences of rainwater harvesting projects and the once-in-60-years drought which happened in 1995, promoted decision-making by the provincial government to launch the "121" project which aims to support each household within the 1.2 million rural population with a subsidy of $80 to build one rainwater collection field, two underground tanks, and one piece of land for courtyard economy.

Within one and a half years, the project has succeeded in supplying water for domestic use of 1.31 million people in 2,018 villages. In addition, a total of 133 square kilometres of land received supplemental irrigation. In terms of the great achievement of the "121" project, a follow-up project was carried out again under the support of local government. By the end of 2001, supplemental irrigation has taken place on 23,600 square kilometres of land and the beneficiaries from domestic water supply have further increased to 1.97 million.

10 Focusing on Key Areas, Promoting Change

Water reuse is becoming an integral part of many national water programmes, particularly in water-short areas

Water reuse is becoming an integral part of many national water programmes, particularly in water-short areas—as shown by a water demand management policies in the Middle East and North Africa, for example, in Tunisia (action 1823) and Bahrain (action 1896). Such efforts require widening the concept of water use efficiency to include basin-wide efficiency and the multiplier effects of water as in Amman Zarqa basin (action 1817). But in some cases severe water shortages can lead to hazardous practices, including the use of improperly treated domestic and/or industrial wastewater for irrigation leading to health impacts and long-term soil contamination. The answer is found in integrating wastewater treatment and reuse, as approached in Tunis (action 3509).

Controlling agricultural pollution

Water actions that address threats to groundwater and drainage are often linked to agriculture. In Lambayeque, Peru, the Regional Environmental Commission has developed an integrated water management plan that includes irrigation uses (action 1846). Pakistan's national drainage programme (action 1157) promotes public awareness of irrigation and drainage issues by strengthening the country's technical knowledge base on waterlogging, salinity, and other water quality issues.

Agriculture-induced pollution can affect groundwater, seawater, or both. In Santa Catarina, Brazil, agricultural pollution is among the threats to groundwater that the Environmental Restoration Plan intends to address (action 1732). In the United States, guidelines are being developed for low-impact applications of pesticides and herbicides, reflecting best practices for water conservation and protection in the state of Colorado (action 2373). The Global Environment Facility has initiated pilot projects to reduce pesticide runoff in the Caribbean Sea (action 745) and in the Baltic Sea (action 1628).

Reforming institutions and governance

Despite the importance of sustainable agricultural development based on balanced plans for resource supplies and demand, many water actions have not considered sustainability during their planning stages. The unfortunate consequences of such projects have forced decision-makers worldwide to review relevant policies, legislation, regulations, and institutions, taking into account the various factors that influence the effectiveness of irrigation and drainage—including the availability of investments for rehabilitating infrastructure and of financing for operation and maintenance. The reforms resulting from such reviews should streamline the development of similar future projects using sound, holistic water management.

Several actions show that agricultural mismanagement and insufficient investment in infrastructure rehabilitation can increase river water salinity and soil salinity and waterlogging, requiring institutional reforms to address these issues and avoid similar risks in the future. The Aral Sea Basin provides a dramatic example of what mismanagement can lead to, and the Aral Sea Basin Project (action 1158) shows how the international community is working with national governments to mitigate the disastrous environmental effects.

Water for agriculture

> *Water is used to expand agricultural land to produce enough food. But people are not aware that this is causing a water shortage.*
> —Bahrain

Stakeholder participation provides a variety of views and helps gain public support and the political and financial backing required to sustain projects and deal with problems

Severe problems have also emerged in China's Yellow River, which runs dry up to 200 days a year up to 600 kilometres from its mouth. Corrective measures introduced by the Yellow River Commission seem to have improved the situation recently (action 819).

The strategic plan for South African agriculture (action 2363) recognizes the need to increase commercial production, build international competitiveness, and address the historical biases that resulted in skewed access and representation. Similar institutional reforms are taking place worldwide, including in Indonesia (action 2023) and Romania (action 934). Of particular interest is the attempt to foster private sector involvement in Morocco (action 424).

Better management, operation, and maintenance are crucial elements of new institutional arrangements and are evident in a number of water actions. In Indonesia (action 780), central and eastern Nepal (action 790), and Tajikistan (action 802) the Asian Development Bank is providing support for rehabilitation through a range of activities, including farmers' participation and institutional reforms, to ensure further operation and maintenance. Institutional changes must address the crucial need for dialogue between the agricultural and environmental communities. Globally, recognition of this need led to the dialogue on water, food, and the environment (action 70). But local initiatives are rare. The low-flow management programme for the Neste River in France (action 2451) provides an example of the needed approach.

Enhancing stakeholder participation

Inadequate stakeholder participation is one of the main challenges for water and agriculture management. Such participation provides a variety of views and helps gain public support and the political and financial backing required to sustain projects and deal with problems.

To reduce risks of inefficient and inequitable performance, decentralization and subsidiarity reforms in the agriculture sector may include irrigation management transfers, which reassign to farmers the main responsibilities for irrigation, including community issues and full or partial cost recovery initiatives. But attempts to equitably distribute water among rural populations may be hindered by the underrepresentation of women in water resources development and management. Accordingly, recent water management efforts that take gender issues into account have used integrated frameworks that address the interactions between gender and social equity, acknowledging the key role that women play in providing food for their families.

Several of the world's water actions try to increase stakeholder participation, understanding that participation contributes to effective development. Stakeholder consultations contributed to Ukraine's irrigation policy (action 1095) and have been initiated in the Indian state of Maharashtra (action 235) and in Jordan (action 167); Pakistan initiated the largest South Asian pilot experiment related to farmers' participation (action 1147). The World Bank recently analysed the benefits and second-generation problems of an irrigation management transfer policy initiated in Mexico 15 years ago (action 1208). Egypt's irrigation management transfer programme (action 1087) focuses on the secondary level; in fact, water user management seems more complicated to implement compared with the tertiary level. Tank management for irrigation is being considered in the Indian state of Karnataka, with a programme favouring decentralized, community-based management (action 2040). CARE has initiated a similar approach in Zimbabwe (action 1826).

At the project level Yemen's groundwater and soil conservation project (action 1142) aims to improve management of groundwater and increase irrigation efficiency,

10 Focusing on Key Areas, Promoting Change

Lack of information and knowledge can aggravate the effects that irrigated agriculture has on the environment and accentuate the threats of climate change to agriculture

agricultural productivity, and small farmers' livelihoods using a participatory water management approach. To reduce poverty among small farmers and raise the living standards of rural populations, Nepal's community groundwater irrigation project (action 1057) seeks to increase the participation of farmer groups, NGOs, private suppliers, and financial institutions in the provision of shallow tubewell irrigation services. A similar example can be found in Mauritania (action 1618). And when projects allow for analysis, the results can be impressive, as in Katepurna, India (action 689).

Some of these projects explicitly try to take a gender-sensitive approach to stakeholder participation in irrigation management. This is the case regionally through the Southern African Development Community (action 365) and locally through a number of actions—as in Cape Verde (action 1578), Pakistan (action 967), India (action 3045) and Nepal (action 3503).

Raising awareness and developing information systems

Lack of information and knowledge can aggravate the effects that irrigated agriculture has on the environment—for example, contributing to groundwater and drainage problems—and accentuate the threats of climate changes to agriculture. The challenge is to minimize negative impacts and promote positive impacts, fulfilling the seventh Millennium Development Goal of ensuring environmental sustainability.

Groundwater has tremendous value in both rural and urban areas for poverty alleviation, livelihoods, drought security, agricultural yields, domestic water supplies, and the environment. But indiscriminate exploitation and its consequences, along with pollution, threaten groundwater resources. Similarly, irrigation without drainage, excess irrigation, and inefficient irrigation and drainage systems can result in severe waterlogging and salinity problems, which lower crop yields and agricultural productivity. Such problems, as well as those associated with climate changes, are unlikely if awareness about hazardous practices and preventive measures is widespread throughout different levels of the decision-making hierarchy and among farmers.

Some water actions have developed online information systems, knowledge bases, and networks to promote awareness about successes and failures worldwide. These include the knowledge bases affiliated with the global dialogue on water, food, and the environment (action 70) or with the Food and Agriculture Organization (actions 3507 and 439).

To address the potential effects of climate change on agricultural production, information on related uncertainties has been expanded and public awareness raised on possible risks and responses. A global assessment of the impact that climate change would have on food production (action 1640) developed models of the sensitivity of world agriculture to potential climate change. Results suggested that moderate climate change might have a small overall effect on world food production, with reduced production in some areas balanced by gains in others.

But the study also found that developing countries—most of which are in lower, warmer latitudes—are much more vulnerable to climate change. Costa Rica created a unit in its Ministry of Agriculture to address this issue (action 1962).

Water for agriculture | 10

Human resources development plays a crucial role in determining the outcomes of irrigation-related water management programmes

Developing human resources

Though institutions can make the difference between success and failure in agricultural development, laws, regulations, and organizations may be ineffective without well-trained, motivated individuals to enforce and administer them. Thus human resources development plays a crucial role in determining the outcomes of irrigation-related water management programmes.

Major capacity-building programmes are well under way or have been initiated around the world. Examples include the Southeastern Anatolia Project (GAP) in Turkey (action 380), RIPARWIN in Tanzania (action 1366), and the Wet Zone Drainage Improvement Project in Sri Lanka (action 448). In Addis Ababa, Ethiopia, training is a prerequisite recognized by an NGO that helps pastoralists start agricultural activities (action 1054).

Water education and capacity-building needs can also be fulfilled through training centres established for such reasons—such as the Asia Drainage Programme for the Humid Tropics (action 2424) and the African Regional Drainage Training Centre (action 830), which aims to strengthen the capacity and skill of water professionals in planning, designing, operating, and maintaining agricultural drainage systems. In addition, international initiatives—such as CAP-NET (action 65) and the United Nations Educational, Scientific, and Cultural Organization's WETWAVE (action 2364)—will provide training and education, networking, awareness raising, and support for partnerships in developing countries.

Supporting action-oriented research and adopting innovative technology

Research and technology play crucial roles in agricultural production. Without research, the multidisciplinary concerns associated with development are unlikely to be addressed. Using information technology and evidence on economic evolution, water and food production and needs can be projected. Research can also solve various problems and enlighten the public on the implications of adopting technological innovations. Solutions to food production problems in water-scarce areas, for example, include high-yielding, drought-tolerant crop varieties and improvements in crop genetics. Finally, research is responsible for envisaging the role of water relative to future agricultural demands, suggesting structural adjustments to secure funds and attract investments in agriculture, and working out the transition costs of such adjustments.

The Actions Database includes several action-oriented research projects. Using mathematical modelling, the International Water Management Institute assessed the impact of interventions in primary and secondary canals on water deliveries to tertiary canals in Punjab, Pakistan (action 1149).

Efforts are also being made to increase cooperation on research and development, as with research partnerships in Kenya (action 2278) that seek to exchange information between scientists and farmers for irrigation development.

10 Focusing on Key Areas, Promoting Change

The economic implications of long-term food imports should be evaluated, as should the global implications of national agricultural subsidies

> We have asked for government support to construct irrigation facilities and have expressed our willingness to participate in construction, operation, and maintenance. Nothing has happened yet.
> —Lao PDR

What remains to be done?

For agriculture to feed the at least 2 billion more people in the world in 2025, water allocated to agriculture must be used more efficiently and new water resources developed. Although many actions have been initiated in this regard, a lot remains to be done. Many organizations and groups will have to choose water use and development priorities—and carefully consider the difficult tradeoffs between water for agriculture and water for the environment.

Shared understanding of the problems and their consequences, solutions, and the interconnections and tradeoffs among these groups is crucial if actions are to achieve common objectives. The starting point must be developing common awareness and understanding among current and future decision-makers around the world. This must be done in schools, in the media, and in workshops, meetings, and conferences—allowing those affected to make the decisions. Appropriate actions must then be taken on economic policy and trade, investment, infrastructure, institutional reform, research, and capacity building.

Developing more consistent, comprehensive water and food policies

Governments in both industrial and developing countries need to intensify efforts to prepare medium- and long-term water and food policies at the local, national, and regional levels. Such policies must be more consistent than they are today. National dialogues on such policy-making should be initiated and strengthened among those responsible for and affected by the development and use of water resources. Associated reforms and capacity building in irrigated and rainfed agriculture should be deepened, providing the main stakeholders with voices and choices in determining their futures. Trade in "virtual" water (water embedded in key water-intensive commodities, such as wheat) offers potential for making water allocations more efficient. It can also help integrate water and food policies, especially at the regional level.

Promoting equitable trade

To achieve adequate nutrition, food must be accessible, affordable, and absorbable. Thus trade arrangements should encourage water-scarce regions to produce and export high-value crops and import water-intensive staple crops. Trade regimes must also make special provisions for countries not yet able to compete in global markets for their food supplies. The economic implications of long-term food imports should be evaluated, particularly in food-deficit countries and regions—as should the global implications of national agricultural subsidies. Trade regimes should also be adjusted to promote socially equitable food production and distribution, and to support agriculture-based rural development initiatives in low-income, resource-poor countries.

Expanding water storage and improving water quality

More water storage—at or below the surface—is essential to achieving the water volumes required for food production and other purposes. Water storage and harvesting techniques should also be further developed to enhance productivity in rainfed agriculture. Work to contain agricultural pollution is also urgently needed because the effects take years to materialize in groundwater. Such efforts should be consistent with other pollution control policies, and policies that provide incentives to pollute should be eliminated—especially subsidies that encourage high-yield practices, which often result in highly polluting agriculture. Improving the quality of agricultural return flows requires developing affordable and effective technologies such as lower impact pesticides and herbicides (including biological agents) and livestock feed. Strategies are

Water for agriculture

Surface and groundwater management need to be better integrated

needed to phase out more persistent agricultural chemicals around the world.

Shifting the focus of irrigation development

The focus of irrigation development should change. Many large projects have been implemented, but more resources should be devoted to small irrigation systems that provide supplemental irrigation and to rainfed agriculture. Small-scale technology, such as treadle pumps, can provide many benefits in poor rural areas; developing them should be a top priority in the least developed countries. Innovative technology that enhances affordable small-plot irrigation can be one of the most effective ways of raising incomes, increasing land productivity, and achieving household food security, liberating the world's poorest and hungriest people from poverty and hunger.

Making irrigated agriculture more productive

Raising the productivity of irrigated agriculture is essential given that growing competition for water will undoubtedly increase tensions in many parts of the world. The main challenge is determining how much water should be used to preserve downstream water quality as well as the aquatic ecosystems needed to guarantee that quality. Methods are available to make such determinations and should be widely implemented. In addition, making irrigated systems more productive requires increasing the efficiency of hydraulic systems and enhancing agronomic performance through decent cropping practices and appropriate crop choices.

Because pumping water is a common way to increase the flexibility of irrigated systems, surface and groundwater management need to be better integrated. Such efforts should rely on individual farmers and irrigation agencies, which must work hand in hand.

Reforming irrigation and drainage institutions

Reforms of irrigation and drainage agencies should shift these agencies towards service-oriented management based on the principle of charging for services, to secure funding for sustainable service provision. Water pricing and cost recovery mechanisms have to be improved significantly to cover costs of operation and maintenance and certain investments. This approach is feasible only if appropriate, effective accountability mechanisms are in place, if decision-making is transparent and participatory, and if the services provided are sufficient.

Developing information systems and knowledge networks

Internet-based information systems and knowledge networks are needed to update users on the latest innovations in agriculture, to increase awareness of the potential of updated designs and modern technologies, and to provide examples of good and bad practices. Such information also helps raise people's awareness about the consequences of harmful practices and about coping with the risks associated with various uncertainties, such as climate change and its possible effects on water availability.

Improving water education and building capacity

Water education and capacity building for individuals and staff at all levels should be considered integral elements of all programmes aimed at improving agricultural management and development. These elements include knowledge about water in a framework that responds to sectoral and societal needs. Human resources development can be carried out in different ways, including incorporating training in agriculture projects, establishing specialized training centres, and developing relevant education programmes.

10 Focusing on Key Areas, Promoting Change

Public funding is required for research on locally important crops that are not likely to attract private investment and on better drought resistance and salinity tolerance of major cereals

Increasing research

More research is required to develop new and situation-adapted technologies that maximize water productivity and poverty alleviation in irrigated and rainfed areas. This should be accompanied by research on developing institutions for management, operation, and maintenance. Biotechnology research is required to increase crop yields. Private genetic research supports growth in the yields of tradable cereal and horticultural crops. Public funding is required for research on locally important crops that are not likely to attract private investment, such as coarse grains and tubers, and on better drought resistance and salinity tolerance of major cereals. Research should also investigate the effects of developing and using genetically modified crops.

11. Water, ecosystems, and biodiversity

Unsustainable consumption and production patterns are degrading ecosystems and reducing their ability to provide essential goods and services to humankind. Reversing this threat and achieving sustainability will require an integrated approach to managing water, land, and ecosystems, one that takes into account socio-economic and environmental needs. It will be essential to encourage participatory ecosystem-based management, to provide the minimum flow of water to ecosystems for conservation and protection, and to ensure sustainable use of water resources.

Many actions are being taken to protect, conserve, and restore water resources, and many countries are developing participatory ecosystem-based management and pollution control activities. But more must be done—in establishing environmental flow requirements, abating water pollution, building a systems approach to water management, and integrating the management of land, water, and ecosystems (including biodiversity). And serious reforms are required to regulate the allocation of water between human needs and ecosystem needs.

Present situation

Freshwater and terrestrial ecosystems (including biodiversity) are an integral part of the water cycle, and protecting them requires careful management of the entire ecosystem. For freshwater and terrestrial ecosystems and biodiversity, this means integrated planning and management of all land and water use activities in a river basin, from headwater forests to coastal deltas. *World Water Vision: Making Water Everybody's Business* (Cosgrove and Rijsberman 2000) affirms that ecosystems should be protected through integrated management of land and water resources in a river basin approach, along with full-cost pricing for water services and reforms in the management of water delivery and wastewater disposal. The "Ministerial Declaration of The Hague Conference on Water Security in the 21st Century" (Council of Ministers 2000) also recognizes the need to take actions based on an integrated water resources management approach, "to ensure the integrity of ecosystems".

11 Focusing on Key Areas, Promoting Change

Access to freshwater is an indisputable need for the maintenance and functioning of valuable ecosystems and landscapes in which human activities are an integral part

> In addition to thinking about human needs, we should also think about the other species living on Earth.
> —India

The ecosystem component of the *World Water Vision* is presented in the *Vision for Water and Nature: A World Strategy for Conservation and Sustainable Management of Water Resources in the 21st Century* (IUCN 2000). This document delivers four key messages about protecting our planet's ecosystem and proposes actions for doing so (box 11.1). Its central message is the critical need to preserve the ecosystem's intrinsic value—and its ability to continue to provide goods and services to humankind.

Ecosystems and water are mutually dependent. Both freshwater ecosystems and coastal and marine areas need freshwater of appropriate quantity, timing, and quality to maintain their functioning and their production of environmental goods and services—and many freshwater and terrestrial systems are essential for providing water (such as clouds, springs, and aquifer recharge zones). Freshwater is a finite and vulnerable resource, needed in all aspects of life.

Agenda 21, a comprehensive global, national, and local plan of action in all areas of human impact on the environment (see www.un.org/esa/sustdev/agenda21.htm), recognizes that in developing and using water resources, priority should go to meeting basic needs and the safeguarding of ecosystems and biodiversity. It recognizes the importance of integrated water resources development and management and calls for incorporating technological, socio-economic, environmental, and human health considerations into that management. But water is often managed by several sectoral agencies whose activities are poorly coordinated, hampering the development of a balanced, integrated management system.

Moreover, the water needs of ecosystems are not always recognized, since many people do not regard water for ecosystems as a social and economic use. Yet access to freshwater is an indisputable need for the maintenance and functioning of valuable ecosystems and landscapes in which human activities are an integral part. Ecosystems are also important in securing good health, because they provide services fundamental to our life support system—such as control of pests and detoxification and decomposition of waste. They contribute to the production of food (crops and fish), medicines, and other goods. They provide water treatment, recreation, and waterway transport. And terrestrial ecosystems help balance rainwater infiltration, groundwater recharge, and river flow regimes.

Box 11.1 Key messages in the *Vision for Water and Nature*

- The current and predicted extinction of freshwater species, and decline in ecosystems that are vital for our water resources, destroy the basis for sustainable development of communities and societies. In the past century alone more than 50 percent of the developed world's wetlands has disappeared.
- Ecosystems and the life they contain have a right to the water they need to survive, both to preserve their intrinsic values and to enable them to continue to provide goods and services to humankind.
- If humanity continues to misuse and destroy water resources and the ecosystems on which these depend, individuals and societies will ultimately suffer social and economic insecurity engendered by severely degraded rivers, lakes, and groundwater reserves, and will be confronted with increasingly serious conflicts in times of scarcity.
- This is an unacceptable future. Experiences from around the world show, however, that an alternative is at hand. Building on known sustainable practices and conservation measures, human behaviour can be changed to realize the world vision presented here. This will require us to take immediate and effective actions.

Source: IUCN 2000, p. x.

Water, ecosystems, and biodiversity   11

In the greater competition for water that results from accelerating population growth and unsustainable consumption and production, ecosystems—and biodiversity—tend to be the losers

Accelerating population growth and unsustainable consumption and production patterns have increased the demand for water. In the greater competition for water that results, ecosystems—and biodiversity—tend to be the losers. But people are the losers too. Activities that reduce biodiversity jeopardize economic development and human health through losses of useful materials, genetic stocks, and potential medicines. As ecosystems and biodiversity are degraded, their ability to lend resilience to the biosphere declines, and communities and human health suffer. The decline in the quantity and quality of water flows has reduced the productivity of many terrestrial, aquatic, and coastal zone ecosystems and led to losses of biodiversity. In remote areas this degradation of ecosystems has devastated fishing, agriculture, and grazing and undermined the survival potential of rural communities relying on these activities.

Agenda 21 recognizes that both the quantity and the quality of water should determine its use. Water pollution adversely affects both human water use, such as for drinking water and food production, and ecosystem water use. Upstream water uses may disrupt downstream uses, not only by reducing the water available but also by polluting it. Thus there has been growing agreement on the need for a water management approach based on a river basin, watershed, or aquifer. The functioning of ecosystems needs to be an integral part of such an approach. This need has been recognized at international meetings such as the Second World Water Forum in The Hague in 2000, the International Conference on Freshwater in Bonn in 2001, and the World Summit on Sustainable Development in Johannesburg in 2002.

What needs to be done?

To move from recognizing the challenge of protecting ecosystems to taking action requires that we appreciate both the intrinsic value of ecosystems and their ability to provide goods and services to humankind—then take the steps needed to protect them. The *Vision for Water and Nature* (IUCN 2000) explains these steps:

- *Adopting a participatory ecosystem-based management approach* to water resources (based on a river basin, watershed, or aquifer), which provides a framework for addressing environmental needs.
- Providing ecosystem security by *leaving enough water in ecosystems* to sustain both the ecosystems and their ability to provide services.
- Protecting surface water and groundwater from pollution by *controlling pollution and waste*, including through the enforcement of existing policies.
- *Reconsidering infrastructure development* by decommissioning existing and designing new, predominantly small- and medium-scale approaches to sustainable water resources management.

11 Focusing on Key Areas, Promoting Change

Protecting ecosystems requires integrating biodiversity conservation and ecosystem management into local and national economies

These four actions also require:

- Strengthening the participation of stakeholders in decision-making by raising awareness and building capacity.
- Developing and exchanging knowledge by using soft technology, appropriate clean technologies, indigenous crop varieties, and ecosystem-based management know-how in combination with traditional and appropriate social and economic mechanisms.
- Valuing water in a way that accounts for the functions and services of ecosystems and charges polluters for the full cost of the harm they cause to the system.
- Building knowledge about biodiversity and its role in the functioning of ecosystems.
- Approaching the management of biodiversity in a socio-economic context.
- Integrating biodiversity conservation and ecosystem management into local and national economies.

What is being done?

Many different activities around the world are protecting ecosystems. An assessment of these activities shows that conserving, protecting, and restoring water resources—rivers, wetlands, coastal zones, lakes, and groundwater—and protecting biodiversity are the key issues in managing the environment (figure 11.1). The actions also include some capacity-building projects on lake, river, groundwater, and water quality issues.

While the relative emphasis on issues varies, in nearly all regions ensuring water quality and protecting and conserving wetlands are key concerns (figure 11.2). In Africa many actions also focus on cooperation in river basin management and protection of lakes and watersheds. Protection of watersheds is also an important concern in the Americas, while in Asia, Europe, and Oceania coastal zone protection receives considerable attention.

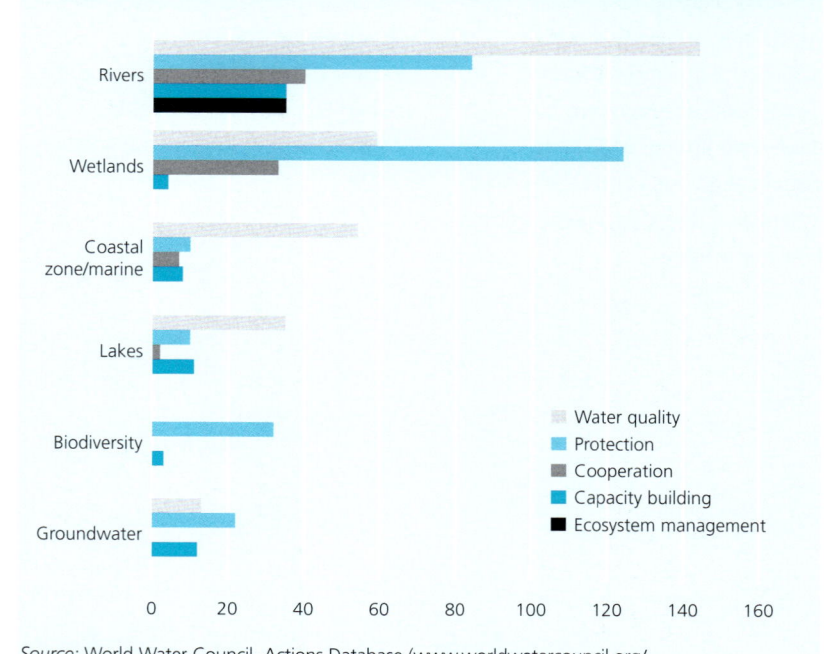

Figure 11.1 Actions to protect ecosystems, by type

Source: World Water Council, Actions Database (www.worldwatercouncil.org/search_actions.php), February 2003.

Water, ecosystems, and biodiversity   11

> *We should protect forests today so that we can have water tomorrow.*
> —Nicaragua

Participatory ecosystem-based catchment management is a fundamentally new approach to using, developing, and conserving water resources

Progress has been made mainly in four areas: wetlands protection and conservation, water quality, coastal zone management and marine protection, and watershed protection. But that does not mean that other issues—such as capacity building, new technologies, water for ecosystems, and participatory ecosystem-based management—are not considered, as shown by some of the actions described in the following sections. "Water for ecosystems" has been accepted as a concept, for example, though decision-makers rarely appear to have included it in national environmental policies. Exceptions include Australia, China, Kenya, and the United States, among others.

The many examples that follow are presented in accordance with the four principles of the *Vision for Water and Nature*.

Adopting participatory ecosystem-based catchment management

Recommendation of the Second World Water Forum. To achieve a sustainable society that cares for its resources, the Second World Water Forum proposed a fundamentally new approach to using, developing, and conserving water resources—participatory ecosystem-based catchment management. This approach requires that we "learn to care" about our water world. The *Vision for Water and Nature* (IUCN 2000, p. 20) explains the meaning of participatory ecosystem-based catchment management:

> The interdependencies between land, water and segments of human society require NGOs, governments, local groups, private companies and donors, in consultation with stakeholders, to jointly develop and implement an ecosystem-based catchment management approach in order to sustainably manage water resources. The augmenting pressure of increasing water demand and resulting conflicts, together with the greater variability and uncertainty in global environmental and hydroclimatological conditions, underlines the urgency of establishing such an approach. The notion of participatory ecosystem-

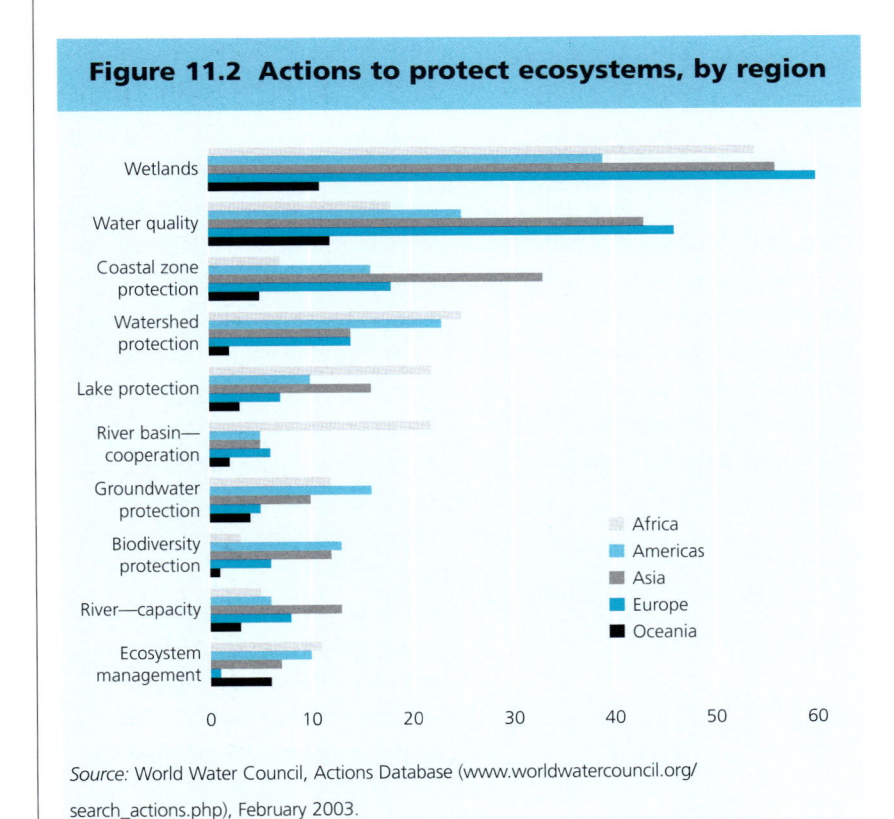

Figure 11.2 Actions to protect ecosystems, by region

Source: World Water Council, Actions Database (www.worldwatercouncil.org/search_actions.php), February 2003.

11 Focusing on Key Areas, Promoting Change

The European Union's Water Framework Directive emphasizes new ecological and integrated management approaches to river basins

based catchment management incorporates the opportunities and limitations provided by ecosystems, societies and economies, rather than relying on conventional single-use, top-down planning and management. In terms of nature conservation, this approach promotes the protection and rehabilitation of upper catchments, rivers, lakes, groundwater reserves, riparian zones, wetlands, floodplains, and coastal areas.

Analysis of Actions Database. Developments in participatory ecosystem-based catchment management are evident in many parts of the world. At the global level the Water and Nature Initiative (action 95) led by IUCN–The World Conservation Union and the work of the IUCN–The World Conservation Union Commission on Ecosystem Management (action 1246) are an essential attempt to identify the advantages of this approach to water management in places throughout the world. This effort focuses on demonstrating conservation and ecosystem management, empowering people through public participation, providing economic and financial analysis and tools, creating and sharing knowledge, carrying out baseline analysis, and providing structured learning to raise awareness.

At the regional level the European Union's Water Framework Directive (action 1169) emphasizes new ecological and integrated management approaches to river basins. The directive puts forth environmental regulations designed to achieve a "good" status for all bodies of water in the European Union by 2015. The directive sets objectives for an integrated policy on water protection, emphasizing a need for "water solidarity".

An ecosystem-based management approach to large marine ecosystems has been developed by projects and campaigns initiated by such international organizations as the Global Environment Facility, IUCN–The World Conservation Union, United Nations Environment Programme, United Nations Development Programme, and World Bank. These actions promote cooperation between the countries concerned, and some have created commissions or steering committees to solve problems in a participatory way—such as the Benguela Current Commission (action 516) and the Baltic Sea Regional Project (action 421).

Other actions have also emphasized cooperation between countries in dealing with ecosystem-based management: Building Partnerships for the Environmental Protection and Management of the East Asian Seas (action 155), Programme for the Bay of Bengal Large Marine Ecosystem (action 158), Protection of the Canary Current Large Marine Ecosystem from Land-Based Activities (action 171), Reversing Degradation Trends in the South China Sea Gulf of Thailand (action 519), Yellow Sea Large Marine Ecosystem (action 1257), Pollution Reducing Strategy for the Coastal Yellow Sea Area (action 1258), and the Guinea Current Large Marine Ecosystem Phase II (action 1381).

Linked to these regional projects have been a number of river management subprojects. For example, the Senegal River Basin Water and Environmental Management Project (action 221) seeks to ensure sound environmental management of natural resources and rational use of the Senegal River. Another project—Establishing Public Participation for Integrated Water Resources Management in the Senegal River Basin (action 894)—is working to establish an integrated water resources management strategy for the sustainable use of land, water, and the environment. Both projects use a participatory approach. The projects support the programme for

Water, ecosystems, and biodiversity — 11

The ecosystem approach places equal emphasis on the environment, the economy, and the society when addressing complex environmental issues

the Rehabilitation of the Degraded Lands of the Arid and Semi-Arid Transboundary Areas of Mauritania and Senegal (action 226). And because there is a strong link between managing river basins and protecting large marine ecosystems, they also support the Protection of the Canary Current Large Marine Ecosystem from Land-Based Activities (action 171).

The project for Integrated Planning for the Okavango Delta and Basin (action 905) in Angola, Bostwana, and Namibia aims to improve integrated floodplain and water resources planning and management in the Okavango Delta, the world's largest Ramsar site. (Ramsar sites are wetlands designated of international importance; for more detail see www.ramsar.org.) Based on an ecosystem approach and broad stakeholder participation, the project is led by the government of Botswana and has the cooperation of Angola and Namibia as well as local and regional initiatives such as the Okavango River Basin Commission (OKACOM). OKACOM has conducted a transboundary diagnostic assessment of environmental protection and sustainable management for the Okavango River Basin (action 316), which will lead to a strategic environmental programme for the basin.

Canada is increasingly using the ecosystem approach to manage the natural environment. This approach recognizes the interrelatedness of air, soil, water, and living entities, and it places equal emphasis on the environment, the economy, and the society when addressing complex environmental issues. Different programmes are developing the principles of integrated resource management. Initiatives such as the Fraser River and Atlantic Coastal Action Plans, the Arctic Environmental Strategy, and the Northern Rivers Ecosystem Initiative (action 1343) show how federal, provincial, and territorial governments can work with communities and non-governmental organizations (NGOs) to address ecosystem health and sustainable development. This cooperation is also the basis for an improved understanding of the cumulative effects of industrial and municipal development on aquatic ecosystems, under the recently completed Northern Rivers Basin Study. A project focusing on freshwater management in North America (action 2146) has been giving greater emphasis to ecosystem management. The Commission for Environmental Cooperation of North America seeks to develop eco-regional, ecosystem, and watershed approaches to sustainable freshwater management with community participation.

The ecosystem-based management approach was adopted under the Convention on Biological Diversity in 1992 (this convention has thematic programmes with links to freshwater issues: agriculture biodiversity, inland water biodiversity, marine and coastal biodiversity, and others). Even so, environmental policy decisions consistent with the ecosystem-based management approach were recorded in only a few countries in 2000–02, such as Australia, Botswana, El Salvador, Mozambique, Namibia, Niger, Nigeria, South Africa, the United States, and Zimbabwe. Governments, the private sector, and NGOs need a strategy for addressing the problems they will face in water resources protection at the river basin level and for strengthening cooperation. That having been said, it is evident that decision-makers interpret the ecosystem-based management approach in different ways, depending on their social, cultural, and political structures. Some countries give more attention to water quality, some to watershed protection, and others to capacity building.

11 Focusing on Key Areas, Promoting Change

Reducing total demand for water will require both behavioural changes, such as reducing consumption, and technical improvements in water distribution

> Our industries must realize their responsibility for keeping our water resources at the quality necessary for sustainable human use and for the sustainability of the environment that supports us. —Guyana

Leaving enough water in ecosystems to provide services

Recommendation of the Second World Water Forum. The *Vision for Water and Nature* (IUCN 2000, p. 20) urges a reduction in the total amount of water abstracted from rivers and groundwater and states that:

> As the source of water and life, ecosystems must be protected and wisely managed by the industries, municipalities, households and farmers who rely on them. Some ecosystems, such as upper catchment "cloud forests", springs and certain wetlands, directly provide us with clean water. Other ecosystems contribute to the regulation of water resources, reducing flood peaks and removing chemicals. Ecosystems need water to fulfil their basic requirements and maintain these functions.

Allowing ecosystems to perform their functions requires that users let certain amounts of water stay within the ecosystems. Leaving enough water in ecosystems allows them to maintain biodiversity and key characteristics of the habitat—including connections between channels and floodplains and between upstream and downstream areas. Techniques are increasingly available for determining the quantity, quality, and seasonal flows of water needed to maintain rivers, lakes, and coasts. These techniques can establish the reserves of water an ecosystem needs to maintain key processes, habitats, and species.

Leaving enough water in ecosystems will often require reducing the water abstracted from rivers and groundwater systems—and thus the water used for agriculture, industry, and direct human consumption. Reducing total demand for water will require both behavioural changes, such as reducing consumption, and technical improvements in water distribution, such as greater irrigation efficiency and reduced water supply leakage. Measures will also be needed to ensure equitable allocation of the resources that are abstracted.

Analysis of Actions Database. Despite the importance of maintaining environmental flows for downstream ecosystems and their use, few decision-makers appear to recognize that without changes in their attitude, food security and environmental security will decline. Increased consumption will deplete water resources, degrading the aquatic ecosystem. Clearly, a balance is needed between human consumption and the requirements of ecosystems. Few actions address this need, but among those that do, some are significant for considerations of environmental flow requirements, such as the Snowy River Inquiry (box 11.2), which was replicated for other rivers in Queensland (action 1770).

Box 11.2 Snowy River Inquiry (action 579)

This action illustrates the priority of establishing a balance between human consumption and the needs of ecosystems—and also shows what communities and governments can achieve by working together.

Beginning in 1997 with the incorporation of the Snowy Mountains Hydroelectric Authority, the national government of Australia and the state governments of New South Wales, South Australia, and Victoria have entered into many agreements to address the environmental flow requirements of the Murray and Snowy Rivers. All these have had input from farmers, the private sector, and the general public.

Of particular concern has been the Murray-Darling Basin, managed by the Murray-Darling Basin Commission and Ministerial Council. To improve its management efforts, the council is working with communities and the private sector to maintain the health of the basin's rivers and streams. The efforts include restoring a natural flow of water to the Murray River, keeping the river's mouth open, improving the condition of the Coorong wetlands environment, and reducing the impact of salinity and blue-green algae blooms. A water agreement calls for releasing up to 70 gigalitres into the Murray River annually and sets a proposed target of 294 gigalitres for the Snowy River.

Water, ecosystems, and biodiversity   11

In urban areas the main problem is insufficient water infrastructure to treat waste

Wetlands play an essential role in regulating the flow and quality of water and recharging groundwater. The designation of wetlands as Ramsar sites has accelerated: 1,015 were designated in 1974–99, but 215 in the short span from 2000 to 25 October 2002 (though designation as a Ramsar site is not enough if no management plan is developed). Rehabilitating wetlands and allocating water to them is a major concern in China; for example, a new plan has been implemented to ensure adequate water in the Zhalong wetland (action 1502). In 2001, 35 million cubic metres of water were temporarily diverted to the wetland. After completion of the plan, 100 million cubic metres will be provided to the wetland each year.

Awareness of the need for equitable water allocation has been growing in East Africa, especially in the Pangani River Basin (action 893). Using a participatory approach, a new initiative has identified the need for a water allocation system that considers both human and environmental requirements in the context of integrated river basin management.

Some countries have been implementing market-based rules for the protection and recovery of ecosystems, including setting prices for the public services they provide. This approach may offer another way to manage equitable water allocation. Examples of water use charges introduced to pay for environmental services are found in Costa Rica (action 1810), Japan (action 1841) and the Republic of Korea (action 1941).

Controlling pollution and waste

Recommendation of the Second World Water Forum. The *Vision for Water and Nature* (IUCN 2000, p. 21) points out that:

> Degradation of freshwater ecosystems and the resources they provide is due partly to pollution and waste disposal. In many catchments, pollution of watercourses and groundwater reserves needs to be controlled, from specific as well as diffuse sources. Municipalities urgently need to treat effluents from expanding urban areas. In the developing world, sanitation services and wastewater treatment within mega cities should be given a high priority, as cubic kilometres of untreated and polluted discharge is threatening downstream ecosystems now and into the near future.

Analysis of Actions Database. Many actions have been undertaken on pollution and waste disposal, including actions relating to the protection of water quality, restoration and protection of watersheds, and capacity building and cooperation. But given the serious consequences of ecosystem degradation—loss of biodiversity at both the species and the ecosystem level and diminished capacity to provide ecosystem services—these actions are clearly not enough. Actions under way address a number of issues: urban pollution, source pollution, organic pollution, transboundary pollution, clean technology, groundwater pollution, and others.

In urban areas the main problem is insufficient water infrastructure to treat waste. Solutions include constructing proper water supply infrastructure and wastewater treatment systems in parallel with developing capacity (see chapter 7). But real progress requires changing behaviour and adopting water pollution abatement measures. To sustain urban water supply systems, attention also needs to be paid to protecting water sources. Actions to protect forests have positive effects on some urban water sources. One example is the Water Towers Project (action 896), aimed at protecting year-round water sources for mountain communities and

11 Focusing on Key Areas, Promoting Change

Activities to control transboundary pollution have been increasing around the world

downstream users in Costa Rica. Action 764 addresses abatement of pollution caused by irrigation in the Baltic Sea region.

To enhance source protection in China, the government will no longer use natural wetlands for large-scale agricultural activities, abandoning earlier plans to develop 25 million hectares of natural wetlands for agriculture. In 2000 China introduced the National Action Plan for Wetland Protection (action 367). This plan, which includes 39 key projects and covers the next two decades, provides guidance on protecting wetlands and identifies measures for protecting and rehabilitating wetland ecosystems in the Yangtse River Basin, the Yellow River Basin, Three Rivers and Song-Neng River Plains in north-east China, the Lancang River Basin, and lakes, plateaus, coastal areas, and mangroves.

There is a global treaty to protect human health and the environment from persistent organic pollutants—the Stockholm Convention in 2001 (action 2500). The first step towards implementing the treaty is to develop national action plans. The National Implementation Plans for the Management of Persistent Organic Pollutants (action 528), an initiative of the United Nations Environment Programme begun in 2001, supports the efforts of the 12 pilot countries concerned and a monitoring network among them.

Activities to control transboundary pollution have been increasing around the world. One good example is the Transfer of Environmentally Sound Technology (TEST) to Reduce Transboundary Pollution in the Danube River Basin (action 422). This activity has recommended priority projects and measures to address "hot spots" of pollution, such as industry, agriculture, and human settlements.

Cleaner production is being actively promoted. The National Cleaner Production Centre Programme (action 1580), set up by the United Nations Environment Programme and United Nations Industrial Development Organization, promotes cleaner production by enterprises in developing and transition economies. In 2002 nearly 30 national cleaner production centres and programmes were established. Another protective technology is eco-sanitation (see chapter 7).

A number of actions focus on the use and quality of groundwater, which must be protected from pollution and overexploitation to meet the needs of both ecosystems and people. There are actions for groundwater quality in the Americas (especially in the United States) and Africa. In Mexico the Groundwater Stabilization Project (action 1172) aims to protect groundwater by training farmers, improving irrigation technologies, establishing protected areas, and supporting water users organizations.

In other areas most actions are aimed at protecting river basins and watersheds by reducing water quality degradation. Australian governments have broad experience in reducing water quality degradation, from national policy through local initiatives to research (for example, actions 586, 685, 688, 735, 976, and 1391). The United States has many actions in this area, driven in large part by the Clean Water Act, which regulates water quality (for example, actions 667, 668, 873, 874, 877, 879, 882, 883, and 884). Local schemes of payment for forest management and conservation in the upper watershed aim at protecting water quality (actions 2525 in Ecuador and 3102 in Costa Rica).

Water, ecosystems, and biodiversity 11

> *The infrastructure required by the millions of tourists and the coastal settlements are two of the most important sources of coastal pollution.*
> —Brazil

Some actions have led to changes in dam designs to ensure the protection of ecosystems

There have also been successful initiatives to protect lakes in the United States, led by government bodies and involving communities and other stakeholders. In other countries the movement is driven much more by NGOs, including a global advocacy network that initiated the World Lake Vision (action 1126). Launched by the International Lake Environment Committee and other organizations, this action aims to put lake management on the agenda of the water movement. The goal is to overcome four obstacles in lake management: lack of awareness, lack of integrated resources, lack of conflict resolution mechanisms, and lack of meaningful participation.

Reconsidering infrastructure development

Recommendation of the Second World Water Forum. The *Vision for Water and Nature* (IUCN 2000, p. 22) urges reconsideration of infrastructure development to conserve ecosystems:

> Sustainable water management requires a different approach to infrastructure development: an approach that "lives with nature", as opposed to one that "strangles nature". Leaving more space for natural ecosystems will require governments and developers to reallocate financial resources and redesign new or decommission existing infrastructure such as dams and dikes. Avoiding the huge environmental impacts of many infrastructure developments throughout the world will, in many cases, be much more profitable than paying for later repairs. Approaches to water management that take advantage of natural features of the ecosystem are therefore often much less costly than large-scale infrastructure developments. For new infrastructure developments, developers should integrate high-quality environmental impact assessment (EIA) studies into the planning phase, not merely as an add-on to the project development. In this way, the results of an EIA can be directly linked to the design and implementation of avoidance, mitigation and compensation measures. For existing infrastructure, operators will have to comply with modern environmental standards that allow for environmental flows, establishment of migratory species passages, and compensation for affected habitats and species.

Analysis of Actions Database. The Dams and Development Project (described in chapter 8) addresses the impact of dam projects on ecosystems, providing a new process for reconsidering infrastructure on the basis of ecosystems' needs. Environmental impact assessments are becoming a standard component of project preparation, and in some cases community pressure has forced a rethinking of projects. Environmental impact assessments have been implemented in, for example, Project Grensmaas: A New Alternative (action 1789) in the Netherlands and Belgium, Guidelines for Environmental Assessment of Small-Scale Water Supply in Namibia (action 1466), and the Athirapally Dam Project in India (action 254).

Some actions have led to changes in dam designs to ensure the protection of ecosystems, such as the initiative in Kenya, Modifying Mtonga Dam Design for the Environment (action 1290). Some countries are also looking at the social impacts of dams. The controversy surrounding the Yacyreta Dam in Argentina and

11 Focusing on Key Areas, Promoting Change

Today's fragmented sectoral approach to water management creates many obstacles to equitable allocation

Paraguay led to an evaluation by the World Bank Inspection Panel at the request of local NGOs and to mediation initiated by another NGO, Green Cross (action 133).

In Turkey a regional development plan known as the South-Eastern Anatolia Project (action 380) is being revised to strengthen its sustainable human development strategy. The revisions are incorporating a development approach based on integrated water resources management and reflecting economic, social, and environmental issues in the upstream water development. This action demonstrates how an infrastructure development project can move from an engineering-based approach to a people-centred one. Another initiative, for the Perfume River in Vietnam (action 341), is developing a partnership for the sustainable use of the river, its water, and its natural resources, centred on ecosystem-based management. Planned activities include establishing a river management board and developing an integrated management plan that includes restoring critical areas in degraded uplands and reducing poverty through community-based activities.

What remains to be done?

Participatory ecosystem-based management and holistic and integrated approaches to protecting ecosystems feature strongly on the international water agenda. But how this critical issue is approached varies from country to country. Some countries lack an understanding of the need for water for ecosystems, while others give more attention to restoring wetlands, protecting coastal zones, and protecting river basins and watersheds. Still, many countries have shown a tendency to strengthen cooperation in ecosystem protection. Some have a strong tendency to participate in international cooperation. And many have been developing public participation.

Very few actions deal with leaving enough water for ecosystems. That probably reflects how little is being done, in part because of a lack of understanding of precisely how much water ecosystems need and how much they are getting and in part because of the problems of reallocating water to ecosystems from other productive uses. Clearly, what can only be described as a conflict between human security and ecological security continues.

Still missing are water reforms to regulate the allocation of water between human needs and ecosystem needs. Today's fragmented sectoral approach to water management creates many obstacles to equitable allocation. In developing countries, where the degradation of water resources affects poor people especially, unreliable information and traditional social and cultural structures that lead to inequitable water allocation undermine the ability to fully assess the problems and find better solutions. No institutional mechanisms exist for making the trade-offs required between the environment, the economy, and social and cultural considerations. To provide possibilities for ensuring the water allocation to ecosystems that is their "legal right", legal systems must change. Future water laws should place ecosystem maintenance among the water use sectors. Moreover, the water flows required for ecosystems should be scientifically determined and regularly reassessed.

Many new initiatives are under way to improve water quality, and pollution control in watersheds has been increasing. But the water pollution problem remains serious, and water quality is becoming a key factor in water management. Sustaining water quality requires water pollution abatement—policies which encourage less polluting uses of water, such as

Water, ecosystems, and biodiversity 11

Biodiversity needs to be managed in a socio-economic context

clean industrial processes, or agricultural practices that use less fertilizer or pesticide. This approach is far from being widely applied.

Biodiversity needs to be managed in a socio-economic context. People depend on biodiversity and functioning ecosystems for their survival. An integrated approach to conservation, the sustainable use of biodiversity, and the equitable sharing of its benefits are all on the global agenda—recognized in the Convention on Biological Diversity, the *Vision for Water and Nature*, and the WEHAB framework. But biodiversity conservation and ecosystem management must be integrated into local and national economies. That will require building capacity and setting up a network for sharing data and information.

The international community has strengthened capacity building activities, but countries also need to develop and foster such activities at the national and local levels, to build a systems approach. International institutions have a leading role to play in advancing the environmental agenda. There has been good progress in capacity building and the exchange of information between countries and international organizations, but both efforts need significant expansion. Similarly, there has been progress in protecting ecosystems, but the problem needs more attention and greater collaboration.

The *World Water Vision* recognizes that people's roles and behaviour must change to achieve sustainable use and development of water resources and proposes that all actors should work together in this. These approaches are reflected in the recommendations of the *Vision for Water and Nature* (IUCN 2000) on participatory ecosystem-based management and reconsidering infrastructure development. Indeed, behavioural changes have been increasingly evident. Environmental organizations, including those involved in the "green movement", have contributed greatly to these behavioural changes by bringing the degradation of ecosystems to the public's attention. In some areas pressure from environmental activists has forced decision-makers to rethink infrastructure development. In others, it has helped to raise awareness.

All this activity has led to behavioural change in participatory ecosystem-based management (though not enough) and in the international arena. For example, there has been increasing behavioural change in many areas of global research and implementation. The World Commission on Dams (action 73), the Dams and Development Project (action 826), the European Union's Water Framework Directive (action 1169), and the innovative policies of the New Partnership for Africa's Development (action 423) and the Association of South-East Asian Nations (action 1385) are all examples of positive new thinking. Another area of change is financial. The World Bank, in its new water resources sector strategy, looks at policy change in the financing of investments in water management. The next step is to apply these new approaches to local initiatives.

There is a great need to integrate the different actions—on a global, regional, and local scale—that contribute in various ways to ecosystem-based management. The ecosystem-based management approach has many aspects—ecosystem protection, sustainable resource use, ecological security, watershed management, a participatory approach. Some projects cover all aspects, and some do not, creating a need for a global assessment of which strategies and institutional, behavioural, or policy options are used to implement ecosystem-based management, how effective they are, and how we could integrate them.

149

11 Focusing on Key Areas, Promoting Change

There is a clear need to protect coastal and marine environments by promoting concrete action at the local and national levels to address the deposition of sewage into waterways

To promote a more holistic approach to water management, the principles of integrated management of freshwater and coastal zones and marine areas should be incorporated into integrated water resources management. In particular, there is a clear need to protect coastal and marine environments by promoting concrete action at the local and national levels to address the deposition of sewage into waterways. The Global Programme of Action for the Protection of the Marine Environment from Land-Based Activities takes such issues into account.

Climate change calls for a systems approach, from the local and national level up. There is a consensus within the scientific community that water resources and wetlands cannot be managed without taking climate change into account. But global and national policies to address this problem have not yet been developed. Water management, including the risks from climate change, should be part of the national planning and budget process. And the resilience of wetlands and water resources must be analysed at all levels. To help address these issues, IUCN–The World Conservation Union has launched the Water, Wetland, and Climate Change Project (action 898). This project will initiate regional efforts to improve the capacity of countries to cope with climate vulnerability in the water and wetlands sector. Identifying the most appropriate solutions will also require more intensive studies, to provide the information needed to improve awareness and understanding of the constraints and enabling conditions for coping with climate change.

Much attention has been paid to capacity building and to raising awareness about protecting lakes and rivers, both key efforts for creating and strengthening participation for improving water quality. These efforts need to be extended to other areas, such as groundwater, biodiversity, coastal zone protection, and clean technology.

3

Taking Stock,
Advancing Change

12. The Third World Water Forum and the future agenda

This chapter takes stock of the debates and progress at the Third World Water Forum on understanding water issues, identifying effective water actions, and making new water commitments. What activities were proposed on issues on which there was consensus and on issues on which there was not? What new issues emerged that require more debate and investigation? And where do we stand after Kyoto?

What happened at Kyoto?

The Second World Water Forum in The Hague in 2000 engaged many thousands of people from around the world in a visioning exercise based on *World Water Vision: Making Water Everybody's Business* (Cosgrove and Rijsberman 2000) and a discussion based on the associated action plan, *Towards Water Security: A Framework for Security* (Global Water Partnership 2000). Discussions dealt with the state and ownership of water resources; their development potential, management, and financing models; and their impact on poverty, social, cultural, and economic development, and the environment. Concurrently, the Ministerial Declaration identified seven key challenges: meeting basic water needs; securing food supply; protecting ecosystems; sharing water resources; managing risks; valuing water; and governing water wisely.

The Third World Water Forum in Kyoto, Shiga, and Osaka in 2003 took the debate a step further within the context of the new commitments to meet the goals established at the Millennium Summit of the United Nations in New York in 2000, the International Freshwater Conference in Bonn in 2001, and the World Summit on Sustainable Development in Johannesburg in 2002. The Millennium Development Goals became a powerful instrument for more constructive and results-oriented international discussions and policy development.

The Third World Water Forum was the largest meeting ever convened on water, with nearly 25,000 attendees, including some 1,200 journalists. Forum participants represented 182 countries, and 170 countries sent official delegations. The large number of participants ensured that a broad variety of stakeholders and opinions were represented in the search for agreement on a common way forward.

The Third World Water Forum and the future agenda   12

The enormous outpouring of interest during the Third World Water Forum is a clear demonstration that water is considered one of the major issues of the century

The forum programme included 351 sessions under 38 themes, promoting open debate. An important innovation was that anyone could propose a topic and arrange a session. Having so many sessions, however, made the task of synthesizing the discussions and scaling up statements and recommendations for action more difficult. Nevertheless, a summary statement was produced for each session, and these were incorporated into a draft Forum Statement. The draft was placed on the web for comments, as well as the resulting Summary Forum Statement (Secretariat of the Third World Water Forum 2003).

The enormous outpouring of interest during the forum is a clear demonstration that water is considered one of the major issues of the century. It is also an indicator of success for the organizers, especially for the host country, Japan, which devoted considerable effort and resources to organizing this large event.

What issues emerged at Kyoto?

Many of the issues discussed at Kyoto gained clarity, marking the way for further action.

Water as a human right

In 2002 the United Nations Committee on Economic, Cultural, and Social Rights declared that water to meet basic needs is a human right and a social and cultural good, not just an economic good. What does this mean in practice? For the poorest people it will have real meaning only if countries enshrine this right in their constitution, legal framework, and policies. The issue received little attention at the forum, where it was generally admitted that responsibility is now in the hands of politicians. But not even the Ministerial Conference could reach agreement on incorporating this principle in the Ministerial Declaration. The water community needs to continue to work on this issue, to persuade policy-makers to implement this principle. This may be a task for the next forum.

Financing water infrastructure

Panel on Financing Water Infrastructure. Despite the important links between water security, development, and poverty alleviation, investment in water resources management has been seriously neglected. According to the Vision and other estimates, developing and transition economies will need $180 billion annually to achieve global water security over the next 25 years, along with greater efficiency, better financial management, and new models for mixed funding from the public and private sectors, donors, and non-governmental organizations (NGOs). Achieving the Millennium Development Goal targets on water supply and sanitation alone will require connecting 400,000 people a day to water and sanitation systems for the next 12 years. That requires applying the full range of options, including local, low-cost solutions.

The topic sparked some of the greatest debate at the forum, in part because of the broad agreement on the need for a substantial increase in resources to achieve the water and sanitation targets of the Millennium Development Goals. The work of the Panel on Financing Water Infrastructure, whose results were announced at the forum, received considerable exposure.

According to the panel, governments alone cannot achieve the required increases in annual investments in water. Other resources, including those of the private sector, are needed to fill the gaps. Meeting the Millennium Development Goals for poverty, hunger, health, and the

12 Taking Stock, Advancing Change

Improvements in governance are an important priority to enable enhanced and effective water sector financing

environment will call for large additional financial flows to irrigation, water resource management, wastewater treatment, and related areas.

Improvements in governance are an important priority to enable enhanced and effective water sector financing since in many countries the sector is exposed to considerable political and monetary risks (changes in legislation, currency fluctuations, and even cancellation of contracts). The panel presented an impressive list of proposals addressed to all actors, while recognizing the lack of commitment from several actors at the national level. The panel did not support the creation of new specific water funds but recommended that existing structures be made to fulfil their intended role.

The policies and operating practices of the multilateral financial institutions such as the World Bank, regional development banks, and the institutions of the European Union, also received attention. There were calls to reform these policies and practices to increase their support for water in the context of increased decentralization with its associated consequences for public finance.

Critics of the panel's report argue that it should focus more on the financial priorities for reaching the poor. Only a tiny share of financing now goes to low-cost water and sanitation projects directed to the poorest people in rural and peri-urban areas, who constitute the largest share of people without access to water and sanitation services.

The panel's estimates of required resources of between $20 billion and $180 billion also aroused controversy. Critics of the total figure of $180 billion often lost sight of the fact that this amount included not only water supply and sanitation but also agriculture, pollution prevention, and other uses of water.

This issue of required financial resources deserves careful attention. To be convincing, the water community needs to arrive at a narrower range of values. Getting more detailed information from countries on their own experiences will be important for improving estimates of the financing needed to achieve various objectives. Also important is distinguishing among the needs for financing new investments, operation and maintenance of existing systems, and rehabilitation of inefficient systems.

A more fundamental difficulty is that there were only two visions of the future of water services: one of water services relying on strong community involvement in the management, using low-cost technologies, and one of water services based on more conventional management and technologies. The first type of low-cost community-based water services is based on the experience of NGOs, often working in rural areas. The second rests on experience in urban areas. Many of the assumptions behind these two approaches need to be clarified.

The water and sanitation needs of rural areas received little attention from the panel which focused mainly on water and sanitation infrastructure in urban areas. Incorporating the needs of rural areas, including their different water management mechanisms and the role of communities and farmer organizations, could alter the conclusions of the panel. This important facet of the financing of water infrastructure needs to be incorporated in the next phase.

Cost recovery. A major breakthrough on the cost recovery debate was made at the forum. Whereas full cost recovery was advocated at the Second World Water Forum, the concept of sustainable cost recovery emerged in Kyoto. Because not all beneficiaries of water management interventions can be identified and because considerations of solidarity and the public good nature of some uses of

The Third World Water Forum and the future agenda

No one in the Third World Water Forum supported full privatization in terms of private sector ownership of water resources and full control over pricing

water may call for subsidies for certain categories of consumers, public support may be required. Participants acknowledged the need for subsidies as long as funding schemes allow operators (whether public or private) sufficient resources to operate and maintain the infrastructure.

Among the concepts that have gained acceptance since the Second World Water Forum is payment for environmental services. Several case studies showed that this approach is being successfully implemented and that wider geographical coverage is required.

Private sector participation

Public–private partnerships were another major controversy at Kyoto, much of it motivated by misunderstanding of what "privatization" would mean in the water sector. No one in the Third World Water Forum—neither the forum participants, nor the World Water Council, nor even the private sector—supported full privatization in terms of private sector ownership of water resources and full control over pricing.

Still, the discussion in Kyoto of private sector participation reflected the ideological concerns of the anti-privatization groups related to globalization and trade liberalization. These groups also feared possible conflicts of interest in the management of water utilities and water resources. The discussion focused mainly on ownership and management of public resources like water, the guiding principles for pricing policy, and the ethical question of making a profit on public services.

The position of the World Water Council in this debate reflects the opinion of the large majority of participants. A wide range of solutions may be possible for successfully managing water utilities, and local authorities should make their own choices, taking into account their capacities and the wishes of their constituency. Local communities need to be involved in the process. Helping the local private sector strengthen its capacities is also critical to economic development.

There was considerable progress made in these discussions since the Second World Water Forum, and a broad agreement, if not consensus, on several issues:

- As a public good, water resources ownership and control must remain in the public domain.
- Private sector involvement is a matter of national policy, and international financing institutions should not pressure governments to privatize utilities by making this a condition for loans and grants.
- The prospect of including water services in the General Agreement on Trade in Services creates serious concern because of their public nature. Deeper and more precise investigation and debate are needed on the meaning and consequences of such inclusion.
- The role and capacity of local authorities, which are in charge of more than 95 percent of water services worldwide, need to be strengthened.

Nearly all the discussion of private sector involvement focused on private sector participation in water supply (and, to a lesser extent, sanitation), probably because there is much less interest in private investment in public irrigation, flood control, and eco-management schemes, where returns to investment are much more uncertain. And yet the irrigation sector is undergoing privatization on an enormous scale as management authority is being massively transferred to farmers groups and water user associations.

Governance

Governance was central to the discussion of nearly all the themes during the Third World Water Forum, and nearly all sessions produced recommendations for improving the legal and institutional framework to ensure greater transparency and

12 Taking Stock, Advancing Change

The forum agreed on the importance of water storage for meeting the Millennium Development Goals for water supply, agriculture, and poverty eradication

accountability. Governments need to promote good governance in water management and service delivery, ensuring cost-efficiency, transparency, and accountability through increased stakeholder participation, public–private cooperation, twinning arrangements, private know-how, and other options for reforming public water institutions.

The Camdessus Panel on Financing Water Infrastructure, among others, argued that strong, equitable, and transparent legal and institutional systems are a prerequisite for sustainable financing. Similar statements were made in thematic discussions on water allocation and ecosystem protection. The water sector is particularly sensitive to the quality of public governance, and the associated risks for sector managers and financing institutions are consequently greater. The high levels of capital investment in water infrastructure and the associated financing mechanisms explain some of the heightened sensitivity. More important, the changes in decision-making processes called for by the water community are far-reaching and often challenge existing political systems, requiring behavioural revolutions rather than cosmetic modifications.

The role of local water authorities was discussed in the sessions on financing water infrastructures and private sector involvement and is covered in the Ministerial Declaration, a step forward from the Action Plan of the World Summit on Sustainable Development, which does not mention local authorities. Decentralization of responsibility to local water authorities has begun in many countries, with the centre establishing the framework and local authorities in charge of implementation and management of water utilities.

In this new institutional context, governments, donors, and NGOs need to focus their attention on capacity building so that the decentralized water agencies can work effectively in a participatory, service-oriented approach with user groups, communities, and households. Yet capacity building, this critical element in water development, is often treated as an afterthought, tacked on to programmes with scant regard to local capacity building or to long-term commitment. The donor community should commit a greater share of funds to establish better water governance systems, with particular support to help countries with sound socio-economic policies implement laws and build administrative capacity for efficient public institutions.

Central agencies also have to be transformed, so that they can take up their new roles and responsibilities. Local water authorities are critical for the future of water, but effective decentralization remains a big challenge for the near future. In many developing and emerging economies, the recommendations by the panel on financing water infrastructure to expand lending at the subnational level is not yet possible, because decentralization has barely begun.

Dams

The Third World Water Forum considered water infrastructure from many perspectives: financing, planning, operations and maintenance, environmental, economic, and social. The forum agreed on the importance of water storage for meeting the Millennium Development Goals for water supply, agriculture, and poverty eradication, as laid out in the papers of the World Summit on Sustainable Development on WEHAB (water supply and sanitation, energy, health, agriculture, and biodiversity).

Taking into account both positive and negative impacts, the forum endorsed measures to improve decision-making on the planning, design, construction, and operation and maintenance of large dams and called for an increase in financing to meet global needs, especially those of developing

The Third World Water Forum and the future agenda

Forum participants again called for preparation of integrated water resources management plans by 2005

countries. There was consensus among participants that dams should be considered one of many infrastructure elements in water resources development and as such should be developed in an economically, socially, and environmentally just and sustainable way. While there is still far to go, considerable progress has been made.

The debate on infrastructure stressed the need for balance between supply-driven and demand-driven policies. As pointed out by participants from several institutions (Blue Plan, World Bank), it is generally less expensive and more sustainable to invest in increasing the efficiency of water systems than to build new ones. For instance, Blue Plan estimates that demand management policies could save about 70 cubic kilometres of water (out of 300) in the Mediterranean. The greater the water scarcity, the greater the benefits of demand-driven policies.

Integrated water resources management

Integrated water resources management was invoked frequently at the forum, but few sessions adopted the broad view required for a true integrated water resources management approach. The sectoral organization of themes and the lack of interaction between some of them—such as agriculture and environment—showed that there is still a long way to go before the sectors that proclaim the need for integrated water resources management really collaborate on water issues.

Integrated water resources management involves political decisions on often opposing water-related interests, which must be considered, balanced, and decided on. Progress has been made in some countries or some river basins. There is broader understanding of the importance of decentralization and stakeholder participation in water management.

But including all stakeholders in the decision-making processes, though crucial, can be difficult and controversial. While the number of stakeholders participating in various consultation processes continues to increase, the decision-making process is often fuzzy and protracted, and decisions are frequently delayed or reversed. Education on integrated water resources management needs to continue and to reach all stakeholders. Greater attention should be given to water education in primary and secondary school, while higher level education and training need to be reoriented towards integrated water resources management.

Forum participants again called for preparation of integrated water resources management plans by 2005, following the implementation plan of the World Summit on Sustainable Development. The Summary Forum Statement (Secretariat of the Third World Water Forum 2003) asserts that primary responsibility rests with governments to make water a priority. But integrated water resources management is about more than identifying and weighing interests. It is also about making choices, the hardest part of the decision-making process, requiring time and skill.

Groundwater

Accelerated groundwater development over the past few decades has resulted in great social and economic benefits, providing low-cost, drought-reliable, and (mainly) high-quality water supplies for urban and rural areas and for irrigation of (potentially high-value) crops. However, investment in groundwater resource management has been seriously neglected. Further development and protection of the underlying resource base will be vital for the achievement of the Millennium Development Goals.

In many countries groundwater reserves have been degraded by pollution and depleted in a non-sustainable way by overexploitation. In

12 Taking Stock, Advancing Change

The quantity, quality, and timing of environmental flows are an essential component of catchment management

some areas the consequences are severe—falling water-tables, continuing poverty, irrevocably salinized or polluted groundwater, land subsidence, and reduced flows to wetlands. Effective solutions are not readily available because of the inherent variability of groundwater systems and of related socioeconomic situations.

Government agencies need to become "guardians" of groundwater, working flexibly with local stakeholders as partners in resource administration, protection, and monitoring, while also acting on broader water resource planning and management strategies, and adopting specific objectives (like the Millennium Development Goals) to reverse the current trends. The challenge is whether such objectives can be worked out before the next forum.

Knowledge about groundwater resources and how to manage them is still partial. Much remains to be done to identify aquifers and to determine their sustainable use. Developing both short- and long-term mechanisms to increase the economic productivity of groundwater use, while renegotiating and reallocating existing abstractions, will be important components of an overall strategy. Greater public awareness and improved scientific understanding and local capacity building are also key elements for improving groundwater management.

Time is of the essence. Many developing countries need to acknowledge their social and economic dependence on groundwater and to invest in institutional capacity for improved groundwater management before it is too late and groundwater resources are irrevocably degraded. Participating organizations pledged to put much greater effort into promoting constructive dialogue on groundwater policy and disseminating international best practice for aquifer management and protection.

Water and ecosystems

Ecosystems are not only water users, but water service providers. The quantity, quality, and timing of environmental flows are an essential component of catchment management. While the Second World Water Forum acknowledged the conflict between environmental and human demands for water, debate at the third forum was informed by new information on ecosystem water needs, thanks to studies by IUCN–The World Conservation Union, the International Water Management Institute, and the Centre for Environmental Systems Research of Kassel University.

Estimates of environmental water requirements in river basins range from 20 to 50 percent of the total renewable water resources. On average, at least 30 percent of the world's water resources need to remain in the environment to maintain healthy freshwater ecosystems worldwide. At least 1.4 billion people live in basins where water use is already impinging heavily on environmental water requirements. With the combined environmental and human needs for water already greater than available resources, a multistakeholder approach is vital for decision-making on water allocation priorities.

The lake community reacted to its low profile at the Second World Water Forum and prepared actively for the Third World Water Forum. The World Lake Vision was launched to provide a framework for addressing the management challenges facing lakes. Now, the vision needs to be translated into action on individual lakes, under the Lake Basin Management Initiative.

Addressing the impact of climate variability and change

Whereas there was little discussion of water-related risks at the Second World Water Forum in 2000, risks and disaster management were specifically highlighted in many themes of the Third World Water Forum in 2003.

The Third World Water Forum and the future agenda

Organizers called for participating organizations to use the forum as a platform for launching projects, campaigns, and initiatives of all kinds to improve management of water

Discussions resulted in several tangible commitments, which include establishing a global network of organizations concerned with water and climate, launching the Global Flood Alert System Project, and initiating a Drought Network for South Asia. Funding for disaster preparedness activities and adaptation to climate change has been very limited, so the planned creation of a Special Climate Change Fund by 2005, committed to by the Global Environment Facility, is a positive step. But more immediate and comprehensive financial schemes are needed to promote and enhance such activities.

As the Summary Forum Statement (Secretariat of the Third World Water Forum 2003) notes, increased vulnerability to water-related disasters diminishes prospects for economic and social development, poverty alleviation, and environmental sustainability. The Ministerial Declaration highlights "the need for a comprehensive approach", including structural and non-structural measures, in considering the growing severity of the impact of floods and droughts. It also calls for enhanced exchange of knowledge and greater collaboration among stakeholders.

Although the Ministerial Conference of the Second World Water Forum encouraged countries "to set feasible and quantifiable targets for reduction in water-related risks", few have done so. Risk management is often left out of national water policies. To set tangible targets on water-related disasters, water and disaster managers must win legislative and financial support to conduct vulnerability assessments and then create strategies for implementing preventive disaster management measures.

Other emerging issues

The Third World Water Forum addressed several new topics that reflect new actors and a broader scope: water and transport, water and energy, water and culture, and water and medicine. Two received particular attention.

Water and culture, little explored until now, is important because how water is valued depends heavily on cultural aspects, including closely related legal and institutional frameworks. Discussion at the forum highlighted the need to align legal and other institutions with culture.

Water and energy, another critical issue for the future of water, received attention at the forum, particularly the use of water to produce energy (hydropower). Other important aspects are the use of energy to transport water and the increasing water withdrawals in developed countries linked to energy production.

What started in Kyoto?

Action and tangible commitments were the focus of the Third World Water Forum. Organizers called for participating organizations to use the forum as a platform for launching projects, campaigns, and initiatives of all kinds to improve management of water. These objectives were expressed in the session reports, thematic statements, and press releases; on the stands in the Stakeholders Corner; and in the Portfolio of Water Actions (a process set up by the Secretariat of the Ministerial Conference for participants to provide information on important voluntary water initiatives).

The number of new commitments is impressive. Because some of these channels reported second-hand information, the World Water Council began the process of compiling information on commitments that seemed new, tangible, and financially secure; of getting official confirmation from the relevant organization or government of the precise nature of the commitment; and of incorporating the confirmed commitments in the Actions Database using the specific keywords "commitment 3rd Forum". The process was still ongoing at the time of publication of this report; the CD-ROM lists the commitments still to be confirmed as well as those that have already been confirmed.

12 Taking Stock, Advancing Change

Participants acknowledged the designation of water as a basic human right

Confirmed commitments include the following, with the number of commitments shown in parentheses:

- Financial commitments, official development assistance (13).
- Networks, partnerships, and knowledge sharing (40).
- Research, studies, and assessments (25).
- Development and modernization of infrastructure (8).
- Development and reform of institutions (6).
- Capacity building (16).
- Policy (11).
- Communication, awareness (12).

Financial commitments were lower than hoped for, in part because budgetary processes are lengthy and procedural requirements do not allow for launching financing commitments at an event such as the forum. Similarly, infrastructure projects were unlikely to be announced at the forum because such decisions are not made on the spot but are the result of a long process of recognition of needs and evaluation of options.

More worrisome is the continuous decline in overall funding for the water sector. While the visibility of water issues was greatly enhanced by the preparatory process of the Third World Water Forum, the forum, and follow-up activities, financial commitments did not increase concomitantly.

Thus water professionals mainly committed to new partnerships and networks, for which the forum was a very productive setting, and to initiatives on gender and capacity building (mainly building on existing programmes). The general feeling was that, without additional financing, few commitments can be made to improve governance.

What remains to be done?

When there is an emergency, such as a house fire, the first step is to become aware of the danger. The next is to take action—quickly. That describes the global freshwater situation. The World Water Forum series, the World Summit on Sustainable Development in Johannesburg, and the G-8 Summit in Evian have all helped build awareness and have made water an important topic of political agendas. The Third World Water Forum has now taken the first tentative steps to action. But the world needs to move more quickly to avert a full-blown global water crisis.

Translating water as a human right and the Millennium Development Goals into national development targets and programmes for water

Acknowledging the designation of water as a basic human right, participants called on the Ministerial Conference to include that recognition in the Ministerial Declaration. The Ministerial Declaration did not do so, however. While the United Nations Committee on Economic, Cultural, and Social Rights formally recognized the right to water, this recommendation has no legal consequence for countries. Many are reluctant to go further in this direction.

The Third World Water Forum and the future agenda

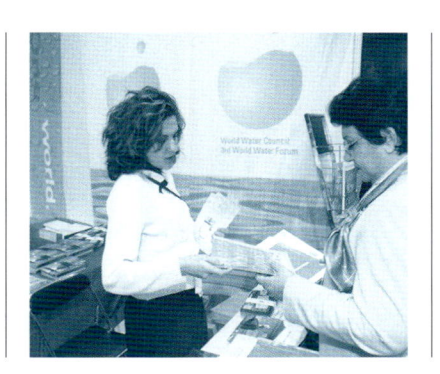

The practical steps to achieve the Millennium Development Goals have to be taken at the country level

The difficulty of reaching the Millennium Development Goals and of motivating decision-makers to focus on achieving these goals drew attention to the importance of monitoring, a point made in the water and poverty thematic session, in the Camdessus report, and in speeches by President Chirac and several ministers. However, the practical steps to achieve the goals—preparing plans, arranging financing, providing assistance, and monitoring activities—have to be taken at the country level. This calls for an explicit translation of the global Millennium Development Goals into country-level targets and programmes. The world water community and the United Nations Commission on Sustainable Development should call for such efforts because without concrete targets and programmes, the Millennium Development Goals are unlikely to be achieved.

Developing linkages through monitoring

As is obvious from this report, exact and complete data on what has been going on since the Second World Water Forum are unavailable. The main reason is that monitoring systems are not focused on achievement of development goals and successful water management interventions. While the Third World Water Forum stressed the need for monitoring progress on achievement of the Millennium Development Goals, care must be taken to ensure that monitoring does not drain too much of the sector's already limited financing.

The first edition of the *World Water Development Report* (WWAP 2003), a joint undertaking of 23 United Nations agencies and convention secretariats, announced that in addition to existing processes within the World Water Assessment Programme, new initiatives will aim at the production of national or regional water development reports. The first will be the African Water Development Report, to be produced by end of 2003 under the leadership of the United Nations Economic Commission for Africa. In addition, the World Water Council announced that it will launch a follow-up to *World Water Actions* and the associated Actions Database, in coordination with other major monitoring initiatives so as to optimize efforts.

Recognizing water's many values and the benefits of sound water management

Sustainable development is built on economic, social, and environmental pillars. Until recently, water investment and management decisions have generally taken only the economic values of water development into account, undervaluing or ignoring other values. Such decision-making requires a broader overview and detailed quantification of the many values of water and the overall benefits of better water management and water investments.

The World Water Council is taking the initiative, in cooperation with other interested organizations, to improve understanding of the tangible and intangible, direct and indirect benefits of water and to develop methodologies and associated tools for incorporating calculations of these benefits in planning, economic analysis, and decision-making. Valuations of ecosystem services and linkage to river basin management will help to improve insights into the ecological benefits.

The direct values of water are usually recognized, but translating that recognition into action by societies and governments is harder. Awareness raising and education campaigns need to be developed and institutionalized. The ongoing dialogues on water, food, and environment and on water and climate are making significant contributions to a new water ethic.

The importance of culture to water resources management must be taken fully into account in the development

12 Taking Stock, Advancing Change

Donors need to stand by their commitments to increase aid for water

and management phases of water systems. Water solutions should combine local culture and traditional knowledge with modern technology and management. Solutions need to be complemented by initiatives like the Water Education Programme for African Cities of the United Nations Human Settlements Programme, aimed at changing attitudes among water consumers and providers and developing a new water use ethic in society.

Mobilizing finance and investment

Governments need to translate water laws, strategies, and plans into realistic budget estimates and financing plans for water in all WEHAB sectors. While national governments and local authorities both need to take adequate measures to reduce risk and improve cost recovery, so as to encourage investment, primary responsibility for investment rests with national governments.

Donors need to stand by their commitments to increase aid for water. In allocating support, multilateral and bilateral donors should give priority to countries that are establishing strategies for integrating and coordinating water issues for all water-related sectors and that are increasing investments based on sound planning. In their investment strategies, governments and donors should give particular attention to pro-poor, affordable, and appropriate technologies and approaches. Governments, donors, and the private sector will need to develop an array of public financial instruments that local water managers can use for developing and managing infrastructure that can provide water to poor people at an affordable cost.

These principles for water finance and investment were agreed at the Third World Water Forum and endorsed at the G-8 meeting in Evian.

Clarifying the role of public–private partnerships and strengthening the capacity of local authorities in management and regulation

Because water is everybody's business, optimum use should be made of all available options. That means that community organizations, NGOs, the private and public sectors, local administrations, and national governments should work in partnership to achieve the best in water management. National governments need to provide a regulatory framework to facilitate operations in an accountable and transparent way under public oversight and to ensure that water services are provided to poor people at an affordable cost. Partners should cooperate in developing and using new instruments to mitigate risk and reduce overhead cost, using objective benchmarking and performance monitoring systems.

The government of the Netherlands has announced that it will support dialogue on public–private partnerships. On-the-ground experiences should be inventoried, synthesized, documented, and disseminated, so that the lessons of public–private partnerships can be made available to the public and to decision-makers, to inform the dialogue. Strengthening the public sector can be a suitable first option in some cases. Capacity building of local authorities will be essential for managing and regulating public and public–private water services.

Promoting comprehensive approaches for managing water more efficiently

All options for augmenting water supply, including increased storage, must be considered. Increasing water use efficiency and improving demand management are essential. But that may not be sufficient to meet the growing demand for water in most developing regions, particularly in urban areas.

The Third World Water Forum and the future agenda

Civil society groups intend to lobby for exclusion of water from the General Agreement on Trade in Services and other trade agreements

A comprehensive approach is required, incorporating demand and supply management, especially for water for food production. On the supply side, this would include supplementary irrigation and water harvesting and wider adoption of good practices, to avoid unnecessary risks, environmental and social costs, and delay. On the demand side, water management policies would include making strategic decisions about food imports and exports, including decisions to import food to save water. Trade in food products (or virtual water trade) needs to be better understood, especially the consequences for equity, poverty, water resources, environment, and geopolitical conditions at local, national, and regional levels. Case studies are needed at each of these levels. These would also be useful as inputs to discussions on the effects of the World Trade Organization and the General Agreement on Trade in Services on development in general and poverty, water resources, and the environment in particular (see below).

As just one example, accelerated groundwater development over the past few decades has resulted in great social and economic benefits. But excessive resource development, uncontrolled urban and industrial discharges, and agricultural intensification have also resulted, causing widespread degradation of surface waters and aquifers. In turn, this has hindered economic and social development, poverty alleviation, and sustenance of ecosystems. More efficient and comprehensive water management is needed.

Understanding the effects of trade liberalization and including water services in the General Agreement on Trade in Services

The theme on governance recommended that external influences on water management at the country level, such as international trade agreements, be carefully considered. The next round of World Trade Organization negotiations will take into account the impact of water resources availability on countries' trading positions, food security and food sovereignty, and development programmes. Civil society groups intend to lobby for exclusion of water from the General Agreement on Trade in Services and other trade agreements.

The World Water Council will need to develop a position on the globalization of trade in agricultural products; free trade arrangements, with their impacts on poverty, water, agriculture, rural development, and the environment; and the effect of water services becoming part of the General Agreement on Trade in Services. All of this is crucial for a better understanding of the links with the Millennium Development Goals related to poverty, water supply and sanitation, and hunger, so that appropriate actions can be undertaken.

Developing active alliances, partnerships, networking, participation, and dialogue

Governments, civil society, and the private sector should continue to seek ways of collaborating that take advantage of each other's strengths and skills, together creating a new ethic of responsible water use through advocacy, information sharing, and education. This can succeed only if governments have clear priorities and strategies for the water sector, and plan accordingly. NGOs, international finance organizations and donors, companies, and others will assist, but there has to be real political ownership by governments to make this work.

Local authorities, government representatives, the research community, farmers, industries, women, and minority groups need to be fully involved in the development of basin and aquifer strategies, agreements, and institutions. Stakeholder representatives and local authorities need a permanent and official role in decision-making and implementation.

12 Taking Stock, Advancing Change

It is vital to the world's well-being that by the time of the Fourth World Water Forum participants will be able to report on significant progress in making water flow for all

The water-related knowledge, practices, rights, and contributions of communities in all cultural contexts need to be recognized and better integrated in water management and environmental stewardship. Private companies can contribute to achieving the Millennium Development Goals through twinning and other kinds of capacity building.

Strengthening international cooperation in transboundary waters

The notion that water has greater potential for cooperation than for conflict, promoted at the Second World Water Forum, received new emphasis and drew much attention from the media. Especially important is the need to:

- Change the focus from sharing water to redistributing shared benefits at the national level, including poverty reduction.
- Respect the integrity of transboundary ecosystems.
- Increase stakeholder participation and capacity building, including the training of mediators.
- Increase, adapt, and coordinate the funding of activities related to internationally shared water bodies.

Countries need to establish institutions and build capacity to manage transboundary waters in ways that contribute to socioeconomic development and protect ecosystems.

The proposed Water Cooperation Facility, a UNESCO–World Water Council initiative, would link these two institutions with two other pivotal institutions for water, the Permanent Court of Arbitration and the Universities Partnerships for Transboundary Waters. On request, the facility will provide complementary services to improve the governance of transboundary waters—the necessary resources, favourable environment, political backing, professional support, and judicial mechanisms for preventing and resolving water conflicts and building consensus on the use of shared water resources.

* * * * *

The overall consensus of the forum is that much has been accomplished to increase recognition of the importance of water for sustainable development—and that much remains to be done. Several organizations are dedicating efforts to achieve substantial progress on priority issues. It is vital to the world's well-being that by the time of the Fourth World Water Forum participants will be able to report on significant progress in making water flow for all.

Photo credits

Pages xvii, 1, 3, 4, 7, 9
Richard Mas

Page 10
David Boucherie

Pages 12, 15
Richard Mas

Page 17
Shiga Prefectural Government, Department of Lake Biwa and Environment

Page 18
Richard Mas

Page 21
PhotoDisc

Page 23
Richard Mas

Page 25
Shiga Prefectural Government, Department of Lake Biwa and Environment

Pages 27, 29, 30, 33, 35, 39
Richard Mas

Page 40
Shiga Prefectural Government, Department of Lake Biwa and Environment

Pages 43, 45, 46, 49
Richard Mas

Page 51
Japan International Cooperation Agency/JICA

Page 52
PhotoDisc

Page 54
Richard Mas

Page 57
Shiga Prefectural Government, Department of Lake Biwa and Environment

Pages 58, 60, 62
Richard Mas

Page 65
Southeastern Anatolia Project

Pages 67, 68, 71, 72, 75, 76, 79, 80
Richard Mas

Page 83
David Boucherie

Pages 85, 86, 89, 90, 93, 95, 97, 99, 101, 103
Richard Mas

Page 105
Shiga Prefectural Government, Department of Lake Biwa and Environment

Pages 108, 111, 114, 117, 119, 120, 123, 124, 126
Richard Mas

Page 129
Japan International Cooperation Agency/JICA

Pages 130, 132, 135
Richard Mas

Page 136
Southeastern Anatolia Project

Page 139
Richard Mas

Page 140
Andrea N Dion

Page 143
Richard Mas

Page 145
World Water Council

Page 146
PhotoDisc

Pages 149, 150
Andrea N Dion

Pages 151, 152
Richard Mas

Pages 155, 156, 159, 161, 163, 164, 166
David Boucherie

References

Abramovitz, J. 2001. "Unnatural Disasters." *Worldwatch Paper* 158. Worldwatch Institute, Washington, D.C.

AFP (Agence France-Presse). 2001. "Mozambique Well Prepared for Flooding: UK Researcher." 22 March. Johannesburg [www.reliefweb.int/w/rwb.nsf/f303799b16d2074285256830007fb33f/374c105a5352b19ec1256a170054f617?OpenDocument]

Averous, L. 2002. "Financing Water Infrastructure." Lehman Brothers, London

Barbier, E., M. Acreman, and D. Knowler. 1997. *Economic Valuation of Wetlands: A Guide for Policy Makers and Planners*. Ramsar Convention Bureau, Gland [www.biodiversityeconomics.org/pdf/topics-02-01.pdf]

Beach, H. L., J. Hamner, J. J. Hewitt, and others. 2000. *Transboundary Freshwater Dispute Resolution: Theory, Practice, and Annotated References*. United Nations University Press, New York [www.un.org/Pubs/unu/003a7.htm]

Benn, J. 2003. "Water Aid and Development: Improving the Flow." *OECD Observer* No. 236, March [www.oecdobserver.org/news/fullstory.php/aid/936/Water_aid_and_development_:_Improving_the_flow.html]

Briscoe, J. 1998. "The Financing of Hydropower, Irrigation, and Water Supply Infrastructure in Developing Countries." *International Journal of Water Resources Development* 15 (4)

Brook, P. J., and A. Locussol. 2001. "Easing Tariff Increases: Financing the Transition to Cost Covering Water Tariffs in Guinea." In P. J. Brook and S. M. Smith, eds., *Contracting for Public Services: Output-Based Aid and Its Applications*. World Bank and International Finance Corporation, Washington, D.C. [http://rru.worldbank.org/Documents/08ch3.pdf]

Brundtland, G. H.. 2002. "Water for Health Enshrined as a Human Right." World Health Organization press release. 27 November. Geneva [www.who.int/mediacentre/releases/pr91/en/]

CEDARE/IFAD (Centre for Environment and Development for the Arab Region and Europe and International Fund for Agricultural Development). 2001. *Regional Strategy for the Utilization of the Nubian Sandstone Aquifer*. CEDARE, Cairo [http://isu2.cedare.org.eg/nubian/project/publications.htm]

Conner, A. M., J. E. Francfort, and B. Rinehart. 1998. "U.S. Hydropower Resource Assessment Final Report." DOE/ID-10430.2. Lockheed Martin Idaho Technologies Company, Renewable Energy Products Department, Idaho National Engineering and Environmental Laboratory, Idaho Falls, Idaho [http://hydropower.inel.gov/state/DOEID-10430.pdf]

Cosgrove, W. J., and F. R. Rijsberman . 2000. *World Water Vision: Making Water Everybody's Business*. Earthscan, London [www.worldwatercouncil.org/Vision/cce1f838f03d073dc125688c0063870f.shtml]

Council of Ministers, Second World Water Forum. 2000. "Ministerial Declaration of The Hague Conference on Water Security in the 21st Century." Second World Water Forum, 17–22 March. The Hague [www.worldwaterforum.net/Ministerial/declaration.html]

Desvouges, W. H., and V. Kerry Smith. 1983. *Benefit-Cost Assessment for Water Programs. Vol. 1*. Research Triangle Institute, Research Triangle Park, NC

FAO (Food and Agriculture Organization of the United Nations). 2002. "Draft Declaration of the World Food Summit: Five Years Later." 10–13 June. FAO, Rome [www.fao.org/DOCREP/MEETING/004/Y6948E.HTM]

Federal Republic of Germany, Federal Ministry for the Environment, Nature Conservation, and Nuclear Safety and the Federal Ministry for Economic Cooperation and Development. 2001. *Conference Report: Water, A Key to Sustainable Development. Report of the International Conference on Freshwater, 3–7 December, Bonn*. Lemmens Verlags Et Mediengesellschaft mbH, Bonn [www.water-2001.de/ConferenceReport.pdf]

Freeman, P. K. 1999. "Gambling on Global Catastrophes." In *Investing in Prevention: A Special Report on Disaster Risk Management*. Disaster Management Facility, World Bank,

Washington, D.C., pp. 4–5 [www.worldbank.org/html/fpd/urban/urb_age/disastermgt/catast.htm]

Gómez-Lobo, A. 2001. "Incentive-Based Subsidies: Designing Output-Based Subsidies for Water Consumption." *Public Policy for the Private Sector* Note 232. Private Sector and Infrastructure Network, World Bank, Washington, D.C. [http://rru.worldbank.org/viewpoint/HTMLNotes/232/232Gomez-531.pdf]

Gujarat State Drinking Water Infrastructure Company. 2000. *Gujarat Jal-Disha 2010: A Vision of a Healthy and Equitable Future with Drinking Water, Hygiene and Sanitation for All*. Gujarat State Drinking Water Infrastructure Company, Gujarat

Global Water Partnership. 2000. *Towards Water Security: A Framework for Action*. Global Water Partnership, Stockholm [www.hrwallingford.co.uk/projects/gwp.fau/documents.html]

Hawken, P., A. B. Lovins, and L. H. Lovins. 1999. *Natural Capitalism: The Next Industrial Revolution*. Earthscan, London [www.natcap.org/sitepages/pid5.php]

IFRC (International Federation of Red Cross and Red Crescent Societies). 2002. *World Disasters Report 2002: Focus on Reducing Risk*. IFRC, Geneva [www.ifrc.org/publicat/wdr2002/]

IPCC (Intergovernmental Panel on Climate Change). 2001a. "Climate Change 2001: Synthesis Report." IPCC, Geneva [www.ipcc.ch/pub/SYRtechsum.pdf]

IPCC. 2001b. "Technical Summary, Climate Change 2001: Impacts, Adaptation, and Vulnerability." IPCC, Geneva [www.ipcc.ch/pub/wg2TARtechsum.pdf]

IPCC. 2002. *Climate Change and Biodiversity*. IPCC, Geneva [www.ipcc.ch/pub/tpbiodiv.pdf]

ISDR (International Strategy for Disaster Reduction). 2002a. "Mobilizing Local Communities in Reducing Disasters." ISDR, Geneva [www.unisdr.org/unisdr/ISDRInf%204.pdf]

ISDR. 2002b. "Disaster Reduction for Sustainable Mountain Development: 2002 United Nations World Disaster Reduction Campaign." ISDR, Geneva [www.unisdr.org/unisdr/Final%20mountain%20booklet.pdf]

ISDR. 2002c. Living with Risk: A Global Review of Disaster Reduction Initiatives. July draft. ISDR, Geneva [www.unisdr.org/unisdr/Globalreport.htm]

IUCN–The World Conservation Union. 2000. *Vision for Water and Nature: A World Strategy for Conservation and Sustainable Management of Water Resources in the 21st Century*. IUCN–The World Conservation Union, Gland [www.waterandnature.org/english/WaterAndNature/Documents.html]

IWMI (International Water Management Institute)–Tata Water Policy Programme. 2001. "Energy-Irrigation Nexus: The Interplay between Energy Policy and Food/Livelihood Security in South Asia." [www.cgiar.org/iwmi/iwmi-tata/projects/energy.htm]

Lecornu, J. 1998. "Dams and Water Management." Presented at the International Conference on Water Management and Sustainable Development, 19–21 March, Paris [www.icold-cigb.org/article-barrages-an.html]

Marin, Philippe. 2002. *Output-Based Aid: Possible Applications in the Design of Water Concessions*. World Bank, Washington, D.C. [http://rru.worldbank.org/documents/OBA%20Water%20Concessions%20PhM.pdf]

McIntosh, Arthur. 2003. *Asian Water Supplies: Reaching the Urban Poor*. Asian Development Bank, Manila [www.adb.org/Documents/Periodicals/ADB_Review/2003/vol35_1/opinion.asp]

Ministerial Session of the International Conference on Freshwater. Bonn, 2001. "Ministerial Declaration." [www.water-2001.de/outcome/Ministerial_declaration.asp]

Muller, M. 2002. "Funding the Water Sector: A South African Perspective." Paper prepared for the Camdessus Panel on Financing Water Infrastructure, 25 November, Department of Water Affairs and Forestry, Pretoria, South Africa

Oxfam. 2002. *Rigged Rules and Double Standards: Trade, Globalisation and the Fight against Poverty*. Oxfam International [www.maketradefair.com/assets/english/Report_English.pdf]

Pazvakawambwa, G. T., and P. Van Der Zaag. 2001. *The Value of Irrigation Water in Nyanyadzi Smallholder Irrigation Scheme, Zimbabwe*. International Institute for Infrastructural, Hydraulic and Environmental Engineering, Delft [www.ihe.nl/publications]

Puri, S., B. Appelgren, G. Arnold, and others. 2001. *Internationally Shared (Transboundary) Aquifer Resources: Their Significance and Sustainable Management, A Framework Document*. IHP Non Serial Publications in Hydrology. United Nations Educational, Scientific, and Cultural Organization, Paris [http://unesdoc.unesco.org/images/0012/001243/124386e.pdf]

Sadoff, C. W., and D. Grey. 2002. "Beyond the River: The Benefits of Cooperation on International Rivers." *Water Policy* 4 (5): 389–403

Sakthivel, S. R., and R. Fitzgerald. 2002. *The Soozhal Initiative: A Model for Achieving Total Sanitation in Low-Income Rural Areas*. WaterAid, London [www.wateraid.org/site/in_depth/in_depth_publications/]

Schultz, B. 2001. "Irrigation, Drainage and Flood Protection in a Rapidly Changing World." *Irrigation and Drainage* 50 (4) [www3.interscience.wiley.com/cgi-bin/issuetoc?ID=88011960]

Secretariat of the Second World Water Forum. 2000. "Final Report: Second World Water Forum and Ministerial Conference." World Water Council, Marseilles [www.worldwaterforum.net/index2.html]

Secretariat of the Third World Water Forum. 2003. "Summary Forum Statement." [www.world.water-forum3.com/en/statement.html]

Seyam, I. M., A. Y. Hoekstra, G. S. Ngabirano, and H. H. G. Savenije. 2001. *The Value of Freshwater Wetlands in the Zambezi Basin*. International Institute for Infrastructural, Hydraulic, and Environmental Engineering, Delft [www.ihe.nl/publications]

Smets, H. 2002. *Le Droit à l'Eau*. Académie de l'Eau, Conseil Européen du Droit à l'Environnement, et Agence de l'Eau Seine-Normandie, Paris [www.oieau.fr/academie/gege]

Sunman, H. 1999. "Towards an Assessment of Financial Flows in the Water Sector." Background paper prepared for the Global Water Partnership Framework for Action paper

Swedish Ministry of Foreign Affairs. 2001. "Transboundary River Management as an International Public Good." Ministry for Foreign Affairs, Stockholm [www.utrikes.regeringen.se/inenglish/policy/devcoop/financing.htm]

Terry, G., and B. Calaguas. 2003. *Financing the Millennium Development Goals for Domestic Water Supply and Sanitation*. WaterAid, London [www.wateraid.org/site/in_depth/current_research/169.asp]

UN CESCR (United Nations Committee on Economic, Cultural, and Social Rights). 2002. "Substantive Issues Arising in the Implementation of the International Covenant on Economic, Social and Cultural Rights: General Comment No. 15." United Nations Economic and Social Council [http://193.194.138.190/html/menu2/6/gc15.doc]

UN ECE (United Nations Economic Commission for Europe). 1992. *Convention on the Protection and Use of Transboundary Watercourses and International Lakes*. 17 March, Helsinki. UN ECE, Geneva [www.unece.org/env/water/pdf/watercon.pdf]

UN ECE and WHO (World Health Organization). 1999. *Protocol on Water and Health to the 1992 UN ECE Convention on the Protection and Use of Transboundary Watercourses and International Lakes*. 17 June, London. United Nations Economic and Social Council [www.unece.org/env/documents/2000/wat/mp.wat.2000.1.e.pdf]

UN Resident Coordinator, Mozambique. 2001. "Mozambique Floods Final Report, 31 May 2001." [www.reliefweb.int/w/rwb.nsf/f303799b16d2074285256830007fb33f/83c6d399dbb2c2b1c1256a6f005741d6?OpenDocument]

UNDP (United Nations Development Programme). 1997. "Guidance Note on Gender Mainstreaming." UNDP, New York [www.undp.org/gender/policies/guidance.html]

UNDP. 2000. *World Energy Assessment: Energy and the Challenge of Sustainability*. UNDP, New York [www.un.org/Pubs/whatsnew/12jan01.htm]

UNEP (United Nations Environment Programme) and UNCHS (United Nations Centre for Human Settlements) Joint Mission. 2000. "The Floods in Mozambique: The Joint UN Response." UNEP/UNCHS, Nairobi

UNESCO IHP (United Nations Educational, Scientific, and Cultural Organization–International Hydrological Programme) 2003. "Water Security and Peace." Draft for discussion in the Third World Water Forum. Paris and Geneva [http://webworld.unesco.org/water/wwap/pccp/cd/pdf/water_security_peace_report/pccp_report.pdf]

UNESCO IHP and Green Cross International. 2002. "From Potential Conflict to Co-operation Potential: Water for Peace." UNESCO/Green Cross International, Paris/Geneva [www.unesco.org/water/wwap/pccp/pdf/brochure_2.pdf]

United Nations. 1997. *Convention on the Law of the Non-Navigational Uses of International Watercourses*. United Nations, New York [www.dundee.ac.uk/cepmlp/water/assets/images/UNCONV.doc]

United Nations. 2000. *United Nations Millennium Declaration*. United Nations, New York [www.un.org/millennium/declaration/ares552e.htm]

United Nations. 2002. "Plan of Implementation of the World Summit on Sustainable Development." United Nations, New York [www.johannesburgsummit.org/html/documents/summit_docs/2309_planfinal.htm]

USAID (U.S. Agency for International Development). 2002. "Mozambique." USAID, Washington, D.C. [www.usaid.gov/pubs/cbj2002/afr/mz]

WHO (World Health Organization). 2003. *The Right to Water*. WHO, Geneva [www.who.int/docstore/water_sanitation_health/Documents/righttowater/righttowater.htm]

WHO and UNICEF (United Nations Children's Fund). 2000. *Global Water Supply and Sanitation Assessment 2000 Report*. WHO/UNICEF, Geneva/New York [www.who.int/docstore/water_sanitation_health/Globassessment/GlobalTOC.htm]

Wolf, A. T. 1999. "Criteria for Equitable Allocations: The Heart of International Water Conflict." *Natural Resources Forum* 23 (1): 3–30 [www.transboundarywaters.orst.edu/publications/allocations/]

World Bank, Project Finance and Guarantees Department. 1998. "Bidding for Private Concessions: The Use of World Bank Guarantees." *RMC (Resource Mobilization and Cofinancing) Discussion Paper* 120. Washington, D.C. [www.worldbank.org/html/fpd/guarantees/assets/images/120.pdf]

World Energy Council. 2001. *Living in One World*. World Energy Council, London [www.worldenergy.org/wec-geis/publications/default/launches/liow/liow.asp]

World Panel on Financing Water Infrastructure. 2003. *Financing Water For All. Report of the World Panel on Financing Water Infrastructure*. World Water Council/Global Water Partnership, Marseilles/Stockholm [www.worldwatercouncil.org/download/CamdessusReport.pdf]

WWAP (World Water Assessment Programme). 2003. *World Water Development Report: Water for People, Water for Life*. UNESCO Publishing, Paris [www.unesco.org/water/wwap/wwdr/index.shtml]

Index

Albania 42, 62
Algeria 32, 99, 110
Angola 33, 63, 143
Aral Sea 129, 130
Argentina 32, 43, 44, 75, 96, 147
Armenia 29
Australia 30, 31, 33, 67, 79, 96, 100, 110, 111, 120, 129, 141, 143, 144
Austria 101
awareness raising 8, 18, 31, 33, 34, 40, 51, 60, 118, 120, 132, 149, 163

Bahrain 120, 130
Bangladesh 65, 84, 95, 119, 128
basin management 5, 9, 22, 23, 30, 37, 43, 49, 52, 148, 159
Belize 43
Belgium 31, 147
Benin 95, 98
Bolivia 43, 44, 63, 81, 96, 97, 129
Botswana 33, 63, 143
Brazil 27, 30, 31, 44, 81, 85, 99, 103, 110, 130

Cambodia 42, 66, 84
Cape Verde 51, 132
Canada 69, 96, 111, 143
capacity building 9, 22, 24, 33, 34, 62, 68, 69, 75, 81, 92, 98, 102, 133, 135, 140, 150, 158, 162
cleaner production 6, 26, 146
Chad 44, 95, 109
Chile 27
China xxii, 27, 30, 32, 42, 51, 52, 63, 64, 65, 66, 84, 95, 99, 100, 101, 103, 109, 110, 111, 118, 120, 128, 129, 131, 141, 145
climate change 5, 7, 10, 20, 57, 68, 71, 114, 123, 132, 135, 150, 160
Colombia 29, 31

commitments xxi, 80, 154, 161
Costa Rica 17, 31, 132, 145, 146
cultural value 4, 14, 20, 31, 49, 70, 78, 110, 154, 161

dams 25, 31, 32,39, 59, 64, 105, 108, 110, 119, 125, 128, 147, 158
Dams and Development Project 32, 110, 112, 147, 149
Danube 41, 44, 65
data collection 20, 31, 42, 44, 50, 66, 67, 135
decentralization 5, 9, 19, 22, 24, 27, 28, 33, 49, 78, 80, 83, 89, 92, 95, 98, 131, 156, 158
development assistance 24, 75, 80, 85, 162
desalination 23, 25, 99, 109, 111, 128
Dialogue on Effective Governance 35
Dialogue on Water and Climate 34, 68
Dialogue on Water, Food, and Environment 34, 131, 132
Dominican Republic 96, 99
Drainage 32, 64, 65, 126, 128, 130, 132, 135
drought 10, 40, 55, 59, 65, 67, 124, 129, 132, 133, 136

economic value 14, 15, 17, 163
Ecuador 57, 146
eco-sanitation 25, 101, 146
ecosystem restoration 32, 42, 59, 64, 142
Egypt 32, 39, 44, 127, 128, 129, 131
El Salvador 101, 143
environmental flows 32, 125, 131, 137, 139, 144, 148, 160
environmental impact assessment 18, 32, 111, 147, 150
environmental services 15, 17, 157, 163

European Union xxii, 63, 80, 98, 119, 142, 156
Ethiopia 95, 101, 102, 133

Finland 82
flood 32, 42, 55, 59, 64, 67, 114, 126, 161
Food and Agriculture Organization 34, 132
forests 32, 64, 105, 145, 146
France 31, 33, 65, 66, 85, 99, 111, 131

Gabon 97, 99
Georgia 109
Germany xxii, 63, 101
Ghana 95, 102, 118
Global Water Partnership xxi, 6, 29, 34, 83, 103, 150, 154
groundwater 23, 33, 39, 43, 44, 109, 113, 119, 120, 126, 128, 132, 159
Guatemala 43, 65
Guinea 82, 95, 110
G-8 Summit 162, 164

The Hague Conference on Water Security in the 21st Century xviii, xxiii, 14, 55, 80, 123, 137
Haiti 17
Honduras 27, 98
human right xxiv, 14, 16, 18, 78, 88, 116, 155, 162
Hungary 52, 64, 65, 66
hygiene education 6, 34, 50, 53, 88, 90, 91, 95, 97, 102, 114, 118, 119, 120

India 27, 29, 32, 33, 51, 52, 63, 67, 84, 95, 96, 98, 100, 101,103, 107, 109, 110, 111, 128, 131, 132, 147
Indonesia 84, 131

172 **World Water Actions**

interbasin transfer 32, 47, 111
International Conference on Freshwater, Bonn 3, 4, 17, 56, 102, 139, 154
International Water Association 102
integrated water resources management 5, 21, 33, 34, 40, 42, 93, 116, 125, 148, 150, 159
International Water Management Institute 32, 119, 160
Iran 43
irrigation 26, 28, 33, 51, 59, 74, 77, 85, 107, 109, 114, 122 to 136, 157
Israel 44, 99
IUCN–The World Conservation Union 17, 43, 111, 138, 142, 150, 160
Ivory Coast 102

Jamaica 127
Japan xxii, 17, 31, 32, 63, 64, 65, 101, 111, 145
Jordan 27, 30, 44, 120, 130, 131

Kazakhstan 42
Kenya 32, 97, 98, 101, 110, 128, 133, 141, 147
Kiribati 95, 98
Korea, Republic of 31, 33, 145

lakes 29, 42, 43, 52, 68, 110, 140, 141, 147, 160
Lao Peoples' Democratic Republic 42, 95
legislation 6, 9, 14, 25, 27, 30, 47, 50, 63, 81, 94, 130, 148
Lesotho 32
Libya 44
life-giving value 14, 16
local authorities 8, 28, 92, 97, 98, 117, 158
low-cost technologies 25, 69, 75, 78, 94, 98, 156

Macedonia, FYR xxii, 27, 42, 128
maintenance and rehabilitation of infrastructure 25, 55, 64, 74, 77, 82, 93, 108, 109, 119
Malawi 102
Mali xxi, 102, 120
Mauritania 120, 132, 143
Mekong River Commission xxii, 42, 66, 110, 118
Mexico 27, 28, 33, 63, 80, 101, 111, 119, 131
Millennium Development Goals xix, 8, 17, 25, 35, 73, 83, 89, 90, 103, 114, 116, 123, 154, 155, 158, 159, 162, 163, 165
Mongolia 119
monitoring 9, 10, 25, 35, 39, 42, 65, 66, 71, 82, 84, 88, 97, 103, 114, 146, 163, 164
Morocco xix, 32, 51, 66, 98, 127, 131
Mozambique 57, 61, 66, 99, 101, 143

Namibia 33, 63, 143, 147
New Partnership for Africa's Development 30, 149
Nepal 32, 60, 68, 84, 95, 98, 109, 110, 111, 118, 119, 127,131, 132
Netherlands xxi, xxii, 17, 33, 69, 80, 82, 127, 147
Nicaragua 63, 96, 100, 110
Niger 109, 128, 143
Nigeria 65, 102, 143
Nile Basin Initiative xxii, 43, 45
Norway xxii, 43, 65, 101

Oman xxii
output-based funding 81
opposition to new infrastructure 32, 44, 110, 112, 125, 128

Pakistan 33, 51, 52, 99, 103, 110, 127, 130, 131, 132, 133
Palestinian Territory 44
Panel on Financing Water Infrastructures 83, 155, 158
Papua New Guinea 60
Paraguay 44, 148
Peru 31, 33, 69, 118, 130
Philippines 62, 70, 81, 84, 97, 99, 110
Poland 64, 82
polluter-pays 9, 26, 30, 80
pollution 26, 43, 44, 55, 77, 82, 91, 94, 113, 117, 119, 137, 145, 148
poverty 4, 8, 17, 20, 36, 60, 73, 75, 84, 90, 92, 94, 96, 102, 113, 128, 164
pricing xxi, xxiii, 29, 50, 74, 77, 78, 83, 84, 94, 128, 135, 145
private sector xxiii, 24, 44, 74, 76, 81, 82, 93, 100, 103, 157
public participation xxiii, 19, 22, 27, 29, 33, 44, 51, 62, 69, 76, 88, 92, 96, 98, 131, 142
public utilities 25, 28, 29, 82, 83, 84, 90, 93, 96, 102
public–private partnership 25, 92, 118, 157, 164

rainwater harvesting 25, 51, 53, 100, 109, 120, 124, 129, 165
Rhine 41, 42, 62, 65, 67
Romania 65, 66, 82, 111, 131
Russia 31, 42, 76, 96

Saint Lucia 63
sanitation xix, 4, 9, 17, 34, 54, 63, 74, 81, 90, 96, 98, 113, 157
Senegal 99, 102, 118, 120, 143
Senegal River 43, 120, 142
service providers 8, 23, 24, 90, 92, 93
Singapore 120

social value 14, 15, 17, 78, 155, 163
South Africa 16, 51, 61, 80, 82, 85, 88, 97, 99, 101, 103, 110, 119, 120, 131, 143
southern Africa 30, 44, 45, 51, 61, 66, 67, 132
Spain 33
Sri Lanka 30, 80, 84, 95, 100, 101, 128, 133
Sudan 39, 44, 97
Sweden 43, 101
Switzerland 63, 101, 111
Syria 32, 42, 52

Tajikistan 131
Tanzania 52, 95, 102, 110, 133
technology transfer 9, 62, 100, 108, 146
Tonga 51, 100
Tunisia 85, 127, 129, 130
Turkey 42, 110, 118, 119, 120, 133, 148
Turkmenistan 43

Uganda 32, 95, 97, 101, 111
Ukraine 52
United Arab Emirates 129
United Kingdom xxi, xxii, 65, 85, 110
United Nations Centre for Human Settlements 61, 102 others
United Nations Educational, Scientific, and Cultural Organization 45, 133

United Nations Children's Fund 35, 101, 102, 118, 119
United Nations Development Programme 50, 52, 101, 142
United Nations Environment Programme 61, 68, 142, 146
United States 17, 30, 57, 64, 65, 66, 67, 96, 101, 105, 108, 127, 128, 130, 141, 143, 147
upstream-downstream xxiv, 18, 31, 39, 139, 146
urban water 33, 63, 64, 82, 88, 90, 95, 97, 98, 102, 120, 145
Uruguay 44
user associations 28, 33, 85, 97, 99, 125, 157
Uzbekistan 110

Vietnam xix, 42, 52, 62, 64, 65, 70, 82, 84, 101, 110, 129, 148
virtual water 134, 165
Virtual Water Forum xx

Water Academy 16
Water Action Contest xx, 97, 100, 129
water allocation 30, 79, 137, 148, 160
water demand management 22, 26, 33, 109, 128, 130, 150, 159, 165
Water Framework Directive xxii, 30, 31, 43, 142, 149

water re-use 26, 33, 95, 117, 119, 120, 129
water rights 28, 30, 32, 49, 79
Water Supply and Sanitation Collaborative Council 53, 118
WEHAB 4, 8, 17, 20, 78, 102, 123, 149, 158, 164
willingness to pay 50, 94, 99
World Bank 34, 81, 84, 101, 111, 131, 142, 148, 149, 156, 158
World Commission on Dams 32, 106, 108, 110, 112, 149
World Health Organization 101, 102, 116
World Summit on Sustainable Development xix, 3, 4, 17, 21, 80, 89, 90, 102, 123, 139, 154, 158, 159, 162
World Water Assessment Programme 35, 39, 88, 91, 105, 163
World Water Vision xx, 20, 37, 51, 55, 98, 122, 124, 137, 154, 155
World Wildlife Fund 43

Yemen 127, 131

Zambia xxi, 102, 128
Zimbabwe 66, 128, 131, 143

Bulk Discounts for 5+ copies
Buy Both Books and Save 15%

Earthscan Freepost 1
120 Pentonville Road
London
N1 9BR
Fax: +44 (0)20 7287 1142
Email: earthinfo@earthscan.co.uk

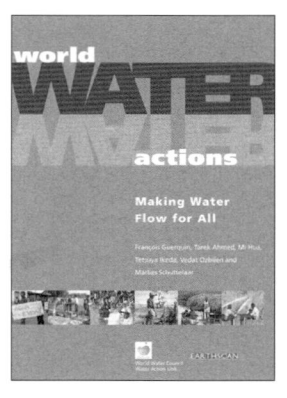

Includes free CD-ROM
Pb £25.00 1-84407-078-6
Hb £60.00 1-84407-085-9

Includes free CD-ROM
Pb £12.95 1-85383-730-X

TITLE	PRICE	QUANTITY	TOTAL £
World Water Actions pb 1–5 copies	£25.00		
World Water Actions pb 6–19 copies	**£22.50**		
World Water Actions pb 20–50 copies	**£21.25**		
World Water Actions pb 51–100 copies*	**£20.00**		
World Water Actions hb*	£60.00		
World Water Vision pb 1–5 copies	£12.95		
World Water Vision pb 6–19 copies	**£11.66**		
World Water Vision pb 20–50 copies	**£11.01**		
World Water Vision pb 51–100 copies*	**£10.36**		
Buy 1 pb copy of both books, save 15%	**£32.26**		
	SUBTOTAL £		
	POSTAGE & PACKING** – within the UK £2.50		
	– airmail £3.60 + £1 per book		
	TOTAL £		

* For 100+ pb (paperback) copies or bulk orders of World Water Actions hb (hardback), please contact Earthscan directly at earthinfo@earthscan.co.uk

** These P&P prices apply to orders of 1–9 copies only. For orders of 10+ copies, please contact Earthscan directly for the correct P&P within the UK or overseas

☐ I enclose a cheque/banker's draft payable to Earthscan Publications Ltd
(in sterling drawn on a UK bank)

☐ Please debit my credit/debit card as follows:

Card type *(eg Visa)* ....
Cardholder name ....
Card number
☐☐☐☐ ☐☐☐☐ ☐☐☐☐ ☐☐☐☐
Expiry date ☐☐/☐☐ Issue number ☐☐ *(only applies to Switch)*

☐ Please send me a pro-forma invoice *(this needs to be paid before the books can be despatched)*

Name ....
Position ....
Institution ....
Address ....
....
....
....
Postcode ....
Country ....
Fax ....
Date ....
Signed ....

☐ **Please add me to your FREE E-NEWSLETTER MAILING LIST, providing new book information** *(write your email address clearly below)*

Email ....
....

☐ Please send me an Earthscan catalogue

☐ As a service to our readers we occasionally make our customer list available to companies whose products or services we feel may be of interest. If you do *not* wish to receive such mailings.please tick this box

EARTHSCAN

Visit our website for special offers, FREE e-bulletin, online catalogue and sample chapters

www.earthscan.co.uk